Custody Down Under

Bound by Loss and Saved by Love

Elizabeth Woolsey

HORSE DOCTOR PRESS

Copyright © [2025] by Elizabeth Woolsey &Horse Doctor Press

ISBN: 979-8-9879635-5-5

All rights reserved.

No part of this publication may be reproduced, distributed, or transmitted in any form or by any means, including photocopying, recording, or other electronic or mechanical methods, without the prior written permission of the publisher, except as permitted by U.S. copyright law. For permission requests, contact the author: ewoolseydvm@gmail.com.

The story, all names, characters, and incidents portrayed in this production are fictitious or have given permission for use.

Book Cover by [Kathy Baldock @ Kathy's Pet Portraits]

Illustrations by [Cathy Walker @Cathy's Cover]

[Edition 1-2025]

To my daughter, Shelley Herbert.
You taught me the critical importance of precise water temperature when bathing young children.
Apparently, bathwater has a temperature range of one degree Centigrade, no more and no less.
I apologize for varying.
Despite this, you survived, and were able to teach me many other important aspects of raising young children.
I know you thought I didn't listen, and despite your reservations about my competence level in raising you,
your existence today proves that I was listening.
I occasionally got it right.
Thanks for helping me with the predawn mare inseminations.
Our success and pregnancy rates prove that
doing it in our pajamas needs to be a written protocol.
To those that think Maddison Taylor couldn't be that bright,
you obviously don't know my daughter.

I am standing upon the seashore.
A ship at my side spreads her white
sails to the morning breeze and starts for the blue ocean.

She is an object of beauty and strength.
I stand and watch her until at length
she hangs like a speck of white cloud
just where the sea and sky come
to mingle with each other.
Then, someone at my side says;
"There, she is gone!"
"Gone where?"
Gone from my sight. That is all.
She is just as large in mast and hull
and spar as she was when she left my side
and she is just as able to bear her
load of living freight to her destined port.
Her diminished size is in me, not in her.
And just at the moment when someone
at my side says, "There, she is gone!"
There are other eyes watching her coming,
and other voices ready to take up the glad shout;
"Here she comes!"

And that is dying.

Chapter 1

Maddison, Yorke Peninsula, South Australia

"Oh, God," were the last words from Daniel Monroe as his car slid off the dirt road and flipped. He couldn't keep his daughter from propelling out of the car window.

Was it seconds or minutes before the little girl approached the car? "Daddy, you need to wake up. Please wake up. You're upside down, and I'm scared. Please wake up. My arm hurts. Daddy? Please?"

Waking her father was not unusual for Maddison Monroe. At six years of age, Maddison dressed herself, made her father's coffee, and caught the bus to school. If she overslept, she didn't go to school. In a role reversal, Daniel never woke his daughter. It was her job to wake him.

This child loved school. It was her escape from the burden of caring for her only parent. She would kiss her father before leaving the house. He rarely kissed her back, but she knew it was a traditional gesture between parents and children. The kiss annoyed him and worked well to make him rise each day. The goodbye kiss was his alarm clock.

Maddison previously lived on an outback station in Western Australia where she'd begun her education, so when her father moved to the Yorke Peninsula in South Australia and away from the sheep station, she went straight to grade one. She knew the basics, had been taught to read, and could add and subtract. The station manager's wife spent time with her and one Aboriginal boy who lived at the station. Mrs. Donovan also taught her to cook and perform basic household duties.

She loved the station and her "extended family" who lived on the outback sheep station. She and her father lived in a small house with their Kelpie, Tag. Kelpies are known as one of the best Australian herding breeds. Tag was the reason her father had employment. Worth his weight in gold, Tag could do the work of several men. He mustered the sheep all day long and saved the stockmen countless hours of work.

At night, he slept on the porch, but when Maddison was four, she was often alone and would let Tag into the house. Tag protected her, and when her father returned from the pub, Tag would not let him into Maddison's room.

Maddison didn't remember her mother. She knew her mother had moved away when she was a year old. Her father had destroyed any link to her mother's past. There was a single picture she found and secretly kept. Maddison's mother was a tall, blonde woman with long, straight hair and broad shoulders.

With long blonde hair, Maddison was a miniature version of her mother. She was aware that her father was reminded of her mother when he stared at his daughter. There were differences. Maddison's mother's face was gaunt, and she had a small scar below her right eye. On the rare occasions Maddison went to town, she secretly searched for her mother. Maddison read about the larger cities in magazines, such as Sydney and Melbourne. She longed to travel there and hunt for her mother. She knew her mother's name was Isla.

Six months ago, Maddison's father moved from the station to a location closer to a town with a school and chose Moonta, South Australia. He rented a small house at the caravan park and was employed by the owner. At night, he worked at the local pub. Maddison's father was different, and Maddison was sadly aware of her father's demons. He was not like other fathers. He preferred to work alone. He barely tolerated physical contact. Maddison's awareness made her self-reliant and independent.

Maddison missed her friends at the station, but she could go to the caravan park's swimming pool. She was gregarious and made friends quickly. On Saturday, she would finish her housework and head to the pool and find a target. Maddison was attracted to mothers with children. She would hang out with them until the families left. Maddison would then find a new target or return to the caretaker's accommodation and help her father with his tasks.

The school year would end in a few weeks. She dreaded leaving her teacher, Miss Osborne, and especially her new friend, Jarlee. Jarlee was an Aboriginal boy from the APY Lands, or the land of the Anangu Pitjantjatjara Yankunytjatjara people. Jarlee and his family came down to Moonta last year so he and his brother could be on the footy team. The boys were stars on their respective Australian Rules junior teams. Jarlee was to travel back to the APY Lands when school ended for the year. He would return in February when the new school year began.

Jarlee's family lived near the road where her father slept in the overturned car. Tag crawled out of the car as Maddison ran to Jarlee's house to summon help. Jarlee's mother saw Maddison and could see the car in the distance. She called the emergency services and told Maddison to wait in the house while she ran to the road. Jarlee's mother didn't notice Maddison's lacerated and bruised arm.

Many minutes later, the ambulance and other emergency vehicles arrived. Maddison watched from the porch and soon saw the ambulance travel up the driveway to the house. Maddison was relieved. Her father must be awake if it only took them a minute to finish with him. A woman in a green jumpsuit approached the porch and saw Maddison's bleeding arm. She placed Maddison's arm in a sling, which caused Maddison more pain, and then asked her to get into the ambulance. No one talked to her about her father. They took her to the local hospital, farther down the peninsula, to the town of Maitland. Her arm was radiographed. It was not fractured, so Maddison was given a short-acting sedation, and the laceration was sutured and bandaged.

It was light outside when Maddison woke up in a hospital bed. No one was around, and she had to pee badly. She got up from the bed and opened the door that led to the toilet. She relieved herself and saw the mirror above the sink. She was sure she had a great shiner and was eager to get to school so she could tell everyone about her evening. She stood on tiptoes to catch a glimpse in the mirror. It was a beauty.

Maddison reentered the room with the bed and went out into the hallway, where the nurses drank coffee. They were talking to a policeman. They hadn't noticed her approaching them. "Excuse me. I need to get to school. Is my daddy here? I think our car is crashed, and I need a ride. Can you call my daddy?"

That night and that accident didn't just change the life course of a little girl. It transformed the lives of family and friends around the globe.

CHAPTER 2

BEN TAYLOR, CHARLESTON, SOUTH CAROLINA

"Doc, the Kilpatricks are still waiting. Should I tell them you're on level four of your video game and don't want to see them until you hit level six?" Lara Hansen was annoyed. She knew she was fighting a losing battle for her boss's attention. Lara was employed as a vet nurse at Crossroads Animal Clinic for ten years. She loved her job even though her boss, Dr. Taylor, had finally lost interest in veterinary medicine and was counting the hours to retirement.

Dr. Ben Taylor was sixty-eight and had lost his wife to cancer four years ago. After Tania passed, his heart was not in veterinary medicine, but the bills from his wife's illness kept him practicing. He'd been a brilliant veterinarian when Lara signed on. He had a referral practice that drew clients from across state lines.

He was still fit, and his black wavy hair was only gray at the temples. Ben's eyes were a deep blue, and his cleft chin was the subject of much talk at the clinic among the nurses. His Oklahoma accent and looks reminded everyone of James Garner. The staff was sure he would remarry in a few months, but Ben Taylor saw no interest in dating. He still grieved for his wife. He went through the motions of work and life, but he'd lost the satisfaction of repairing a fractured limb or successfully treating an arthritic dog or cat.

The orthopedic veterinary clinic was famous for cruciate or knee surgery and spinal surgery, which his partner, Dr. Jan Berry, performed. Dr. Berry agreed to buy out Dr. Taylor's interest in the new year. She had to find a replacement for Ben Taylor before he could retire. This took more time than either veterinarian had planned, but a new orthopedic surgeon would join the practice after the first of January. He was experienced, and Ben knew he would not need to train his replacement.

Lara walked around the desk to encourage Dr. Taylor. She was surprised to see photos of tropical islands and not Candy Crush. "Cool, Doc. Is this where you're heading when you retire?"

Dr. Taylor didn't respond. He put on an old white lab coat with a frayed hospital logo and headed to the examination room. The Kilpatricks stood and reined in Brutus, a six-year-old German shepherd who jumped and wagged his tail at the sight of Dr. Taylor. "Hi, Ben. Thanks for seeing us at short notice."

Ben Taylor bent down and patted the dog's head. The Kilpatricks were long-standing clients and breeders. They were known for producing healthy and sound working dogs for law enforcement and the military. The dogs had to be strong and trainable. Brutus had none of those qualities and remained with the Kilpatricks as a pet.

"We think his toe's been fractured. It's swollen, and he keeps licking it. We know it isn't a big deal or an emergency, but we're leaving town tomorrow and wanted to get it checked out, so we didn't worry the kennel man."

Dr. Taylor bent down and asked Brutus to shake hands. The dog quickly extended his sore and swollen paw, which Dr. Taylor gently took and examined. Between the toes was a small red hole. Brutus allowed the paw to be squeezed without resistance. As the pressure of the squeeze increased, the dog yelped and put his muzzle down on Dr. Taylor's hand but didn't bite him. The hole opened slightly, and the pus flowed out, which Brutus immediately licked. "Grass seed or I'll give you the farm."

"Oh, thank God." The relief of the Kilpatricks was clear.

Dr. Taylor smiled. "Yes, some people have called me God, but this is a slam dunk. Come on, Brutus. Let's go meet the staff."

Brutus was taken to the pre-surgery room, where several veterinary nurses were prepping animals for surgery, changing wraps, and administering medicine to cases that required hospitalization.

"Dr. Berry, can I steal one of the nurses for a minute? Brutus has a foxtail in his paw. I'm sure I can get it out without anesthesia. I need someone to hold him for a second."

Jan Berry grimaced. She would be so glad when her partner retired. She would never remove a grass seed from a German shepherd without anesthesia. The risk was too significant for someone to get hurt. The new protocol was for any animals that needed excessive restraint to have a physical examination, with or without pre-anesthetic blood tests, and then, at the very least, receive a short anesthetic that can be reversed.

Dr. Berry shook her head and pointed to Alex, the long-term kennel man. He'd restrain Brutus while Dr. Taylor probed the tract and attempted to find the migrating barbed grass seed.

"I'll have Alex back in fifteen minutes, tops. Thanks." Dr. Taylor knew what they were all thinking. He may have been slightly old-fashioned, but he knew his practice style was on its way out. *Hell, I'm on my way out. A few more weeks, and I'll never do surgery or see a case like this again.* He dreamed of the tropical island he would explore as soon as he hung up his scalpel handle. *Tahiti, here I come.*

"Alex, you know the drill. Just cradle the dog's head and extend his arm. Brutus is a great big teddy bear. He should let me get this out without too much fuss." Dr. Taylor swabbed the area with a disinfectant and gently probed the wound with alligator forceps. The thin end could open like an alligator's jaw and yet not stretch the skin of the entry point. With one probe into the space between the digits, Dr. Taylor pulled the forceps from the dog's interdigital area, bringing the tiny sliver of grass to the surface. He wiped the end of the forceps on a four by four, removed the spear, and returned to the wound. The second time, he retrieved a humongous foxtail, and Alex smiled.

"Atta boy, Doc." Alex loved Dr. Taylor. They'd worked together for thirty or more years. Alex witnessed the transition of veterinary medicine, and while understanding the need for change, occasionally missed the "old ways."

Ben Taylor probed the wound again until he was sure the offending foreign body was gone. He squeezed some antibacterial ointment into the hole, returned him to the Kilpatricks, and dispensed oral antibiotics that would need to be given for five days. The Kilpatricks' kennel help could administer the tablets.

If it were his dog, Dr. Taylor would not have bothered with the antibiotics. Still, he knew the additional antibiotics were a prudent addition to prevent any issues with the State Veterinary Board. The Kilpatricks would never cause a fuss, but it was cheap insurance.

In another twenty minutes, he was back doing Google searches of tropical islands and thinking about how his life had gone so wrong. This was not how it should end. He fantasized about trips with Tania in Europe and finding Daniel, who'd found his way in life and was engaged to be married.

Chapter 3

Nigel Buckby, North Island, New Zealand

Nigel Buckby was going fishing. He was taking his neighbor and had the car loaded. The North Island of New Zealand was his home for thirty-five years, and it was the rivers and lakes that kept him when he arrived from the UK to do a post-doctorate in reproductive medicine. He'd finished his lectures for the year, and the final exams were completed. Better yet, he would meet his soon-to-be-ex to discuss the final divorce division of the assets this evening.

He'd done the very thing he was warned to avoid. He'd remarried impulsively following the death of his wife five years ago. His soon-to-be-ex had been a godsend until she found someone wealthier and younger. C'est la vie—the fish await.

Nigel knew he was punching above his weight with Celeste. He was fifteen years older, and their interests had never intertwined. He loved rock and roll, and she was a classics woman. He enjoyed the outdoors, and she adored museums. Celeste had recently recommenced smoking, and it wasn't tobacco. He detested the smell and the effect it had on her. She detested his stodgy attitude toward her lifestyle choices.

Her children were continually hitting her up for money, and he was "the bank." His own daughter had gone AWOL when she was eighteen. Isla was arrested for drug dealing and was out on bail. Where she went was a mystery. The police searched for her for months, then years, before she was declared dead.

Nigel was sure she was still alive until a mysterious package arrived with her deceased mother's ring and a New South Wales Australian driver's license, with the address etched off the card. His wife must have given her the ring before she died. There was no return address or explanation, but the postmark was from the Northern Territory of Australia. Nigel had assumed the worst. It brought no closure, but after an inquiry into deaths in the Territory, which had not found a trace of his daughter, he stopped searching.

As he was loading the car with his fishing gear, he noticed mail sticking out of his old box. If it rained, it would get wet. Nigel walked over and pulled the mail from the box. Along with a professional journal on reproduction, he found a letter addressed to him from Australia. That was when his life changed.

The letter was from an agency in South Australia. A man was killed in an automobile accident, and a six-year-old girl was now orphaned. Papers were found in the house linking this child to his supposedly deceased daughter, Isla. The agency was seeking family members so the child could be cared for by relatives, and he was asked to contact the agency.

Nigel walked next door and explained he had to cancel today's trip. "Jock, I may have found my daughter."

"Mate, that's wonderful. Are you sure it's worth giving up a day of fishing, though?"

Nigel and Jock laughed at the absurdity of this idea. He knew Nigel had spent years searching for her. Nigel laughed, but he only shook his head. "I'll let you know later. I have a few phone calls to make."

"Are we still on for dinner?" Nigel's neighbor knew the answer, but it didn't hurt to make sure.

"I may fly out. I think I better pass on that tonight." Nigel knew he was heading to Australia as soon as he could. A flood of memories swarmed in his mind. He quickly returned to his house to wait. It was only seven in the morning in South Australia.

He went to his daughter's room and stared at the pictures of the girl through the years. He used his camera to record the last picture they had of her. Taken a month before she disappeared, her decline was obvious. Her prominent cheekbones and unkempt hair spoke volumes. Nigel's deceased wife, Bette, had removed the rock and roll posters and had the walls covered in Isla's pictures. She had been a precocious, beautiful little girl with long blonde hair. She played sports, rode horses, and even fished with her father when she was little.

Nigel realized the room needed dusting. His soon-to-be-ex rarely ventured into the room. Her children were grown and never stayed at the house. He went to the hall closet and took a cloth and returned to the room. He opened a drawer and saw her brush. He immediately knew it contained vital information. DNA! He took the brush and placed it in a bag. He'd take it with him to Australia.

Nigel considered he may have a granddaughter. He could only hope this would lead him to his daughter. He cleaned and vacuumed the room and then called Celeste. Nigel left a message informing his soon-to-be ex that he was heading to Australia, and he would be unavailable for any negotiations or signing of court documents.

He was relieved he hadn't replaced their dog with a puppy yet. He wanted to travel and fish, and he would find a new dog when the fishing season was over in April. He missed Tink, but she was always Celeste's, and he was never her favorite. It was funny, as Tink was Nigel's dog until he married Celeste. Bloody turncoat. No woman would ever steal his dog again. He was sixty-three. He'd resigned himself to living out his last days as a single man.

He estimated the Department for Child Protection in Kadina, South Australia, would be open. He dialed, and the call was immediately answered. He asked to speak to the person in charge of the case of the child whose father was killed in the automobile accident. "Oh, and were you a relative?"

Chapter 4

Maddison and the Department of Child Protective Services

Maddison Monroe knew her last name was really Taylor. She also knew her mother was probably alive. She answered every question as best as she understood. Her goal was to get back to the station and Mrs. Donovan. She didn't know any relatives except she had a grandfather, but she thought he was dead. She said she thought her mother was dead too, as that was what her father always expected her to say. She suspected otherwise.

She and Tag were staying with Jarlee's family. The woman, who said she was now Maddison's temporary custodian, was kind and, despite protests from others, said she could stay with Jarlee and his family. A white girl staying with an Aboriginal family was unusual, but in modern times, it wasn't out of the question. She was comforted by Mrs. Yarran. Staying with Jarlee gave her a sense of normalcy. After a few days, she even went to school.

The lady who said she was looking out for her interests had taken Maddison to an office in Kadina and asked her a hundred questions. She wasn't allowed to go back to the cabin where she and her father lived. Her personal items were collected by Harry Grant, the caravan park owner. He needed the unit for a new employee. It was late November and the start of the busy season. He took all of Maddison's father's personal items and put them in a storage shed. He brought Maddison's clothes to the Department for Child Protection. The caravan park owner was not happy with where Maddison was living. He kept the possessions, so they weren't sold. He offered to keep the child, but the agency declined his offer.

There were only a couple of boxes. Harry missed the child. She was bright, fed his cat, and was no bother. She even played with holiday guests and entertained the children. He knew she was an exceptional child.

Maddison was questioned repeatedly about her father and parents. She told them what she knew and finally admitted her father's last name was Taylor and not Monroe. That might be the key to finding Maddison's mother.

She was later told she had family, including two grandfathers. She asked about them, but she received no firm answers. She was told the lady in charge of her case, who she now knew was Mrs. Harding, would vet them, and if they were legitimate, then the department would decide where she would live the rest of her life. She didn't say vet, even though she'd heard the Donovans use that expression daily.

Where was Mrs. Donovan? Maddison was desperate to return to the station. If she could only find Mrs. Donovan, then she would be safe again, and she and Tag would never leave her beloved second family and homestead. Mr. Donovan could use Tag to work the stock. Where were they?

Chapter 5

Daniel Taylor's Story

Ben Taylor never imagined he would be a widower when he retired. He and Tania had lived the dream. They'd married when he finished vet school, with only the occasional hiccups in their lives until their son was born.

Their son, Daniel, had gone AWOL from their lives when he finished high school. He had issues throughout most of his life. His most significant challenge was that he was on the spectrum, which interfered with his education. He'd been diagnosed with Asperger's disorder in primary school. He was later reclassified as autistic. In those days, it was not treated, and he floundered in the educational system. He barely finished high school, and Daniel vanished from their lives when he was eighteen.

Tania blamed her husband. Ben never accepted Daniel's hopeless diagnosis and prognosis. Ben's attempts to break through to his son, to encourage Daniel to try harder and to allow tutors to help, had made their relationship worse.

After their son's disappearance, Tania and Ben sought help in finding him, but they were unsuccessful. When Tania was diagnosed with pancreatic cancer, Ben hired a private investigator to help find their son. The PI could show their son had migrated to New Zealand and then Australia, but the trail had gone cold, and Tania died without seeing her son again.

Now Ben was facing the rest of his life alone, losing his life's purpose in veterinary medicine and his family. His only close friend was his vet school classmate, Rob Deiner, who had retired several years ago. Rob was a general practitioner whose veterinary clinic was bought out by a corporation. The corporation rehired Rob for two years and finally cut him loose. Rob introduced Ben to skin diving and fine whiskey. They agreed never to drink alone. Ben only drank socially. Tania had a drink every night. Ben wondered if this had led to her cancer. It was moot. His fun, beautiful, and smart wife was dead, and so was his heart.

Rob suggested Ben explore a corporate buyout to retire and introduced him to the organization that bought veterinary practices, but Ben's partner resisted. Dr. Jan Berry did not want to go the corporate way, and since they had a specialty clinic, there was little interest in the practice from any veterinary corporations. Finally, Ben drew a line in the sand and sought a replacement. Jan Berry bought Ben out with the provision that Ben would stay and train the new vet.

As D-day approached, Ben was advised by his golfing buddies that if he didn't find a passion or a new woman, he would be dead inside a year. Ben thought travel and his new enthusiasm for skin diving might be the answer, and so he took some lessons. The swimming pool lessons went well, but Ben's goal was to dive in the tropics. Retirement was approaching, and Ben planned to travel to Tahiti or Bali in the Southern Hemisphere. He also planned to go to New Zealand on the remote chance he could learn more about what happened to his son.

Ben now marked time at work by searching online for resorts specializing in skin diving adventures. He considered Australia's Great Barrier Reef, but that seemed to be too touristy for his liking. At the end of work, Ben went to the store, bought a frozen dinner, and went home. It was cold and raining. He would eat his dinner, read his latest crime novel, and wait for the next day to begin. Ben knew he was in a funk and would be dead in a year like his friends predicted, and he didn't mind.

He pulled into his driveway and took his dinner. The newspaper ceased to be delivered several years ago. The mailbox would only contain bills now. Christmas was approaching, and there would be the odd Christmas card from old friends.

His brother-in-law always sent a picture of his family. Tania's brother was on his second wife and had a blended family. Their children were all grown and had children of their own. The group picture of the family was yet another reminder of how empty Ben's life had become.

Yep, there it was. The family all skied in Colorado. The photo was taken a year ago, but there was no mistaking the feelings and happiness this family unit had for one another. Ben hated them. They never invited either Tania or him on any family adventures or vacations. Tania cried every year she received the Christmas letter. She tried to hide it from Ben, but he knew.

There was a second letter that appeared to be from Australia. Ben's heart skipped. He hoped that one day his son would contact him. This letter appeared to be from an official source. It was from the Department for Child Protection in South Australia. The rain was pelting down, and he ran to the house with his dinner and the unopened letter.

Ben waited before opening the letter. He placed his frozen dinner in the oven, poured himself a glass of milk, and sat down in his recliner. He'd received hopeful letters and dead leads over the years. A few years ago, before Tania died, they had their DNA analysis done in case a body was discovered or a missing persons or cold case unit wanted to identify a body.

Finally, after several bites of his chicken. He opened the letter.

Dear Mr. and Mrs. Taylor,

We have been trying to contact you regarding your son, Daniel Taylor. We ask that you contact us immediately. I'm the caseworker assigned to your granddaughter, Maddison Taylor. I can be reached by email or by phone.

Sincerely,

Fiona Harding

Ben shook as he reread the letter and considered the implications. He checked the time in Australia. It was seven in the morning. Ben went to his laptop. It had not been opened in days. He did all his internet surfing at work and watched sports at night on television. He opened the email and found the usual spam and veterinary emails with offers of continuing online education and new equipment for sale.

He carefully addressed the email to Ms. Harding.

Re: Daniel and Maddison Taylor

Dear Ms. Harding,

I received your letter today. I'm eager to respond and get any information about my son, Daniel, and his daughter, Maddison Taylor.

As you can imagine, I would like to contact Daniel as soon as possible. I don't think he knows his mother, Tania, passed away two years ago.

I will attempt to call you when you are in the office in another hour, but if I cannot make contact, my phone number is with my address below.

Thank you for any information.

Benjamin Taylor DVM

He reread what he wrote and pushed send. Ben waited for a minute to make sure the email didn't bounce. He finished his dinner and waited for a response. He turned on the television and found only football replays. Ben rechecked his computer and finally attempted to make the call. Ben had to find the country code for Australia. The call went to voicemail. He announced his name and the subject and mentioned he had emailed.

He then remembered the envelope had a postmark. It was dated November 12th, two weeks ago. His heart sank. Why hadn't they tried to call him? He waited another thirty minutes and called again. Again, the call went to voicemail. He left one more message, and went to bed at ten o'clock, but set his phone on charge next to his bed.

He didn't receive a message all night. He opened his computer and noticed he had received an automated reply saying Fiona Harding was out of the office and would not be back until Monday morning. He checked the time on his computer and realized it was a Friday evening in Australia. His heart sank. He had to wait until Sunday night before he could expect to make contact.

He did a quick search on the internet for either a listing for Daniel Taylor or Maddison Taylor. Daniel was thirty-four, and one could assume he had a daughter who might be as old as fifteen. He didn't have Facebook. Tania had a Facebook account, hoping to find Daniel through social media, but Ben never attempted to access the account. He didn't know the password or have any login details for any other social media apps that Tania may have set up.

Ben went to work in the morning and considered calling his long-departed private investigator. He had two surgeries to perform in the morning and a recheck of a cruciate repair from the week before. He considered talking to his business partner, Jan, but she had the morning off so she could take her daughter to the dentist.

The only other person he could speak to about such a personal problem was the office manager, Sarah Jenkins. Sarah was in her mid-fifties, raised beagles, and was employed for over twenty years. Sarah was an unstoppable force. She was a no-nonsense businesswoman. She was married to Shawn, and they had several side businesses, including buying and reselling various items on eBay.

Ben performed his surgeries like the master he was. The anesthetic nurse asked if Ben was feeling all right. "Doc, you seem a little quiet. You okay?"

"Never better, Nancy." Doc smiled under his mask.

"I'm Lara." She shook her head. "I'm taking your temperature when we get done."

"I'm fine. I have a bit on my mind today. May I have the 2-0 suture material, and let's turn off the gas." *Why would a government agency want to talk to me?* "Is the consult here? I want to finish up early."

"Hillary Tatum isn't coming in until one-thirty, Doc, but you have nothing after that." Lara removed the instruments and took them to the autoclave room. "You know, I think she has the hots for you."

Love and romance were so low on Ben's list of priorities. He pretended to care, but he was still in love with his deceased spouse. "Maybe I'll extend the consult. What does she do? I've forgotten." He was going through the motions to please the staff.

"I think she's a social worker. She works at some level of the child welfare system."

Ben lifted his head. "Can you ask Sarah if that's true?"

"Now? Your dog is ready to crawl off the table."

Ben placed his last suture and removed his gloves. He headed straight to the front office. Sarah was sipping her third or fourth cup of coffee. "Hey, Doc, how was the surgery? I think you're done except for the consult after lunch. Do you want to run out and have some food?"

"What do you know about Australia?" Ben bent over Sarah's shoulder and glanced at the computer screen.

"Not much. Why?" Sarah pivoted in her chair and studied his face. Since Tania's death, her boss had aged. Still, he was one of the lucky ones, with a full head of hair and the physique of a man half his age. But his face appeared drawn, and his eyes were dull. She wondered whether he would ever recover from his loss and move on.

"Read this." He handed her the letter he'd received from Australia.

After reading it twice, Sarah took the letter, stared at her boss, and grinned. "Is this for real? When did you get it?"

"It came last night in the mail. I tried to call, and I left a voicemail. I emailed the lady, but I received an out-of-the-office reply. She won't be back until Monday."

"So, the prodigal son may have surfaced?" Sarah sipped her coffee and leaned back in her chair.

"Maybe." Ben stood to leave but turned and asked Sarah to check the time in Australia. *Oh, please, Lord. Give me one more chance with my son. I'll do anything to make him happy.*

"You know it's Saturday there? They're almost a day ahead of us. It's midnight in Sydney. I don't know where Kadina is. Are you getting on a plane tomorrow?"

"I need to talk to the woman first. But I know how good you are at sleuthing. Can you quickly look around and see if you can find anything on Facebook or something else?"

Sarah handed her boss the company credit card. "You go get us all some pizza, and I'll look around." The phone rang, and Ben headed to the car. The clinic had a standing pizza order on Fridays. The staff usually picked it up, but they were busy.

When he returned, Sarah was on the phone. She had information that would need to be given privately. Now was not the time. She was heartbroken, knowing what she'd discovered. She would wait until Ben finished his consultation. He stared at her, and she shook her head. "The damn phone hasn't stopped. I'll get on it as soon as I can, Doc."

"Hillary Tatum's here, Doc. She's in room three." Hillary's dog had cruciate surgery last week, and the sutures needed to be checked. A follow-up was necessary to make sure the internal fixation still held.

Ben entered the room and noticed Hillary appeared worried. "Hi, Dr. Taylor. We may have a problem. I'm struggling to keep Marky confined, and he's sore today."

Ben could see signs that Hillary's dog was licking his incision. "Are you keeping the Elizabethan collar on Marky?"

Hillary appeared embarrassed. "He hates it, Dr. Taylor."

"How about if Marky stays with us over the weekend?" It was rare that the clinic hospitalized orthopedic cases over the weekend. It was expensive and stressful for both the owner and the animal, but clearly, this woman was not coping with the aftercare.

"I'm supposed to go skiing this weekend, and the snowpack has increased, so it should be a good weekend. I was going to cancel, but maybe for all concerned, it might be better if I left him here." She bent down and patted Marky's head. "You'll hate me, old man, but it might be for the better."

Ben took Marky out of the consulting room, handed him to one of the nurses, and asked her to replace the Elizabethan collar. "Put him in a cage where he can't jump and stand on his hind legs." He returned to the consulting room. "Hillary, do you mind if I ask you a question about your line of work?"

"Sure. I can't comment on specific cases, but I can discuss general topics."

"Have you had any experience with the Australian social service network?"

"No. I don't deal with international issues. We have a section that does, but mostly it's been for South America and Mexico and the rare Canadian issue. What's the problem?"

Ben hesitated to discuss it further. She wouldn't be able to help. "I'm not sure. I have a son. I haven't seen him for many years, and I received a letter showing I may have a granddaughter. The letter's from Australia. The agency that sent the letter is closed over the weekend."

"I'm sorry I can't help you. If you get any information and you think you need help, I can direct you to my boss. She would be the person I would contact." Hillary handed Ben a business card. "Call me anytime. Thanks for your help with Marky. I understand you're finished and retiring soon. I can't thank you enough for what you've done."

Ben sat in the exam room until a nurse entered to clean it. His partner, Jan, had returned for a few neurological and orthopedic consultations, and they needed the space. Ben was done, and he could leave for the weekend.

He went to the front office, where Sarah chatted on the phone. Ben gave her the signal that he was leaving. Sarah pointed a finger in the air, showing she wanted a word with him. He half hoped she had information to help him get through the next two days before the Australian office would open. He sat down on the chair behind Sarah as she finished her phone conversation.

Sarah turned to Ben. "We need to talk, Ben. How about we use the staff room where we can talk alone?"

Chapter 6

Nigel Crossing the Tasmin

Nigel booked a first-class ticket to Adelaide, South Australia. It was another two-hour trip by car to Kadina on the Yorke Peninsula. Most of the travel he'd made in the last few years was for work, and he only traveled first class as part of his compensation. It was one of the perks that an emeritus professor received when traveling for conferences. He paid for this one, but he had so many miles on his Air New Zealand account that he'd never returned to economy.

The attendant recognized him. "Hi, Doc. Another speaking gig, or is it your old rock and roll band reunion? What can I get you? The usual?"

If Craig hadn't had his name tag on, Nigel wouldn't have remembered. "It's a little early in the morning, Craig. How about some tea and maybe a scone if they're fresh?"

"If they're fresh? Doc, I'm wounded." Craig held his fist to his chest. "Scones coming up." He turned to his colleague. "Lucinda, do we still have the scones from last week?"

He turned and winked at Nigel. "We aim to please. Now fasten your seatbelts and get ready to rumble. The trip may be rough."

It was. The flight across the Tasmin Sea from Auckland to Adelaide was unpredictable. The seatbelt signs never went off, and the woman sitting next to Nigel gripped her armrest for the entire trip. Nigel tried to talk to her, but she didn't look his way or respond. He was glad to walk off the plane and head to the car rental. He was headed to the Yorke Peninsula to meet his granddaughter.

Nigel spoke to Fiona Harding several times before booking his flight. While she wouldn't discuss details until they were face-to-face, she said the child was six and appeared to be well cared for and highly intelligent. He thought about the last time he saw his daughter. Was she still alive?

Nigel arrived at the Department for Child Protection in downtown Kadina. Theresa Barber and Fiona Harding were waiting for him.

"We're so sorry for your loss. Did you know your son-in-law?" Fiona was tall and probably in her mid-to-late fifties. She had gray hair, but her face was smooth. "Can we offer you tea or coffee?"

Nigel considered her offer but wanted to get straight to the point. "I want to meet my granddaughter. I'm not even sure she's mine. I've had no contact with my daughter for several years, and this is all a shock to me. Can I meet the little girl today? Is she all right? Was she in the accident?"

Theresa Barber appeared to be younger than Fiona, but it might have been her dyed brown hair. The gray roots showed. She was not as tall as Fiona but had an athletic build. "Dr. Buckby, your granddaughter has injured her arm and has stitches, but otherwise, she's fine. We don't want to upset her, and we'd like to get some confirmation to verify that you're indeed her relative. As you can imagine, the case is complicated, and our primary aim is to ensure the child's safety."

"I've brought a picture of my daughter, which was taken when she was in school, and the last photo we had of her. I brought hair samples so we could check DNA. I have Isla's birth certificate. What else would you need?"

Nigel handed the pictures to the women, who stared at the images and nodded. "I think that's probably all we need. Your granddaughter has a strikingly similar profile to her mother. The DNA might be important, but at this stage, I think we can say you're Maddison's maternal grandfather." Fiona saw similarities in Dr. Buckby. He was tall and had reddish-blond hair that was mostly gray. He had a bald spot, and his hair receded above the temples. Dr. Buckby appeared fit but had a slight paunch typical of older men. He spoke with a British Cockney accent in contrast to his status as a university professor.

"Maddison's staying with a local family. Their son is in her class, and she asked to stay with them. They were able to accommodate both her and her dog."

"May I go see her?"

"No, not tonight. We've arranged a visit for you tomorrow morning. Fiona will bring her to you, and you can meet her at the rental house we secured for you. The child appears to show little emotion, but we are sure she's grieving."

Theresa interjected. "We've located Maddison's other grandfather. Since it's Friday, we may not be able to speak to him until Monday. It seems he's a veterinarian from South Carolina. I'm sure you understand we can't give you custody before we've made all the inquiries, including possibly finding your daughter if she's still alive."

Nigel's heart jumped at the thought. "Do you think there's a chance that Isla is still alive?" Nigel did not expect to take on a six-year-old at his stage of life. *Damn Isla would do that as her final "screw-you" to her mother and me.* Nigel was all over the map. He desperately wanted grandchildren, but he couldn't imagine being the primary caregiver.

"We can find no record indicating she's dead. We found an arrest warrant issued four years ago for petty theft, but she was never found. After seeing your photograph, it would seem she would be easily found if she were alive. She's quite the looker."

"Our daughter was a gifted athlete and at the top of her class until her last year in school." Nigel shook his head, remembering the unstoppable downward spiral he and his wife had witnessed. "Do you know anything about the other grandfather? What was Maddison's father like?"

"We can't share any details about Dr. Taylor. We know nothing, really. As far as Daniel Taylor is concerned, we understand he kept to himself and worked menial labor jobs. Maddison was not abused as far as we can tell, but she was left alone in the caravan park when Mr. Taylor worked at the local pub. It seems she would lock herself in the cabin with her dog until her father returned after midnight. She appears to be quite used to this lifestyle and exhibits no emotional problems. In fact, she may lack the emotions you would expect in a six-year-old and may be on the spectrum, if you know what I mean."

"Asperger's or autism?" Nigel could see this playing out. Will I be saddled with another disturbed child who will make my final years hell? His thoughts and emotions bounced from elation to desperation.

"I'm not sure, but probably not either. She's in shock and maybe in denial. She wants to go back to the cattle station she left last year. She keeps talking about the Donovans, who managed the station. We haven't been able to find them yet."

Nigel was directed to the residence where he would stay until everything was finalized. The house Nigel had rented was arranged by Fiona Harding. She knew the owners, and it was on the beach and would allow a dog on the patio, but not in the house. The rent was high, but it had a view of the beach, and Nigel loved the idea of living near the beach. He'll see his granddaughter tomorrow. He could hardly wait. He drove to the town of Wallaroo and bought provisions.

Chapter 7

Family Ties

"Will I see my father's father or my mother's father on Saturday?" Maddison hid her grief. Her concern was for her future and her dog. She'd repeatedly asked to speak to Mrs. Donovan, but the people in charge said they couldn't find a station where a Mrs. Donovan worked.

"She doesn't work there. She owns it. Mr. Donovan runs sheep and cattle. My father and Tag worked for them. We moved here so I could go to a proper school. I know they'll take me in if they know my daddy's dead." *These people are as dense as custard.* "Google them!" *That is what Mrs. Donovan would say.* Maddison wasn't sure how to do that but she knew Google could answer most questions.

"We have, and we can't seem to locate them. I'm sorry, Maddy."

"My name is Maddison—Maddison Monroe."

"Maddison, I'm sorry for your loss and for all the mix-ups, but I think you know your real name is Taylor. Do you want to tell me why you're called Monroe?"

"I don't know." But she did. She and her father were hiding from her mother.

"It doesn't make any difference now. So, why don't we call you by your proper name?"

"Okay?" But it wasn't okay. As much as Maddison wanted to find and meet her mother, she knew her mother was dangerous. Her father told her that, if she came back, she might want to take Maddison from her father. Well, was that so bad now?

"Did your father ever talk to you about his parents or maybe your mother's parents?"

"No." Maddison stood up and walked behind the desk. She peered at the computer screen. "My father said my grandparents were all dead." Maddison suspected this wasn't true, but she never questioned her father. She knew the subject upset him. "Do I have a family? Do I have any cousins? I know my father is a Yank and my mother is a Kiwi." Maddison had wished for cousins. She'd met the Donovans' grandchildren and would have loved to be in their family.

Fiona Harding took Maddison and lifted her onto her lap. She was sure Maddison couldn't read the words on the screen. She was wrong. She leaned forward and read two names. Dr. Nigel Buckby and Dr. Benjamin Taylor.

"Do I have a grandmother, or an aunt, or any cousins?"

Chapter 8

News About Daniel

"It's not good, is it?" Ben sat at the staff table where they'd had pizza an hour ago. He could feel his heart rate rise. His blood pressure was checked at his last doctor's visit, and so far, he had escaped any issues with that aspect of his health.

"Ben, God, I hate to tell you this. I'm sorry, but it looks like your son was killed in a car accident. You may have a granddaughter who's orphaned. I don't see anything about the child's mother in the newspaper article. That's all I know."

Ben had expected this news for years. It didn't lessen the shock. His eyes brimmed, and he turned away. He didn't reply.

"Ben, I'm so sorry. I found a number for the police in the town where it happened. I attempted to call but was diverted to the central police office for the state. They wouldn't release any information to me, but they said they would speak to you. I couldn't find anything out about the girl, other than she's six years old and her name is Maddison Taylor." Sarah was heartbroken and hated delivering the news.

"They said she's in foster care. Ben, I think you can call, and they'll give you more information than they would give me. The town is Kadina, in South Australia. I looked it up on a map, and it looks like the nearest airport is in Adelaide, South Australia. It happened a few weeks ago. Maybe they've found her mother, or she's with her mother's family. I can dial it for you if you like."

Ben didn't reply. Sarah set down the notes she had collected and printed a copy of the news article and left the room. She stood outside the door for a moment. She thought she heard a sob, so she remained at the door so no one would disturb her boss.

Ben sat down and stared at the news article. It showed a car that had flipped on its side and was leaning against a tree. Was the child also injured in the accident? He regained some composure and then stared at the phone number. He opened his phone and Googled the time in South Australia. It was now eight-thirty in the morning. This was strange. Ben had never heard of a place that was not at least on the hour and not the half hour.

He took a deep breath to compose himself and dialed the number for the police station in the town where the accident occurred. The phone rang for several seconds—or was it hours? Finally, a woman with a heavy Australian accent answered. She explained she was at the central office in Adelaide, and they answered the phones at night and during the weekends.

Ben prayed she could direct him to someone who could help him. The prayer went unanswered. Constable Jacobs took his information and phone number but said she would only be able to transfer it on Monday when regular office hours recommenced.

"You don't seem to understand. There may be an orphaned child involved. I received a letter from the Department for Child Protection, and it seems my son was killed in an accident, and he has or had a daughter. The office is searching for me. I want to get in touch with the people caring for a child who may be my granddaughter. Can you understand the urgency?" Ben continually wiped tears from his eyes as he spoke. His voice was stilted as he tried not to cry.

"Yes, sir. I have no way of contacting any of these people until Monday. I'm truly sorry, and I understand your frustration. I can leave messages, but that's all I can do."

Ben gave her his mobile, office, home number, and email address. He sat down and stared at the news article once again. He dialed the private investigator he had used many years ago, but a transport company now owned the phone number. He wiped his face with a paper towel and went to the front office. He thanked Sarah and explained he was going home to wait for more information.

"Want me to book a flight to Adelaide?" Through the years, Sarah had handled most of Ben's travel plans. "Is your passport up to date?"

"Yeah, I renewed it a few months ago. I think I'll wait until I know what's happening, but thanks."

"Marcel and I are having a quiet weekend if you want to come for dinner tomorrow." Sarah had invited Ben to dinner many times since Tania had died, but Ben rarely accepted. She knew he would refuse, but she hated the thought of him sitting alone at a time like this.

"Thanks. I should stay close to my home phone just in case."

"See you Monday?" Sarah thought it was unlikely.

"Sure. Only a few weeks to go. I wouldn't miss it for anything." They both knew he was lying. Ben patted Sarah's arm. "Thanks. It's just..." But he couldn't finish his thought. Even before this new revelation, Ben was ready to leave and never return. He was counting down the hours. Ben went to the store to get a pre-made deli dish for dinner. He would only have to heat the lasagna and add salad from the prepackage packet. He watched television and read himself to sleep. Ben would have a long, fitful night. It would be a prolonged forty-eight hours waiting for someone to call him.

Ben thought of this poor child sleeping in a strange bed and crying for her mother and father. He opened his laptop and searched for flights to Australia. Since the pandemic, flying overseas hasn't been easy. The market was opening, and the restrictions for flying were being lifted, but because of the backlog, there was a high demand, and the next available flight was not for two days. No matter when he booked, there were no next-day flights to Australia.

Ben and Tania had gone to Australia several decades ago. They'd received information about their son and went there to seek any evidence that he was nearby. They knew their son would shun the typical tourist destinations. The report was sketchy at best, but the source, a backpacker, had provided a picture and claimed to have worked with Daniel during a grape harvest.

In a moment of inspiration, Ben searched for veterinarians working in South Australia. He found several, but the one who stood out appeared to be an American horse veterinarian who owned a clinic north of Adelaide. Ben Googled her and her clinic and discovered she'd been in South Australia for twenty years and had her practice for at least fifteen of the years. He found the clinic was based fifteen miles from where the accident occurred.

Ben checked the time. It was eight in the morning in South Australia. He dialed the number, and immediately a woman answered. "Copper Coast Animal Hospital." There was a pause, and Ben suspected the person answering realized this was an overseas call.

"I'm trying to reach Dr. Lindy Smart. Is she available for a quick chat? I'm just after some information. I don't need professional help. I'm a vet too, and I'm calling from the US." He paused and gripped the phone, hoping to cross the first barrier.

Dr. Lindy Smart was accustomed to early morning calls. As the only horse vet in the area, she was called day and night. She took the good with the bad. It was lucrative, and her life was full of adventure. In her mind, there was no bad.

Her children disagreed, but they were launched and were following their own dreams.

Lindy's life had taken a significant detour when she met Jamie thirty years ago at a veterinary conference. Four years later, with a son and a second on the way, Lindy found herself in a rural Australian town without the support of her family and friends. She hardly thought about it. She was deliriously happy. She and Jamie owned the Copper Coast Animal Hospital. They served the Yorke Peninsula and coastal area west of the Adelaide Plains.

Jamie's diagnosis of pancreatic cancer three years ago burst the bubble. He didn't even make it to the predicted three-month survival period. One month later, Jamie was dead. The children had planned to come in two weeks for his birthday, but they didn't arrive in time to say goodbye. Life was not fair.

Lindy spent the last few years grieving and depressed. She, or her office manager, Sandy, hired a succession of veterinarians to work in the clinic while Lindy attempted to pull herself together, but no one stayed for long. Veterinary medicine in a rural town with no other vets to share the load was a tough gig.

Lindy described her career as a frog in a pot of cold water where the heat was increased incrementally, and the frog just didn't notice. Jamie and Lindy were each other's support. In a role reversal that was becoming more frequent in modern times, Jamie was the small animal vet, while Lindy cared for the large animals. They each spelled one another, and once a year, they closed the clinic down and took the kids to the States to see Lindy's parents and take them to Disneyland.

Lindy's parents died, and the boys grew up and moved to the States. After Jamie died, Lindy buried her grief in work. She finally found a local kid who'd finished veterinary school and wanted to come home. Gary Hancock, or Gaz, was cut from the old school. He would take over the practice. He loved the people and the area, and he loved veterinary medicine. His parents were the local GPs. They maintained their family practice in Kadina.

Lindy didn't back off, but she concentrated on the horses and left the cows, sheep, and small animals to Gaz. Her after-hours calls decreased when they set up an answering system. which directed everything except the horses to her associate. Lindy knew when the phone rang early in the morning that it would be a client with a horse in distress. Her clients were trained; especially after Jamie died—no one would call at night without a genuine need.

The phone rang once and then again. She realized it was her private phone, and the call was from America. It might be about her children. She heard the man explain he was a vet and wanted verification that he was talking to another vet.

"That's me. Do you realize what time it is? Where're you calling from?"

"Isn't it eight in the morning? My name is Ben Taylor. I live in South Carolina, and it will only take a second. If it's a bad time, I can call back."

"It's five in the morning. Go ahead. How can I help?" She should have been annoyed, but with South Australia on a half-hour difference from Sydney and with the difference in daylight savings, this vet was not the first to get the time zone wrong.

"Oh geez. I must have mistaken the time zone. I'll call back. I'm so sorry, Dr. Smart."

"Lindy, and sadly, I'm awake. Go ahead." Lindy sighed.

Ben gripped his phone. "I'm sorry if I woke you. I'm trying to reach the authorities about a potential family member. My son was killed in an automobile accident, and I've been told he has a daughter. I think she may be very young. Are you sure this is a good time?"

Lindy immediately knew who this vet was referring to. There was a sign on the highway leading from the town of Port Wakefield to the coast and the Yorke Peninsula showing the number of days since the last fatality. Lindy knew the last fatality was twenty-five days ago, and the deceased was a single father who left an orphaned daughter. The child was placed in a home near Port Hughes until a family member could be found.

Lindy knew the family and had met the child when she attended a sick pony owned by the family who fostered the little girl. Her heart sank when she realized this man must be the grandfather. She understood how painful this must be for him.

"Dr. Taylor, I know about your son and his daughter. I think some relatives may have been found. Maybe it was the mother or a relative of the mother. I'm not sure, but I know the little girl is in a good temporary home."

"So, the girl exists, and do you know her? How old is she? Was she involved in the accident? Did you know my son?

I'm sorry to ask so many questions, but our son, Daniel, fled from our lives many years ago, and we've tried to find him over the years. My wife died, never knowing he was alive." The tears ran down Ben's cheeks as he wiped them with a towel. He felt a hard knot in his throat and could no longer speak.

"Dr. Taylor, her name is Maddison Monroe. Maybe he isn't your son who died? The girl is six years old, but she may have a birthday coming up. Her father was killed instantly when he went off the road, and the car rolled. Maddison wasn't wearing a seatbelt, and she was thrown clear. She injured her arm, and that was addressed. She's staying with a family friend, but it was only until they could find a relative. I don't know where the mother is, but I think they found a grandfather. He's from New Zealand. He came over here, and he's staying in a rental property at a place called North Beach. I don't know his name."

Ben took notes as he listened to the story. "Is there anything else you know?"

"I know Maddison is under the care of the Department for Child Protection. My girlfriend works there, which is all I feel comfortable telling you at this stage. I can ask her if she'll talk to you today. You know we're ahead of you, and today is Sunday here." Lindy sat up and took her phone off the charger and headed to the kitchen to start some coffee.

Ben cleared his throat. "I can give you my number and email address if it's easier. If I could confirm this is even my son, I would be grateful. My son had several problems, and we've not heard from him in years. We weren't even sure he was alive. Did he use the name Monroe for himself as well?"

"I think so. I met him a few times, and if you send me the most recent photo you have of your son, I could probably identify him. I'll call my friend. It may not be her case. I think email is best for now."

Ben and Lindy exchanged email addresses, and Ben hung up. He quickly emailed the vet with his son's picture and waited for a reply. He fell asleep in his old recliner.

There was an email from Lindy the following morning, which confirmed it was probably his son who was killed. He'd changed his last name to Monroe, but a former employer said it was Taylor. She sent a second email that gave her friend's personal number and said to call her anytime. "So sorry for your loss." Such a trite and inadequate response. How many times had Lindy heard that phrase?

He dialed the number and was surprised to have the call answered in one ring. "Dr. Taylor?"

"Yes, it's me." Ben knew the phone number would have alerted the woman.

"I'm Teresa Barber. My friends call me Terri. I'm not in charge of your granddaughter, but the caseworker is under me, so I'm aware of the situation."

"Oh, thank you. So, what can you tell me? I guess you know this is all a shock and new to me."

"Dr. Taylor, what we know about Maddison is kind of sketchy. We found her maternal grandfather, and he's over here and staying nearby so he can hopefully take her back to New Zealand. Maddison's mother hasn't been found, and she's sought no help from the government for years unless she's under an assumed name. We're unable to trace her.

There're several people looking for her, but we suspect she's moved to another country or, I'm sad to say, is deceased.

"From what we can find, your son was Maddison's primary caregiver since she was a few months old. We talked to the pub owner where he worked, and he thought the mother was addicted to something and was not fit to care for Maddison. He thought Mr. Monroe changed his name from Taylor to hide from her and to care for the child. We still don't have a birth certificate. The mother's father seems certain she's dead. If you want, I can ask him if he would be happy to talk to you?"

Ben was relieved. "Oh, that'd be wonderful. Can you tell me anything about him?"

"I won't give you any specific details yet, but he taught at the University of Auckland School of Medicine and is retired. He met Maddison, and the meeting went well. He's unsure of his ability to care for a six-year-old, and he's assessing his commitment. He's suggested someone younger might be better suited to care for the child."

"Terri, I'd like to meet the child. I'll book a flight ASAP and be there within the week. I'd like to ask you not to decide until we all can meet and discuss the situation. Can I ask you to do that?"

Terri whispered a prayer and crossed her fingers. She rarely had responsible family members involved in any of her cases. This is a dream come true. "Oh, there'll be no decisions made for several weeks. I think it will be good for all concerned if we get together to discuss the child's future. I will say she's staying with a family, and the family will leave for the Christmas school holidays next week. We'll have to find a place for Maddison to stay during that time. I know her other grandfather said he would stay and care for her, but are you willing to do the same?"

"In a heartbeat. I'll get there as soon as possible. If you can pass on my number to the child's other grandfather, I would be ever so grateful." In a heartbeat? What was he thinking?

Chapter 9

Spitting Image

Maddison was dreading the day. She would meet her grandfather for the first time. She would have rather stayed with Jarlee's family. She and Jarlee were enjoying the last few days before he and his family returned to the APY Lands to see his father. She would miss them and prayed they would return after a few weeks.

Maddison knew her father was dead. She felt a stone in her stomach and knew this stone was weighing her down. Maddison cried most nights when she was alone in her bed. She was used to sleeping without her father, but she could not have her dog Tag when she was at the first foster home.

Once she was placed with Jarlee's family, they allowed her to sleep with her dog, and her stone was lighter. The stone emanated a pulse that came and went. It expanded when she had to talk to people about her father or talk to a counselor, but it reduced in size when she and Jarlee swam in the shallow water of the ocean or when they walked into the town to get an icy pole.

She noticed people staring at her and Jarlee when they were in town. She knew two young children alone in town were an oddity. Their different ethnicity was probably also a concern. Maddison was aware of the prejudices that whites held against Aborigines, but she was taught by her father and the station owners to treat everyone as they found them.

"There are good and bad people in all 'tribes,'" was a common phrase used on the station. She took people as they came. Jarlee and his family were good. The lady who took her to a motel on the night after the crash was bad. She made Maddison shower and took away her dog.

Two days later, she was sent to stay with Jarlee, and there was Tag. It was temporary, as Jarlee's family would leave in the next week or so. The usual temporary foster parents were already full or wouldn't have a dog. She kept asking if she could remain with Jarlee or her teacher, but she was told that wasn't possible. Her teacher, Miss Osborne, visited her several times and brought her workbooks and other material until she came back to school.

Miss Osborne was so kind, and Maddison asked if she could stay with her when Jarlee's family left for the summer, but Miss Osbornewas moving away to be married and was not returning next year—another loss.

Two weeks later, Maddison dressed in her best clothes to meet her grandfather. She was told this man was her mother's father, and she didn't want him to think her father had neglected her. She wore a bright pink dress and new sandals.

Fiona Harding drove up to the old farmhouse and found Maddison sitting alone on the porch with her dog by her side. She smiled at Maddison and waved her to the car. "Are you all ready to meet your grandfather? He's excited to meet you, Maddison. He even said it was okay for you to bring your dog."

Maddison was relieved. She knew she had no choice about where she would live, but that was a good start. She and Tag jumped into the back seat, while Mrs. Harding went to the door and talked to Jarlee's mother. They didn't realize Maddison could hear the conversation. "Maddison will meet her maternal grandfather, and then I'll bring her back this afternoon. Ruth, we can't thank you enough for helping to care for the poor child."

Jarlee's mother, Ruth Yarran, nodded. "She's fine. I'm sorry we're leaving, and she can't go with us. She's no trouble, Fi." The two women had become friends when Maddison asked to stay with the family. Her only other option was traditional foster care. There were no local families who could accommodate Maddison and her dog.

"I'll have her back in a few hours. This is only a meet and greet. It won't last long. I'll have her home for evening tea for sure." Oops. Fiona knew she should not use words like "home," when discussing children in temporary or emergency housing.

Fiona Harding headed to the house where Nigel was staying. It was large and luxurious and had a view of the bay. "Maddison, do you like to be called by your Christian name or Maddy?"

"Neither ma'am. I like to be called Maddison." Maddison wondered what her Christian name was. She knew her father would get mad if anyone called her Maddy. She liked the name Maddy, but she didn't want to upset her father. "My father hates anyone calling me Maddy. It probably doesn't matter anymore." Maddison sighed and put her arm around Tag's back.

They arrived on a narrow road with mostly garages lining the road, while the house's fronts faced the cliff overlooking Wallaroo Bay. They stopped outside a large double garage with a gate alongside the garage. The gate had a bell to signal the arrival of a person entering. Maddison and Tag exited the car, and with Mrs. Harding leading the way, they went through the gate and entered a small garden area with a water fountain. Tag drank from the water that collected in a small pond.

Nigel saw his daughter through the glass door. He had to remind himself it was not his daughter. A flood of emotions washed over him. In an instant, his life and focus unexpectedly changed. *O-M-G, I've been ambushed. Tell me this isn't happening.* Nigel knew that was the moment the rest of his life would not be the same. He felt his entire being shift from himself to the child he'd just met. But was he up to it? Could he help this child, who without a doubt was his granddaughter, find a home and the love and care she deserved? He was sure it wasn't with him. He was too old. Wasn't he? He was, wasn't he? *Am I?*

Maddison saw a tall man with curly red-blond, graying hair and a wide face peering through the sliding glass door. She stared up and gave a small wave. He smiled and opened the door and extended his hand. "Hi, Maddison, or do you like to be called Maddy?"

"I like Maddy. What do you want me to call you?" Maddison wasn't sure, and no one had given her any instructions. She was used to meeting new people at the caravan park. She'd been instructed to call them mister or miss, but she knew this was different. They had grandparents' day at school. Most of her classmates called their grandfathers "Pop."

A few had called them Grandfather or Grampa. She knew to look him in the eye and shake his hand firmly. Mrs. Donovan taught her how to greet people who occasionally came to the station. She waited for a reply.

Nigel stared into the little girl's face. She was an exact duplicate of his daughter. There was no doubt she was his granddaughter. He couldn't stop staring. "What would you like to call me?" He waited and watched her consider the offer.

"I'm not sure. Are you really my grandfather? What makes you so sure? Do you have edivents?"

Nigel immediately realized this child was intelligent. He wouldn't correct her pronunciation today. "I do. Do you remember your mother?"

"No. I have a picture, but I'm not supposed to have it. My father didn't like her. I don't know why, but he didn't."

Nigel went to his briefcase, which was on the counter, and pulled out a picture and handed it to Maddison. Mrs.

Harding came up behind Maddison and saw the likeness to the child. "Your mother was beautiful. She looks so much like you, Maddy."

Maddison realized Mrs. Harding called her by the nickname and quickly corrected her. "My name is Maddison, ma'am. Only my family calls me Maddy."

Nigel turned away and excused himself. He went into the bathroom for a moment to compose himself. Fiona Harding knew the reason for his departure. Maddison looked up at her and shrugged. "Did I say the wrong thing?"

"No, darling. You said the perfect thing." Fiona was ecstatic. She rarely saw moments like this. She knew this child would not be abandoned. The rest was only a formality.

Nigel returned to the front room. "Maddy, I'll let you decide. You can call me whatever you want. Anything is all right with me. Pop, Pops, Grandpa, or anything else you would like to use. Would you like to go down to the beach and take your dog for a walk?"

"Do you have a dog, Pop?"

"I did." Nigel was reminded his ex was taking the dog. "I'm looking for a new one."

Fiona glanced at her phone. She had an urgent request and would have to cut the meeting short. She'd have to leave sooner than planned. "You can walk on the beach tomorrow. I can bring her back tomorrow if that's okay? I'm sorry to make the visit so short."

Maddison was quick to respond. "I have school, but I can miss a day. We're reviewing, and the material is really boring."

Nigel's eyebrows rose. The material? Reviewing? Who is this kid?

Fiona tried to hide her attraction to this man. "I'll call you later, and we can set a time. Maddison needs to get back to the Yarrans."

"No, I don't. I have time to walk on the beach today." Maddison crossed her arms.

"Maddy, you can come and visit again. I think we'd better do as Ms. Harding suggests. I'll be waiting for you." Nigel bent down and hugged his granddaughter.

Nigel watched Maddison wave shyly to him from the back seat of Fiona Harding's car as they drove away.

"He'll do," was Maddison's only comment when they pulled into the Yarran's long driveway.

Chapter 10

Nigel's Course Correction

Nigel walked into his bedroom and lay face down on the bed. For a moment, he sobbed. He turned over, and for the first time in a year, he talked to his deceased wife. "Bette, we have our daughter back." He went to the bathroom and wiped his face. Nigel would see his granddaughter again tomorrow. He could hardly wait. He drove back to Wallaroo and bought provisions, including treats for the dog.

He watched the sunset from the grass verge that ran between the houses along the cliff face and the natural barrier that rose from the beach up to the houses. He saw several people with dogs and children playing in the water where the waves were only a few inches.

Nigel thought about the women who would decide his fate. He prayed they had a reasonable option for the care of the child. He was too old. He couldn't imagine caring for a six-year-old at his age and stage in life. He enjoyed going fishing with his neighbor Jock and Jock's two grandchildren. He took Jock's granddaughter, and they caught a large rainbow trout. Maybe if she likes to fish, we could go fishing once a year.

He remembered her other grandfather's name. Ben Taylor was a vet in South Carolina. Maybe this guy was younger and would be able to care for the child. He opened his computer and found several messages from his ex.

Celeste was furious. She wanted a call, but it was now after ten in New Zealand. He would call her in the morning. If I can be bothered. Why had he not heeded the advice from his colleagues? A relationship, let alone marriage, was way too soon following his wife's death.

He found two Ben Taylors who were vets in South Carolina. One was too young to have grandchildren. The other didn't have much of a profile on the web. He had a clinic outside of Charleston. He appeared to be a well-respected surgeon, and bloody hell, he was a stud. He looked like a movie star. With a deeper dive, he found his date of graduation from vet school. He calculated unless he was a prodigy, Ben Taylor was older than himself. Nigel was officially jealous. Nigel was at least four years younger but looked older. Maybe this was an old picture. Why did he care? He tried to convince himself that Maddison's best interest was with a young family.

Tomorrow, he would meet the little girl once again. With any luck, she'd be so disconnected from an older man, that the agency would seek a fresh foster family. He'd help with her expenses, and he'd immediately set up a college fund, but the idea of visiting her once or twice a year was about as much as he could offer.

Nigel Buckby was watching the last light on the ocean. He knew how lucky he was to secure a first-class rental property on the cliff above North Beach. He looked out onto the beach and could still see some teenagers swimming in the shallow waters off the shoreline. He was about to pull the blinds when he heard his phone ring.

The number on the phone was an undisclosed international call. "Hello." Nigel hoped it might be the child's paternal grandfather. He knew the man had been found, and he would be calling.

"Hello." The phone call dropped out. The reception at North Beach was erratic. He waited to see if the caller would try again.

Nigel had mixed emotions. The little girl was charming, intelligent, and beautiful. Men in his family died before they reached eighty. The money wasn't the issue. He'd saved his money and planned for a secure retirement. His university pension was enough to see him live comfortably, even if he returned to the UK.

The phone rang again. "Hello? Dr. Buckby?"

"Yes, is this Dr. Taylor?"

"Ben. My friends call me Ben. I understand we may have a grandchild in common. I hear you've met the girl?"

"Nigel. Yes, I have." There was a pause while each man considered the other.

"Nigel, I realize there's an issue with the mother. Are you sure you're related?"

"No, I'm not sure, but she sure looks like my daughter. She's a beautiful and intelligent child. She takes after my side of the family."

There was a pause. Ben was already assessing the other man's intentions. "Oh, really?"

"Ben, it was a joke. I guess I shouldn't be joking about this. I'm so sorry for your loss. I use humor in difficult situations. I'm truly sorry."

Ben was taken aback by this man's attitude. Wasn't his daughter dead as well? "I guess your daughter is deceased. Is everyone sure?"

"No, but there is evidence to say she died several years ago. Are you coming over? What are your plans?" Nigel paused and hoped he was coming. He didn't know the man at all, but if there was any possibility of sharing the burden, he would be grateful. "Is your wife coming?"

Ben realized this man had no information about his side of the family. "My wife died a few years ago. How about you?"

"My first wife died, and my second is divorcing me."

"How about we discuss this when I get there? I'll catch the next possible flight. I'll let you know when I've arrived, so we can meet face-to-face. I need a place to stay. I've heard the rentals and motels are full since it's a summer destination. Have you got a source for rentals?"

"Ben, just get here and you can stay with me until you can find something. I'm hoping we can sort this out quickly."

"Yes, I agree." Ben liked the sound of his accent. It was British but somehow different. He'd heard this accent before, maybe in a movie?

"I have your email. I'll send you one tomorrow when I can, and then you can let me know about your flight details." Ben felt relief. At least he didn't blow me off.

Nigel ended the call. He was eager to see the little girl again before Ben arrived. He wanted to establish himself as the preferred relative. Maddison was so much like her mother. *What the hell am I thinking?*

Chapter II

Road Sign

Ben entered the kiosk where the rental cars were held at Adelaide Airport. He chose an SUV. He knew the little girl had a dog, and he didn't want to pay for any damage the dog might do to the car. He'd been told the dog was an Australian kelpie. He'd met a few over the years and suspected the dog was obedient.

When his last dog died, he hadn't replaced him. He occasionally babysat the neighbors' dog, but he knew he wanted to travel. Ben thought he would get the travel bug out, and then he would return to find what he thought would be his last dog.

He promised his wife he would not sell the house in the remote chance their son returned. He now considered the option to downsize. If it was true and his son was dead, Ben had no constraints on where he lived in the future. He knew he wouldn't be caring for the little girl. He was sure the mother's family would take her. The authorities would choose New Zealand over the States.

This was not the first time Ben had driven on the left side of the road, but it still made him nervous. Ben calculated it would take two hours to drive from the airport to Kadina on the Yorke Peninsula. Nigel Buckby had invited Ben to stay with him. Ben initially considered a motel, but when he attempted to find accommodation, he realized the influx of holiday tourists made the stay with a stranger more tempting, and he accepted the offer.

He would arrive in Kadina and had an appointment with Fiona Harding just before noon. He would be introduced to Nigel, and the two of them could talk and discuss the child before he was granted access to his granddaughter.

The drive up to the Yorke Peninsula was not inspiring. The city gave way to dry cropland, with little that would suggest modern times. The crops, which might be wheat, had been harvested, but much of the land looked like it couldn't support any stock. He saw a rare flock of sheep, but the feed was sparse and desolate. There were only a few small rural towns, and they reminded him of the Oklahoma 1930 pictures his family had collected. He wondered why anyone would want to live here. The pastures were interrupted by a large "crop" of solar panels, but then the road became an elevated windy path toward the west and God knew what kind of sea town. Please let this be quick.

Shortly after turning off Port Wakefield highway, Ben saw a digital sign displaying the days since the last fatality on the Yorke Peninsula. He shuddered, knowing his son was day zero. It was depressing to think his son lived here.

Ben passed several small towns, which comprised only a few structures along the main road leading toward the coast. Signs for Kadina appeared. Ben's phone GPS directed him to a small office with a placard that read Department for Child Protection. There was no one at the front desk. He waited for several minutes and finally yelled down the hallway until a woman emerged eating a sandwich.

"Hi, I'm looking for Fiona Harding?" He was sure this woman was not who he was searching for. She was tall and thin, with straight graying hair, and appeared to be in her late fifties. *Definitely a nine on the ten scale.*

"Dr. Taylor?"

"Ben, am I too early?"

"Nope. Never, when it comes to the needs of a child. Come in and sit down."

She set her sandwich back under her desk and pulled out the file she had prepared. "Let me call Dr. Buckby and see if he's close by."

As she reached for the landline phone, a man walked in, and Ben immediately recognized the man from his university homepage photo.

"Ben? I'm your better half, Nigel Buckby." Both Ben and Fiona laughed at Nigel's introduction. Nigel shook Ben's hand.

Ben thought Nigel's voice was familiar. He'd heard the accent before. He tried to remember. It was from a movie. It didn't sound like a New Zealand or Australian accent. He knew the man was educated, but his accent wasn't as cultured as he'd expected. *Cockney? Who does he sound like?*

Fiona stopped and looked at each man now seated across from her desk. She knew they had both realized their one and only child was dead—in Ben's case and probably dead in Nigel's case—and both recently found out they had a granddaughter who was orphaned. Would either of these men step up and accept responsibility? Would they both want custody of the child? Or would neither of them want to be saddled with a young, precocious child?

"So, I feel at some stage we need to discuss what either of you is or isn't willing to do before we go much further. I promised Maddison that she would meet her other grandfather today. Ben, you've come from a long plane ride. Would you like to rest first? I'm willing to let you rest and maybe have a bite to eat, but I thought it would be good for you to meet her alone at first. It was your son who died, and in all this, we need to be mindful of the loss you and Maddison are experiencing. Is there any question that this was your son?"

"I brought my son's birth certificate and the last picture I had of him, but it's been a long time. I was sent a copy of his driver's license, and it looked like him, and there was a scar that seemed to help make the identification. I wish I were wrong."

"So, what I propose is to bring her into town, and you can meet here." Fiona tapped her pen on the desk.

Nigel sat forward. "Why don't I take Ben out to where we'll stay? I need to run some errands, so Ben can meet Maddy alone at the beach house. She and the dog are comfortable there."

Ben was relieved. He knew Nigel was looking at the same prospect he was considering, and he seemed to be a nice guy, and he hoped they could come to some agreement about the care of the child. Yet, he still wondered why Nigel's daughter left her parents. He grimaced inwardly and wondered if Nigel was thinking the same thing about him.

Ben followed Nigel to the parking lot. Nigel gave him the address but said he would go slow so Ben could follow him to the house. He said he'd bought enough food and grog, and unless Ben needed something special, he was sure they could go straight to North Beach. Nigel laughed as he observed Ben go to the passenger side of his rental SUV. He pointed to the other side and observed Ben shrug.

As they left the town of Kadina, the terrain gave way to an area that was dry with a salt-lake. It wasn't inspiring, but they turned toward a cluster of modern one and two-story houses facing the ocean. They drove down the street that was closest to the ocean. Ben hoped they had a view of the ocean and was relieved when Nigel pulled into a beachfront house.

The two-story house sat in a line of houses that perched on a cliff face with the street entry at the back. The living room faced the bay, which featured a pristine beach if you ignored the seaweed that abutted the dunes and cliff. The garage could accommodate two cars and so each man parked in the garage, and Nigel helped Ben with his suitcase and his carry-on from the plane trip.

It was now past lunchtime, and Nigel offered to make a quick sandwich and then leave. He asked if Fiona could call him when it was time to return. Nigel was going crabbing.

It was the wrong time of day, but he thought it would be a pleasant way to pass the time. He planned to go to the Wallaroo jetty. He would fish, set his crab nets, and eat some ice cream from the local kiosk.

"Ben, she's an exceptional kid. She'll have you wrapped around her finger in seconds. I resisted for at least eight seconds. Let's see how you do." Nigel cocked his head. This reminded Ben of an actor. He just couldn't remember which. It wasn't Sean Connery.

Ben moved his belongings into one of four bedrooms. His room was on the second floor and had a small balcony that looked over the ocean and beach below the cliff. Ben could get used to this. "You said she looks like your daughter?"

"Spitting image." Ben could see the pleasure Nigel exuded when remembering his daughter's beauty.

"Forewarned is forearmed, buddy, or do you say mate on the Island of the Long White Cloud?" Ben studied Nigel. They were of a similar age and disposition. They had both lost a wife. Ben didn't know or remember Nigel had remarried and that his marriage was ending. He was caught up in the shock of hearing his only child was dead, and he was a grandfather. There was no wedding ring. Ben didn't notice the pale circle on Nigel's ring finger, which showed a recent ring. Maddison had. She pointed it out to Fiona when they were driving home from the first encounter.

Fiona explained Nigel was in the process of divorcing his second wife. "Maddison, you're a very observant girl."

Maddison hadn't responded. She said nothing about the other things she noticed. She could see the attraction Miss

Harding had for Nigel. Nor did she mention Nigel was wary of Tag. She didn't mention she saw Nigel stare at her and knew he was not seeing his granddaughter. He saw his daughter. She didn't mention she knew he didn't want to care for her. She could see his reservations about any commitment.

Ben was tired, and he quickly showered and shaved after Nigel departed for the jetty. Fiona and Maddison arrived soon after. He heard the knocking at the back door. Fiona Harding stood holding the hand of a beautiful, thin child with perfect features. Nigel was correct. She was the embodiment of Nigel's own daughter.

Ben opened the door and welcomed them. "Hi, Maddison. I'm your other grandfather. I've flown from America to see you. I was your father's father. I'm so glad to meet you, darling."

Maddison extended her hand. "Pleased to meet you, sir. What am I supposed to call you? I call my other grandfather Pop. What would you prefer?"

"What would you like to call me?" Ben had not considered this.

"What do most American children call their grandfathers?" Maddison had a strong Australian accent, that despite growing up on a station, sounded cultured. Ben found it endearing.

"I guess there're many names, but one of the common names is grandpa." *Five seconds and she has me.*

"Okay, Grandpa. Thank you for coming all this way. I looked at a map and saw how far it was. How many grandchildren do you have?"

"Maddison, you're the one and only. Your father was my only child." *O-M-G, is this an adult in a child's body?*

Maddison could see him shiver. "He was my only father, sir. I know how you feel. I'm sorry for your loss. By the way, you can call me Maddy. This is Tag. He's a kelpie. Have you ever seen a kelpie?"

"Yes, I have, Maddy." Ben reached down and rubbed Tag behind the ears. "He's a beautiful dog. Did you know I'm a vet?"

Maddison was surprised. She had asked about her other grandfather. Mrs. Harding hadn't mentioned this. She turned and gave Fiona a look of disappointment. "What else should I know?"

Fiona let Maddison's hand go and walked into the living room, where she gazed out the window and into the ocean below the cliff. The day was hot, and there was no wind. Several children played in the water. "Maddison, how about I sit out on the porch, so you and your grandfather can get acquainted?"

Ben smiled and asked the little girl if she was hungry. "Your other grandfather left some cookies for us." Ben went to the cupboard.

"They're called biscuits over here, Grandpa. My father told me the Yanks have different names for things. I'll help you so you don't look uneducated." Maddison stared up at him with disdain.

"Okay, that will be a help." *This kid is so like her father. Déjà vu all over again.*

"What kind of vet are you? Do you know Dr. Smart? She's a horse vet, but she can do dogs too. She helped my friend Jarlee with his kitten. It was snake-bit. That's something you should know about. Snakes are dangerous here. They have three toxins. One for the blood, one for the nervous system, and one for the muscles. I guess you know the heart is a muscle?"

"I do. How did the cat go, Maddy?" Ben reached for a Tim Tam. Damn, these are delicious.

"Oh, it lived. Cats aren't as skeptable as dogs."

Ben laughed to himself at the mispronunciation of the word susceptible. "I'll keep it in mind." He desperately wanted to talk to the little girl about her father, but now was not the time.

"So how old is Tag?" Ben rubbed behind the dog's ears and realized he missed his old dog had been fifteen years old when he died. When Ben stopped for a moment, the dog nudged him, begging for more.

"Tag's four and three quarters. His birthday is in March, but I don't know what day. He and I celebrate our birthdays together. At the station, Mrs. Donovan made a cake for me. It had five candles and three for Tag. It was lemon. What's your favorite cake, Grandpa?"

Hearing the name "grandpa" made his heart jump. He was falling under this child's spell, and he would drown if it didn't stop. "I like any cake within reach. Is Tag a working dog or a pet?"

"Mostly working. Daddy turned down twenty-two thousand dollars for him. He earned a wage at our station. He almost made more than my father."

Ben found a spot near Tag's ear that made the dog extend his head and scratch his belly with pleasure. This was not lost on Maddison. She observed Tag's reaction to this man.

Ben had so many questions. "Why did your father leave the station?"

"My father wanted me to be a vet. He said it was in my jeans." Maddison gazed down at her pants. "My jeans are too small now, and I borrowed these from Jarlee. He's my friend from school. I'm not supposed to tell you I'm living with Jarlee's family, but they are going back to the APY Lands next week. I have to go to a new home, then, unless you or Pop get permission to keep me."

"Well, hopefully, we can work something out. What are the APY Lands?"

"They are far away. Have you met any Aboriginals? Some people don't like them, but Jarlee is my best friend. He'll be back when school starts. His mother is very kind to me. If I could live with them for the rest of my life, I would choose them. You might as well know it. I'm sorry, but I love them. Someday I might love you too, but for now, you and Pop are just nice, old men."

"Maddy, I can appreciate what you're saying. I, and I'm sure your other grandfather, hope to earn your trust and maybe even your love. We're going to make sure you have the best life you can. I'll make sure if you want to be a veterinarian that you are given every opportunity to become one. It's a rewarding profession. I love my job. Well, I did. I just retired."

"Okay, Grandpa. But what if I wanted to stay with Jarlee's family? Would that be okay?"

"What do Jarlee's parents say?" Ben studied the child's face.

Maddison looked down and didn't reply. Ben had his answer.

"Let's wait and see what we all decide. How about if we can include you in the decision? I promise we won't ask you to choose, but we'll listen to you. Would that be fair?"

Maddison nodded. "Tag comes with me. That's 'no ngotiable.'"

Ben nodded. He would not correct her mispronunciations, which he found charming, but he knew she wanted to sound educated. No doubt, this kid was wise beyond her years.

"Maddy, you know there are words that sound the same and are spelled differently?"

"Like what?" She looked at Ben and cocked her head.

Ben thought about something simple. She probably had a rudimentary idea of spelling. "Maddy, do you know how to spell sail?"

"Do you mean the selling sale or the boat sail?"

O-M-G, this kid is incredible. "Never mind. Anyway, they're called homophones, and the word jeans is one. The pants you wear are spelled j-e-a-n-s. Then there is one g-e-n-e-s. It sounds the same, but it's about your DNA and inheritance. You have inherited your mother's good looks. Now, I would like to think your desire to be a vet may have come from your father's side of our family. Do you understand?" Ben hoped the "our family" reference caught her attention.

"Mrs. Donovan says there are two things that determine who you are. Your DNA stands for deoxyribonucleic acid. But the other is nurture. It's how you are raised. My dad always said he was so proud his dad was a vet. Maybe I got it from both."

"Excuse me for a minute." Ben went into the bathroom and wiped his eyes. *I'll kill anyone who tries to take this kid from me.*

Chapter 12

Ten Seconds

It was close to five, and Fiona had to return Maddison to the Yarrans' farmhouse. She entered the room where she saw Ben and Maddison sitting together looking through a photograph album that he must have brought.

"Time to go, Maddison. I called your pop, and he's on his way back. Maddison, you're heading back to the Yarrans."

Ben wanted to continue showing family pictures to his granddaughter, but he was jet-lagged and understood the little girl needed to get to her foster home and be fed. He wanted to know when they could meet again, but he didn't want to discuss anything in front of the child for fear it would upset her.

Fiona, Maddison, and Tag left as Nigel was returning. Ben could see they were having a brief discussion as their cars passed on the road. He waited for Nigel to park the car.

"I win. It was easily ten seconds. Want to arm wrestle for her?"

"Bullshit." Nigel smiled and nodded. "I was a weightlifter and played cricket in high school."

"Never mind." Ben held up his palms. "I guess this will be difficult."

"I asked to meet Fiona for dinner after she drops Maddy off at her temporary foster home." Nigel went to the fridge and took out two beers. He glanced at Ben and saw him smile.

"No fair. Are you trying to ply Ms. Harding with your charm?" Ben took the beer and examined the label. The worst beer in the world would be acceptable after today. It wasn't bad.

"She turned me down. She's meeting the local vet for dinner. How about we head to the pub and get a quick bite, and then you can get to bed early? I know you older guys need your sleep."

"Yes, I crave some sleep. This beer isn't helping. Let's go." Ben set his beer down and they headed to Nigel's car. They entered a pub on what appeared to be the main street of Wallaroo. They sat at a booth and, while reading the menu, realized Fiona and her dinner companion had also entered the pub.

Fiona saw Nigel and Ben and quietly turned to the other woman. Nigel waved as the women conferred. "Small world. Can we join you?" Fiona stared at Nigel, who stood and greeted the two women.

"By all means, ladies." He moved over to Ben's side of the booth.

Ben and Nigel were introduced to Dr. Lindy Smart. She was tall, with long graying-brown hair, pulled back in a ponytail. She appeared to be in her late fifties, which fit her bio on the clinic's website.

"Ah, the man who woke me from my sleep last week. I believe you're a vet as well?"

"Retired as of four days ago." Ben could see her face had a tinge of grief. She smiled, but he could see it was forced. Ben knew her pain. At least his wife hit her sixties when she died. He thought Lindy's husband was in his late fifties when he passed.

They ordered their food, and Nigel asked Fiona about how she had arrived on the YP, as the locals referred to the Yorke Peninsula. As their drinks arrived, Fiona said her decision was a combination of a love for rural life with a need to flee a relationship that would not proceed. "I was given several destinations, and I guess this was the lesser evil."

Lindy laughed. "The YP isn't for everyone. I thought I would die when I arrived. I was a California girl. It grows on you—kind of like a fungus. I had a husband who kept me here for years, and now I have my clients, friends, and lifestyle. My children left and moved to the States. I'll finish up here, and then who knows where I'll go?"

Nigel was keen to continue the conversation after dinner, but he could see Ben was fading. "I guess we should get the old man home."

Fiona pointed to Nigel. "Remember, I have both of your bios, and I know your age, Dr. Buckby. Despite my reticence in discussing work, when would you like to see Maddison again?"

Both men simultaneously said, "Tomorrow."

"I'll call you in the morning." Nigel and Ben left the pub.

They stopped and paid for the women's dinners. Nigel grinned. "Damn, I hope our generosity in paying for dinner will sway Fiona to let us have her."

"She seems to be a straight shooter with her work. I'll bet she's been burned before." Ben was beyond tired, and he was grateful the dinner didn't last too long. Both women were single and attractive, but he wasn't looking.

The men returned to the beach house, where the last orange light from the setting sun was making the shadows blue against the white walls of the house. Nigel said he would take a walk down to the beach. Ben declined, and when Nigel returned, Nigel could hear the rhythmic, light snoring of his housemate. He eventually retired and read reproductive journals until he crashed. He hardly knew Ben, but Nigel felt he was going to be a stand-up-guy. He could tolerate him in the short-term. Time would tell.

Chapter 13

From the Ashes

Nigel awoke to the smell of bacon and coffee. Nigel drank tea, but he would occasionally go to the "dark side," as he called it. He greeted Ben, who was in shorts and a tee shirt. "You're up early."

"And I already walked on the beach. You scored a great place, Nige."

Nigel smiled. His deceased wife and one other good friend from his university days called him "Nige."

"It's only for the summer. I think things should be sorted by then, and Maddy and I will head back to New Zealand." Nigel knew he was testing the waters.

"Maybe. Do we know if Maddy has citizenship anywhere besides Australia?"

"No. The agency is trying to find more info. I submitted a DNA sample, and they're checking to make sure I'm related. I guess they'll do it with you as well. I gave them some hair from a brush I saved. Did you bring anything to confirm your relationship?"

"Other than his picture, no. I didn't know it was in doubt." Nigel hadn't asked about Daniel Taylor's story. He'd only heard Daniel might be on the spectrum. Nigel had a few colleagues whom he suspected were mildly autistic. They were titans in research. Still, they were single-minded, and only one was married.

"Fiona said she would bring Maddy over around ten. Do you want more time alone with her?" Nigel held his breath, waiting for the answer.

Ben scooped bacon, eggs, and toast onto plates and brought them to the table. Nigel went to the kitchen and brought out a jar of Vegemite. Ben stared at the jar. "I've heard of this, but I thought it had fallen out of favor. Isn't there a chocolate spread most people use these days?"

"Nutella. That's what Maddy prefers. So, do you want some time with her again, or maybe we could take her to town? The poor kid doesn't appear to have much in the way of clothes."

"Nige, what are we allowed to do with her? Are there any limits to where we can take her?"

"So far, Fiona has suggested we keep it simple as we shouldn't form attachments that will be broken when we decide where she ends up. You know, it might not be us. If there was a young family, that might be the best for all concerned."

Ben was surprised, but he realized that two old men might not be the best choice. He wondered about the family where she was staying now. "I guess you can see she's gifted. That comes from my side of the family." Ben had to suppress a smile.

Nigel shook his head and laughed. "Let's see. You have a vet degree. Anything else? Because I have a Ph.D., and I'm an emeritus professor of reproductive biology, and I last lectured at Cambridge."

"Acknowledged, and I'm board-certified in veterinary surgery. Basically, I'm an animal Lego man. I can fix broken bones like there's no tomorrow." Ben tried a small amount of Vegemite—nope.

"So, what happened to you and your son? You don't have to tell me."

Ben took a bite of the food to give himself a moment to consider what he would tell this overly educated man. "Well, Daniel was always a challenge. He had Asperger's. I know they call it autism spectrum disorder now. He was high-functioning, and he wasn't bad on the spectrum, as they say. I knew he was intelligent, but getting him to focus on his education was difficult. I wanted him to try harder, and I had tutors to help him. I knew life would never be easy. According to my wife, I pushed too hard. When he graduated from high school, I knew he could attend college, but he wasn't interested. We had an argument, and the next day, he left without saying goodbye, and we never saw him again. So how about your daughter?"

Nigel wanted to put the best face on her story, but there was no way to sugarcoat the events that led to her demise. "I was up for associate dean of the medical school. My wife was involved in her work as well. To be honest, we dropped the ball. She became friends with some kids who we were concerned about, but one was the son of the local police chief. We thought she would make good choices, but we were oblivious to the drug culture in our city.

"It was a downward spiral, and we were too busy to notice. Drugs were the eventual issue, although she had an abortion in all of it. That's when we woke up and realized we needed to step away from our work and concentrate on our daughter. I would give anything to take back those years. It's my only regret in life."

Nigel and Ben studied one another. Each arrived in Australia with no intention of caring for their grandchild, and with a single encounter, they knew they would do anything to help this child. As they cleaned the plates and tidied the kitchen, each man wondered what the other was thinking.

It was early, and they knew they had an hour before Fiona would ring. Ben was still struggling with time zone issues. To him, it was late at night. The coffee was pulling in one direction and his inner clock in another. They sat down on the porch overlooking the ocean. Neither talked for a while.

Ben finally asked about Maddy's past. "Do you know the lady Maddy refers to who was on the station? Mrs. Donovan? Do we know anything about her, or has anyone contacted the station where Daniel worked? I wonder if we can get some history from her. She seems like she was on the ball as far as Maddy's concerned."

"I tried, but Fiona hasn't found contact information for her. Australia is like New Zealand. Families are supported, and your son should have been receiving child support, but it seems he never applied, so we don't know where this station is or if it even exists. I'd like to meet the woman and thank her for educating my granddaughter."

Ben would not let Nigel assert any possession over his granddaughter. "Our granddaughter."

"Yeah, the station lady needs to be found and thanked, anyway. Do you think the woman who is caring for Maddy might know?"

"I don't have a clue. I've never been allowed to meet her. They don't want us to know where Maddy resides. It wouldn't be hard to find out, but I didn't want to rile Fiona."

"That Fiona is a force. I wouldn't want to get on her bad side." Ben stood and took the binoculars.

He watched for only a second, and he turned to Nigel. "I think someone's in trouble in the water, Nige." He had on shoes, and he immediately took off from the porch and made his way down the zigzagging path along the cliff face, across the dunes, and down to the almost deserted beach. He glanced both ways as he kicked off his shoes and ran into the water. The water felt surprisingly warm, and he continued out without reaching an area deep enough to swim.

The water immediately turned cold, and he fell off the sand and into a deeper pool. He reached the lifeless woman, who lay face down in the water. As he scooped her up, she immediately turned and hit him. "What the bloody hell are you doing?"

That was when Ben realized she wore a snorkel. He trod water and gasped. "Sorry, I thought I was saving your life."

"Well, you goddamn aren't, are you?" The woman was livid. She swam away and resumed watching the ocean floor with her goggles and snorkel.

"Sorry, ma'am." Ben swam a few feet toward the shore, as the woman lifted her head, turned back, and said what he thought was, "Fucking American."

He was sure she could hear him. "Yes, I'm just a Fucking American who thought he was saving your life."

The woman raised her arm, and he recognized the universal middle-finger salute. Ben turned toward the shore where Nigel stood laughing. "You're screwed, mate."

Ben gave him a quizzical look. "I honestly thought she was drowning. Excuse me for trying to save her life."

"That's Terri Barber. She's the head of the children's protection mafia. She's Fiona's boss. She swims down here every morning."

Ben fell back into the water. He had on his shirt and the only shorts he had packed for his trip. He took off his shirt and threw it at Nigel. "Well, the water's perfect, mate. I think I'll join her." Ben emphasized the word *mate*.

Ben's torso was of a much younger man. Nigel gazed down at his ever-increasing midriff. Now that he was retired, he considered getting some exercise and toning up. He would be officially divorced soon, and this time, he would be more cautious, but it didn't hurt to buff up. He thought of Fiona and sighed. She was at least ten years younger, and Nigel knew he was punching above his weight with her in his crosshairs.

Chapter 14

Setting Some Rules

Nigel returned to the patio and watched Ben swim. At one point, he saw Ben and Terri Barber standing and talking. Nigel was alarmed. He was worried Ben would get the inside track on adopting Maddy. Nigel never heard Ben say he wanted her to go back to America for sure, but he suspected that was his intention.

Ben returned and smiled smugly as he headed for the shower. "She's really nice once you get to know her."

"I'm sure." Nigel gritted his teeth.

"No word yet?" Ben asked as he emerged from the bathroom. They didn't need to explain. They were keen to see their granddaughter.

"No," he replied as his phone rang. He walked out onto the porch to take the call, and then finally returned. "Fiona's dropping her off in thirty minutes and said we could take her to town to purchase some new clothes. The school has a uniform policy, so there's no need to buy clothes for school, but she's outgrowing the ones she has, and they appear to be secondhand, anyway."

Maddison arrived without Tag. She was not happy to leave him with her foster family, but she knew he couldn't stay in the car, and he would be happier with Jarlee than left in her grandfather's house.

She went to both men and shook their hands and asked them to be quick so she could return to her dog. There was a Target, which the locals pronounced "Tar-jay."

The three entered the car, and Maddison was sure it was all right if she sat in the front seat. Nigel pointed to the printed warning on the visor that children under the age of thirteen could not sit in the front seat.

"Well, my father allowed me to sit there. I guess you're going to make me wear a seatbelt, too?" Her voice was indignant.

Ben took some of the heat off Nigel. "It's the law, Maddy. We didn't make the rules, but in this case, it's a good rule."

"Is that because I'm your last hope to carry on the genetic line?"

Nigel turned to Ben. "Who is this kid?"

Ben smiled. "An alien, but she gets it from my side, for sure."

"I heard that. I'm not having kids, anyway. There is no way I'm kissing any boys."

Ben and Nigel high-fived one another. Nigel turned on the ignition. "We'll revisit that in ten years."

"You dream, Nige. The Taylors were all early starters." He knew this was not the case with his son. Ben would have been happy to hear Daniel had kissed a woman—ecstatic, actually. Obviously, he had kissed one. Ben glanced back at Maddy—for sure. Maybe Daniel's life wasn't as tortured as he'd imagined. If only Tania had died knowing she had a granddaughter...

They arrived at Target, and the three entered the small department store. To Ben, this store appeared to be a place where the company sold last year's clothing lines. He observed Maddison gaze around the room as if it were Christmas. She was unsure of what was expected. She stood awkwardly without moving in any direction.

"Maddy, we're here to get you some new outfits. Do you know what you need?" Nigel took her hand and headed to the children's department. Ben said he would find some shorts and a swimming suit. He left them and strolled over to the men's section. There wasn't much he would have chosen. He hated shopping. He bought clothes only when his wife was no longer there to dress him. She'd always kept him looking sharp. His personal dress taste was not trendy.

Nigel showed Maddison the clothes that would fit her, and she picked several outfits that could be used for play. Nigel knew there would be a funeral for Maddison's father in the next week and showed her a dress which might be appropriate. Ben joined them, and the three of them chose two nightgowns and some underclothes.

Ben suggested Maddison try on some of the clothes before they paid for them. Maddison was not happy. She asked Nigel to accompany her to the dressing room. Ben was disappointed he wasn't asked. She had only known him for a day and, despite her easy nature, she was still just a child with childlike reservations about strangers.

Nigel asked Ben to come in, and both men realized they would have to go up a size in all the clothes. Ben exchanged the clothes while his granddaughter and Nigel tried on various outfits. A saleswoman finally came to assist them. The sizes were changed again, and the last purchases were made. The two men split the bill.

They headed to McDonald's at Maddison's request. "I want a kid's meal, please. Can I have a Coke?"

Both men glanced at each other. They never let their young children drink Coke at that age. The signal was received. Simultaneously, they shook their heads. "No."

"I figured, but it was worth a try. My father never let me have Coke either. Can we hurry? I want to go home to Tag."

"I think we're supposed to keep you until three. I thought you might like to go to the playground and go on the water slide."

"I lived there. I did that all day long. Can we go horseback riding? I used to ride all the time at the station." Maddy crossed her arms, and both men could see the beginning of a pout.

Nigel shrugged. "I don't know where we can get you a horse to ride."

Ben wondered if the vet, Lindy Smart, might know of a horse. "I'll tell you what. How about I talk to the vet clinic and see if they know where there are horses to ride?"

"Well, that might work. Can we go back and buy some new riding pants?" She crossed her arms and sat back in the seat.

Nigel chuckled. He'd raised this child years ago. She was her mother—thirty-something years later. Nigel knew this was an unfamiliar experience for Ben, who he suspected never had the pleasure or displeasure of a savvy, controlling, wise-beyond-her-years daughter. The manipulation and guile were exactly what he had known in his beautiful daughter. This time, he would see the humor in this child. He knew outwitting her was perilous and futile, but he was up for the challenge.

Nigel was already planning his first fly-fishing trip with his granddaughter. New Zealand had some reservoirs where children could learn to cast and were usually rewarded with a fish. He didn't know anyone who had horses, but he was sure he could find a place for her to learn to ride in New Zealand.

Ben envisioned Maddison and Tag walking along the Appalachian Trail together. He couldn't wait to photograph her at the McAfee Knob. Maddison appeared to be fearless. He would be so nervous while she dangled her legs off the precipice. His heart raced as he imagined the moment. She would laugh and try to scare him by edging closer to the edge of the precipice.

Maddison secretly loved her new clothes, but she didn't want to take them home to Jarlee's family. She knew they were better off than her father, but they never showed off. She didn't want to embarrass them. She asked her grandfathers to keep most of the clothes at their house on the beach.

Maddy wished she could show Mrs. Donovan her dress. She knew she would "shine," as Mrs. Donovan would say when they had the funeral for her father. She dreaded that. Did she have to look at her father again? Would they expect her to kiss his face or talk? She was homesick for the station.

"I want to go home, please. I want to get Tag. I don't mind going back to the beach, but I want my dog."

Nigel immediately called Fiona, who didn't answer. "Let's go over to the office and see if we can get someone to retrieve the dog." They arrived and found Terri Barber sitting at her desk, talking to someone on the phone. She appeared relieved to see the three of them. She waved to them and quickly hung up the phone.

"Dr. Taylor, can I talk to you privately?" She appeared distressed.

Ben turned and glanced toward Nigel, who took Maddison by the shoulders and went back to the foyer.

Teri quietly told Ben. "The little girl's dog has been hit by a car. He's at the local vet. They say his femur is shattered, and they would like to euthanize the dog, but they would like a second opinion from you. Apparently, this is your field of expertise?"

Ben understood the implications, and while most of the time he could dispassionately assess and treat or not treat injured animals, this was different. He remembered when Daniel's dog was terminally ill. He hated to tell his son there was nothing he could do.

Chapter 15

Tag

"Let's go." Ben opened the door, and without explanation, headed to the car. He was putting in the address on his GPS.

Nigel could see something was terribly wrong. He feared Fiona had been injured or worse. He said nothing in front of Maddison and only allowed Ben to direct him through Kadina and then out to the edge of town to the veterinary clinic.

Finally, he turned to the back seat and calmly explained Tag was in the hospital with a broken leg. He minimized the report he received. "Darling, Tag's been injured, and we need to see what we need to do to fix him, so he isn't in so much pain."

Maddison stared, saying nothing. Her tears fell, and she quickly emerged from the car and took both grandfathers' hands and ran toward the clinic door.

They entered the waiting room and saw several people sitting with pets. Ben gave them his name, and the three were escorted into an examination room. Both Dr. Lindy Smart and her associate, Dr. Gaz Hancock, entered the room, and their faces said it all. They had a dark screen and showed them an image that was too small to see properly.

Dr. Smart bent down to be face-to-face with the little girl. "I'm afraid Tag had an accident, Maddison. He broke his leg, and he's in a lot of pain."

Maddison sat wide-eyed and asked, "How much pain?"

"A lot. He's crying." Everyone in the room now heard the dog's cries coming from a room down the hall. Maddison stood to go see him.

Dr. Hancock bent down and put his hand on her shoulder. "Maddison, maybe you should wait here? It's okay if you don't want to see him. I can take you, but maybe it's best not to remember him like he is right now?"

"No, that's what they said about my father. I want to see him."

Ben took Maddison's hand and turned to Lindy. "Can I see the radiographs?"

Lindy hit a button on the screen, and the small image enlarged to show a femur that had at least four distinct fracture sites and many small fragments. There was a fracture of the pelvis on the other side. Amputation was a consideration, but with the pelvic fracture, this would be beyond this clinic's capabilities.

Ben studied the images as Nigel stood to walk Maddison toward the door leading to the room where the crying dog lay. As they entered the room, both Nigel and Maddison gasped as they watched the dog crying and staring back at his left leg. Maddison went to his head and petted him behind the ears. Tag immediately stopped crying, looked at the little girl, and gave one wag of his tail.

Ben knew he had full neurological function. He turned to the young vet and asked what he had in surgical instruments and analgesics.

Lindy smiled and nodded. "Gaz has whatever you need. His parents are the local doctors, and we can always borrow or rob what we need from the hospital."

Ben put his hand on the young man's shoulder. "Let's go trick or treating, Gaz. What is Gaz short for?"

Gaz laughed. "Gaz is short for Gary. It's kind of Australian. Baz is short for Barry."

Ben leaned down and took Maddison's face in his hands. "No promises, Maddy. This is what I did all my life. I fixed broken bones. I won't pretend this is a walk in the park. This is as difficult as it gets. I'll try my best. Your job is to keep your pop entertained while I play doggy Erector set."

Maddy appeared confused. "What is an erection set?"

Ben turned to Nigel. "I'll let you handle that, old man. Hopefully, Maddy can teach you something. Maddy, you can stay and care for Tag until Dr. Hancock's ready to do the surgery."

"Aren't you doing it?" Maddy looked up at her grandfather.

"No, I'll assist him. If this works, you'll owe Dr. Hancock a lot of money. Can you wash windows and sweep floors?" Lindy and Gaz grin. Maddison nodded through tear-filled eyes.

Ben and Gaz went to the utility room, where the instruments were kept. They opened the surgical packs without contaminating them and found most of what they needed. They then took several bone plates from a tray and placed them in the autoclave. It would take thirty minutes to sterilize, and Ben asked what they had for pain control.

Gaz and Lindy discussed various analgesics and tried ketamine, which had helped many dogs in Ben's experience. Lindy returned to the surgical prep room, where Tag and his entourage waited. She gave Tag the dosage Ben had suggested, and the response to the injection was profound.

Lindy asked if anyone wanted anything and offered coffee or tea to Nigel. Nigel gratefully accepted the offer of tea. Lindy noticed Maddison's weight shifting and took her to the toilet.

Lindy placed her hand on Maddison's shoulder. "You're so lucky to have such wonderful grandfathers. One knows how to fix broken legs, and the other knows about…" Lindy paused. She knew little about either man other than what she had heard during her impromptu dinner with Fiona.

"About erection sets. He teaches reproduction. I don't know why they're talking about erections when it's Tag's leg that's broken."

Who is this kid? Lindy laughed and explained what an Erector Set was. She Googled the image on her phone to show Maddison what many children played with before Lego. "It looks like they call it a Meccano set in Australia."

Maddison returned to Tag, who was resting quietly but managed a tail wag when he felt her scratch his head. Several minutes later, Ben and Gaz returned and said they were ready to start the surgery. It would take up to two hours, and Ben and Nigel discussed calling Fiona, who was now back at her office. It would be after five before they could return Maddison to her foster family, and they would ask for permission to keep her overnight.

Fiona knew where they were and was apprised of the dire situation. "I'll call the Yarrans. I'm sure they'll be fine. It was Mrs. Yarran who ran over Tag. She's beside herself. We all thought he would be put to sleep. I'm so glad you're at least trying. That poor child doesn't need another loss in her life right now. Will you call me when things have settled down?"

Nigel felt genuine sincerity and concern in her voice. "I will. Any chance you'd care to join us?"

"I could bring pizza if that's okay." Fiona had more than a professional interest in the family. She'd sworn off men, but Nigel was so humble and caring.

Nigel was excited to share another meal with Fiona. He was not happy that it was Maddison's poor dog's injury that brought them together. "I won't say no. That's for sure."

Chapter 16

Ben in His Element

Tag's leg and opposite hip were shaved and scrubbed. Tag's gurney was rolled out of the prep room, leaving a tearful child. Four and a half hours later, Ben walked into the reception room where Maddison lay on a bench with her head in Nigel's lap. Ben's heart sank, observing how comfortable the child appeared to be.

So much for any chance of being the hero. Ben smiled and nodded to Nigel and Fiona, who sat together, while Fiona stroked Maddison's head as she slept. There were plates with pizza crust, and Ben walked over and took a piece of crust. Nigel put his finger to his lips and pointed toward the door leading to the staff kitchen. Ben needed to relieve himself. He was satisfied with his efforts. He only helped and advised the younger vet, who was more experienced than he would have imagined for a country vet.

Maddy woke up when all three veterinarians walked back into the reception area. "Is Tag going to live?"

Ben wanted to control the information, so there were no delusions and unjustified hope. "Darling, I won't sugarcoat it. It's a nasty injury. Dr. Hancock and Dr. Smart did a wonderful job fixing the fractures. Tag's officially banned from going through metal detectors anymore." Ben wanted to say he could be a model for an Erector set, but he would never joke in front of a client, let alone his precious grandchild. "We won't know for several days, but you need to thank everyone here, including the nurses."

Ben turned to the staff, who were all eating pizza. "You have a brilliant team here. You're lucky to have such efficient nurses." Hopefully, this will reduce the bill.

Gaz took the compliment, but he knew it was Ben who had directed him and shown him the intricacies of the interlocking plate. "We couldn't have done it without your guidance, Dr. Taylor. You were brilliant. Thanks for your help."

Ben was mindful that much of the equipment belonged to the local hospital, and while most human fractures were sent to Adelaide, once in a while they did surgery at the hospital. Gaz's connection through his parents being the local doctors was the key to borrowing the equipment, and he would return the instruments and order the plates and screws he used on the dog.

Maddy stood and went to each of the staff in the reception and shook their hands and thanked them. She walked up to Ben and extended her arms so he could pick her up.

She kissed him and then rested her head on Ben's shoulder. He had to turn away so no one could see the tears in his eyes.

Fiona took Nigel's hand and squeezed it. She whispered, "That little girl is so lucky to have you two."

Ben wins for now, but wait until she's in her thirties and wants to have children. Nigel laughed at himself. He would not be there when she was thirty. Game on, old man. Two can play the "who's my favorite grandfather" game.

There were tears when Maddison was told she could not spend the night with Tag. A compromise was made, and Ben would stay with Tag. Nigel would take Maddison to the beach house with Fiona's permission, ending Maddison's stay with Jarlee and his family. They were leaving in two days to return to their home in the APY Lands for the summer. Fiona would retrieve Maddison's belongings and thank them for hosting the girl. Considering Mrs. Yarran had run over the dog, but knowing it was an accident, it was too much for Maddison to understand.

The memorial service for Maddison's father was in three days, and that was the next hurdle for this family and the agency. Daniel was not a well-known or popular man. He tended bar, but he made the drinks and chatted little with the patrons. Fiona doubted the service would be attended by anyone besides the family. She'd tried to reach the Donovans, who had finally been found. They were leaving for an overseas trip and were not sure they could come. Fiona didn't tell Maddison.

Nigel took Maddison to the house and realized she needed a bath. Her clothes were all covered in Tag's hair, and she smelled like a wet dog. He ran water in the tub and prepared to leave her to bathe herself. It was an awkward age. Some children were still not embarrassed by nudity in front of strangers, and some were. He left her and closed the door.

She called from the bathroom. "How am I supposed to wash my hair?"

"Do you need help?"

"Well, duh." The disdain was unmistakable. Nigel knew that tone in her voice. Ben can have her.

He knocked on the door and opened it. Maddison was naked and showed no evidence of embarrassment. Nigel pointed to the bathtub. "Get in."

Maddison lifted her leg over the edge and dipped her toes in the water and immediately pulled them out. "Are you trying to kill me? That water's way too hot. Don't you know anything about raising kids?"

Nigel was alarmed. He had felt the water. His concern was that it was too cold—not hot. He reached in and felt the water again. He glanced at his granddaughter and turned on the cold water from the tap. It could not have been on for more than a second. He felt the water again and knew the temperature could not have changed. "Sorry, try this."

Maddison slowly entered the water and sat down. "You know, you could have killed a child with that water. You're going to have to learn about this if you expect me to choose you."

Nigel had to turn away, so Maddison didn't see his smile. The manipulation was so much like his daughter. "I'll be guided by you, Maddy. I guess I have a lot to learn."

"Well, burning your granddaughter won't look good on your record."

Chapter 17

Post-op

Nigel woke when he smelled coffee. Thankfully, Ben must have returned. He could care for Maddison while he slept a while longer. It was barely light outside. Finally, he knew someone was in his room.

"Are you going to get up, Pop? Don't make me throw water on you like I did with my father."

"Ben," shouted Nigel. "What the hell are you doing?"

"It's me, Maddy. Get up. I want to go see Tag. If you don't get up now, I'm going to walk to the clinic."

"Where's your other grandfather?" Nigel forgot he'd spent the night at the clinic.

"I don't know. He must be with Tag. What do you like to eat?"

"That's my job, Maddy. What do you want?"

"I always made breakfast for my father. I can cook—cereal or eggs and toast. I don't see any bacon."

Who is this kid? "Tea and toast, thanks." Nigel sat up and rubbed his eyes. He remembered the bath last night and wryly smiled. He would wait and see if she pulled the same thing on Ben. What a schemer.

"How do you take your tea?" Maddison popped her head in the door. He'd left it open in case Maddison had a night terror or called for him.

"White with sugar, thanks. How do you know how to make tea?" Nigel prepared for tea that was too strong or too weak.

"Mrs. Donovan taught me." Maddison turned and headed for the kitchen. A few seconds later, she handed him a perfect cup of tea, using a towel to protect herself from the hot mug.

Nigel took a taste and smiled. "You've had some experience."

Maddison left the room, and he could hear her mutter "duh" again under her breath.

"I heard that." Nigel smiled. He was delighted with this precocious child, but he wouldn't tolerate sniping or back talk from a six-year-old.

There was a knock at the door, and Maddison ran to the back door before Nigel could throw on a robe. He heard Maddison scream, and he raced to the back door where Ben stood holding a limp dog. Was he dead? Maddison opened the door and realized Tag was just sleeping. Ben placed the dog on the divan. A vet nurse followed him with a mat and a box of medical supplies.

Ben thanked her for the ride and offered to pay her, but the nurse refused any money. "I think my bosses would kill me if I took a gratuity. You've done enough, and your payment was more than sufficient to cover the expenses. Dr. Hancock said he would come by tonight after work. I suspect you may see Dr. Smart at some stage as well. As I said, the fodder shop next to the hardware store has elevated dog beds that would be good for Tag."

The nurse turned toward Maddison. "I understand you're in charge here. You are to pet him every thirty minutes. Offer him water at least once an hour. He needs kisses regularly, and you already know he loves to have the back of his ears scratched. Can I trust you to do that?" Maddison was tongue-tied, but nodded. The nurse smiled and extended her hand. "Okay, I'm officially transferring nursing duties to you, Maddy. Don't disappoint me." The nurse turned and left.

As she shut the door, Maddison ran out and gave her a hug. "You can count on me. Thank you."

"The best way you can thank me is to be a good citizen, study hard so if you decide to be a vet, you have the grades to get into uni. Oh, and be kind to your grandfather and let him sleep. He's been up all-night caring for Tag." She gave Maddison a hard look but smiled as she turned away.

Nigel stood at the door and watched this remarkable young woman drive away. That clinic was lucky to have her. He returned, and Maddison was already lying on the couch and petting a very drugged dog. Ben set an intravenous bag above the dog on the back of the divan, and fluids were slowly dripping into the leg vein.

"So, what's it like to have slept?"

Chapter 18

Neighbors

Ben awoke three hours later. He sensed he was being watched, and when he turned and opened his eyes, Maddison was sitting on his bed and staring. "Did you get enough sleep?"

Not hardly. "Yes, thanks for letting me sleep. Any chance you could ask your pop to make some coffee?" Ben checked his phone. It was eleven thirty.

Maddison returned with coffee. The coffee was fresh and delicious. "If you can take over my nursing duties, Pop said he would take me to get a dog bed."

"We'd better get Tag up and see if he wants to pee. He hasn't wet the couch yet, has he?"

"No, sir, but I think he must be busting."

Ben slipped on some new shorts. He glanced down at his chest and saw more of his chest hairs were gray, and his belly was expanding. He hadn't thought about his looks since Tania had passed. He compared himself to Nigel, who lacked any signs of fitness. *I could be worse.*

He took the towel hanging in the bathroom, placed it under Tag, and lifted the dog to the grass verge facing the ocean. He used the towel to support the dog's hind limbs, and Tag immediately urinated and then passed a motion. Tag placed a small amount of weight on his side with the plated pelvic fracture. Ben was amazed by the dog's resilience.

The next-door neighbors were sitting on the veranda. The elderly couple stood and walked over. "Hi, we're your neighbors, Doug and Janet. We're your landlords. I'm guessing the agency didn't tell you about the no-pet policy?"

Ben stared at Nigel. "Uh, no is the short answer."

Nigel appeared sheepish. "I knew. We never planned this. As you can see, he was in an accident."

Nigel formerly introduced Ben, Maddison, and himself. He explained they were both from overseas and came to care for their granddaughter, who owns the dog. "Maddy, will you go in and get a plate of biscuits for our neighbors?"

Maddison knew she was supposed to leave so her pop could tell the entire story. "Will I hurry or take my time, Pop?" She rolled her eyes.

Ben and Nigel shook their heads. Nigel smiled. "Come back when you're twenty-one, darling." Everyone laughed.

Janet pursed her lips. "We have several grandchildren. The good thing is you can always send them home." But then Nigel quickly told them the story, and Janet instantly said they were here to help.

"So, you're a vet?"

Nigel was quick to respond. "No, Ben is. He's a surgeon and did the surgery to fix the dog's fractures."

Ben shook his head. "I assisted the vets at Copper Coast. They did it."

"We're off the land. We bought this place over twenty years ago, so when we retired, we could be near our son and our grandchildren." Janet went over and petted Tag's head. Doug had gone back to the house.

Ben took the lead. "We'll look for a new place right away. If we might keep him here until we can locate a new place to stay, I promise to prevent him from destroying the place, and we'll replace anything you aren't happy about."

Doug returned with a large, elevated dog bed with a porous sling. "If he has a pee, it will go straight through, and he won't get himself dirty or wet. When we moved here, we had two old Great Pyrenees that we couldn't leave. The last one died three years ago. You're welcome to use it."

Maddison returned and held out the cookies to the neighbors. "I do housecleaning and laundry if that will help? This is our first night. If Tag and I can't stay, then I have to go into foster care." Maddison looked at the ground and then turned slightly away from the neighbors and winked at Nigel and Ben.

Ben cleared his throat. "No one's going into foster care. I'm afraid my granddaughter is a con artist. She gets it from his side of the family." He pointed to Nigel, who couldn't hide his smile. "She might get it from both sides. Anyway, we'll start looking today." He paused, waiting for the couple to respond. They didn't. Damn.

Ben took the dog bed, placed it under the patio away from the sun, and took a mat that the veterinary clinic had given him. He used the towel to support the dog back to the bed and then reset the intravenous fluids while Maddison sat down beside him and began her nursing duties once again, with ear scratches.

Ben walked into the house, and as he passed the child, he quietly said, "Con artist."

Maddison replied, "I learned from the best."

Ben wondered who that was. His son was too literal to have conned people. Maybe he'd changed?

A few minutes later, Janet came over holding a banana cake. "I'm afraid we weren't quite honest with you."

Ben and Nigel sat on the veranda, sipping more coffee. "Our last name is Smart. We're Lindy's in-laws. We want you to stay as long as you need the house. We had the beach house booked in four weeks for another couple, but we canceled their reservation. Don't worry, they're relatives too. He's my nephew, and he can stay with us. Half the time he cancels."

Nigel stood. "Well, we're hoping to be out of here in less than a month. Maybe you can still have the house, but thanks. We promise to do our best and be good neighbors, Janet."

"If you can bring some joy to our daughter-in-law, we would be so appreciative. She's been through hell and back. She needs to move on."

Chapter 19

Talking Smack

"We still need some dog food." The banana bread was their only lunch, and so Nigel took Maddison for a trip to the grocery and fodder store to get the dog food the vets recommended for his recovery.

Ben stayed to monitor Tag, who'd been brought back into the living room. His intravenous fluids contained ketamine, which reduced the pain. Ben would wean him off over the next twenty-four hours. Tag was stoic. After the horrific injury, and despite the state-of-the-art repair, he might not be able to walk.

The goal was to allow the bones to heal and to keep his appetite strong. Infection was a worry, but the fractures were not open, and the surgery had gone well. The dog was an excellent patient. He didn't need a cone that is often used around the neck to prevent animals from licking or biting their incisions. Tag had shown no interest in doing any of this.

Ben had not become attached to any dogs since his last one died. Don't do it. It'll be hard enough if you lose Maddy to Nigel. Don't add a dog to your losses. Ben carried the dog out to the grass, and using the belly towel to support the hind limbs, he helped Tag relieve himself once again.

Doug Smart rose from a chair on the porch and walked over to the grass where Ben supported Tag. "Ben, I talked to Lindy a while ago, and I understand your son was the man killed in the rollover. I know what it's like to lose a son. Mate, I'm so sorry for your loss. I know there aren't enough words to describe the grief of losing a son, but then to compound it, I think of that poor child. She's got to be going through a horrific time in her brief life. What a hell of a deal."

Ben considered how to answer him. Doug must know Daniel had been estranged. Lindy would have known and told him and his wife. "Thanks. Yes, it's a shitshow for sure. The memorial is in two days. I'm trying to be strong for Maddy's sake, but it's tough. That's why it's so important we try to save her dog."

"Yeah, that's why we want to help in any way we can. If you need a babysitter or a dog sitter, we're here for you. I'm asking for one favor, though. Do you mind visiting a bit with Lindy? We know she's lonely. She needs to get reacquainted with the living. You'd never know it to look at her, but she needs a good kick in the backside. My son wouldn't be happy with how she's isolating herself."

"Doug, give me a few days, and I'll do what I can. I lost the love of my life as well. It's been a few years, and while I don't want a new relationship, I should probably get out a bit more myself. Thanks for letting us keep the dog here. When we leave, you won't even know a dog has been in the house. Scout's honor."

"You Americans and those damned Scouts." Doug returned to his chair on his veranda.

An hour later, Nigel and Maddison returned with the evidence of a trip to McDonald's as well as food for all concerned. Tag wagged his tail when Maddison lay down next to him and fed him a portion of her hamburger. Tag ate the meat and closed his eyes as Maddison stroked his head and neck.

Ben wanted to walk on the beach and asked Nigel to watch the dog while he was out. He asked Maddison to join him. She agreed, which pleased him. They walked together in silence. He extended his hand and waited. She didn't accept the offer for several minutes.

Maddison walked alongside her grandfather and finally turned her head and began speaking. "What was my father like when he was my age?"

Ben considered his response. "He was different from most kids. He was kind." Ben understood deep down that his son was kind, but he never showed much concern for his family. He justified his "kind" adjective by remembering only the rare times that his son showed any form of caring.

"He loved his dog, Spock." Spock, a lab, was his constant companion and was the calming force in Daniel's early life. Daniel would barricade himself in his room with Spock when he was upset. Spock was more important to Daniel for emotional support than either of his parents. For that reason, Ben had all the time in the world for the emotional support that animals can bring. He knew its true value. That was why it was so important to give Maddison's dog every opportunity to live a pain-free life.

Ben had different goals for the dogs he cared for. Some were to return to work or get back into the show ring, but his favorites were to be an elderly person's companion. Now that he was retired, his only professional endeavor was to heal his granddaughter's dog, so he could help her through the next few years until she formed attachments to other humans.

This little girl showed none of the behavior patterns that alarmed his wife and him when Daniel was young. She understood human emotions and relations and, to his amusement, could play Nigel and him like a fiddle. She could be on the spectrum, but that might be from her unusual father's influence. Ben believed she was probably normal.

"Did my dad have friends?"

"Of course he did." Ben wondered if this exceptional child could sense when he was lying.

"He didn't have friends at the station or at the caravan park. I don't think he had friends at the pub. He said I was his friend—me and Tag."

"Your dad was a little different. He loved exploring and building things, and he was so busy that he didn't play with kids much, but he had two friends in school." Ben didn't want to mention they were the school psychologist and the janitor.

"I think my mother was his friend. Did you ever see a picture of her?"

"Yes, your pop showed me some. She was beautiful." Ben could sense her sorrow.

"I know she's supposed to be dead, but I'd like to see her one more time and talk to her." Maddison bent over to explore an accumulation of small pebbles. She stood and gazed out to sea. "Did you have a brother or sister?"

"One of each. My brother and sister live in Florida. They have grandchildren who are older than you, but someday, I'd like for you to meet your cousins." Ben hadn't seen them since Tania's funeral.

Maddison smiled. "I have cousins?" She stared out at a ship anchored and waiting to be taken into the harbor to be loaded with grain. She took Ben's hand and turned to go back to the house.

"Your grandmother's side has more. When you come to visit, I'll take you to meet them. They would love to meet you, Maddy. Have you seen snow, or have you skied?"

She shook her head. "Am I going to live with you?"

Ben dreaded this question. "Maddy, I'm not sure. Your pop and I both want the best for you, but we don't have the final decision. The agency gets a say as well." Ben squeezed her hand. "I'll bet Tag's missing you." He felt her respond with a returned squeeze.

Chapter 20

Getting to Know You

Tag became more alert. He wagged his tail several times when he saw Maddison. Nigel was preparing dinner. They were having pasta, salad, and vegetables. Maddison looked at the food and shook her head.

Nigel stared at her. "What? Don't you like pasta?"

"Where's the meat? I'm not a sheep." She crossed her arms and assumed a take-no-prisoners stance.

"You know, too much meat may not be good for you." Nigel wanted to say, you'll eat what you're given, but thought better of it.

"You realize I was raised on a station. We raised sheep for a living, not vegetables. I need to support my family." She spread her legs slightly to emphasize her resolve.

Nigel went to the fridge and opened a package of sliced meat. He removed a slice of turkey and handed it to her. "Will that do until I go shopping?"

Maddison took the turkey and gave it to Tag. "You have a lot to learn about raising Australian children."

Ben observed this and shook his head. He whispered quietly to Nigel, "I'll be getting a flight home, mate. She's all yours."

"I'll join you. Is it five o'clock? I need some grog. By the way, will you stay with Maddy tonight? I'm meeting Fiona for a drink. She'll need a bath." Nigel pointed to Maddison. He was sure she would pull the same burning-child stunt on him. Following dinner, Nigel left to meet Fiona. They agreed to meet for a drink and not to discuss business.

When bath time came, Maddison asked for help once again. She tried the same trick on Ben as she did on Nigel. Ben wasn't having any of it. After testing the water, he left the room. "Well, it will cool down in a minute. Let me know when you're ready, and I'll be in the front room." He walked out and left her.

"You know, my father read the stock journal to me while I bathed." Maddison was not impressed with her grandfather. She didn't want to bathe alone. Bath time was one of the few times that she had her father's attention.

Ben reentered the bathroom where Maddison sat in the tub. He knew little about girls, but at her age, they couldn't differ that much from boys. "So, have you read any stories you like?"

"I liked the Black Stallion." She lay down in the water and let her hair swirl as she rolled her head back and forth.

"Yes, that's a good one. How about Black Beauty?"

"Yeah, Mrs. Donovan used to read that to me."

"Mrs. Donovan sounds like she was a wonderful woman. Why do you like her so much?"

Maddison considered the question. She sat up and pointed to the shampoo. "I'm only six. You can't expect me to wash my hair." She covered her eyes with her hands while Ben shampooed Maddison's hair. When she had rinsed off the soap, she stood and, with her eyes closed, stepped out of the bath and held out her hand for a towel.

She dried herself and handed the towel back to Ben as Maddison pointed to her hair. Ben retrieved a dry towel and rubbed Maddison's head and then used a brush to comb out the snarls. "Ouch, dammit, that hurts. I'm going to have to teach you how to care for children, Grandpa."

"And I'm going to have to teach you not to swear. I had my mouth washed with soap if I said bad words when I was your age."

"Daddy just laughed. He told me it was okay when we were alone, but it would 'deflect' on him if I did it in front of outsiders. They might think he was a terrible parent and take me away. Mrs. Donovan smacked me and told me she would whip me good and proper if she heard me say the F-word ever again." Maddison turned away.

"I think I would like Mrs. Donovan." Ben considered what a positive influence this woman must have had on his granddaughter.

"She was all right." Maddison turned away, hiding her face, which was close to showing her grief. Leaving Mrs. Donovan was worse than anything she had endured. She loved her father, but Mrs. Donovan had loved her in a way that her father couldn't.

Maddison didn't understand the difference. Her father took care of her, but Tag was the one who made her feel safe and loved. She put on her new pajamas and came out to the veranda where her grandfather was helping Tag relieve himself. She knew both he and Nigel could love her if she let them, but she knew it was temporary, just like the women her father brought home occasionally. Those women were so nice, and then they were gone. She would not let either of these men hurt her if she could help it. She vowed not to love them.

"Maddy, Tag's doing well, but he isn't out of the woods. We need to be very careful with him. Can you hold him up with the towel while I get his antibiotics?" Maddy came around and inserted herself between Ben and the barely standing dog. She felt her grandfather transfer the dog's weight to her as he released the towel and put his hand on her shoulder.

"Yeah, but hurry back." She was not confident she could hold him for very long.

"I will." Ben quickly got the antibiotics and returned to see Tag bearing a small amount of weight on his fractured limb.

He opened Tag's mouth and placed the medication into the back of his throat. They let Tag have a quick sniff around and returned him to the mat on the veranda.

The sun was setting, and Ben thought it would be nice to watch it with his granddaughter. She walked out onto the lawn and stared out to sea. Ben walked over to her and put his hand on her shoulder. Maddison leaned into him, and they stood together until the sun disappeared.

"Mrs. Donovan used to say death was only a sunset, and somewhere, the light of life moved on. I hope my mother and father are in the sunlight together again."

Ben gazed down at Maddison. "Mrs. Donovan is very wise. Was she married, and did she have other children?"

Maddison didn't answer. Ben didn't press for a response. He was grateful this woman had given Maddison so much wisdom and a sense of what Maddison could expect from life.

They carried Tag into the house, and Maddison went to her bed. Ben followed her, which surprised the little girl. "I'm sleeping now, Grandpa. I can't talk anymore. I'm puffed."

"Does puffed mean tired?" Ben had never heard that expression.

"Boy, you don't know much, do you?" Maddison was annoyed her grandfather didn't know much about words.

"I was wondering if you would like to hear a story. I downloaded a story about a pony from an island off the American coast. It's called Misty of Chincoteague."

Maddison sat up immediately. "Yes, please." She sat mesmerized as Ben read the first chapter.

"Okay, that's enough for tonight. May I kiss you goodnight?" Ben was aware this child didn't have the basic routines that most children received from their parents.

She leaned over, and he kissed her. "Thank you for helping Tag and me. My father was lucky to have you."

Ben recalled the drama he and his wife had in getting their son to sleep. He knew this child was the reward for the tears and anguish their son had put them through. He and Nigel had a second chance at parenting. The question was, were they up to the task?

"Sweet dreams, Maddy. No, we're the lucky ones. See you in the morning."

She didn't reply. Ben heard her rhythmic breathing. He wanted this to last forever.

Chapter 21

Fiona

Nigel waited at the bar for several minutes before Fiona arrived. He was nervous. Fiona was lovely, but he realized this might be interpreted as trying to influence the decision of his granddaughter's placement. That was not his intention. He genuinely liked Fiona, and he wanted to get to know her. She was cheerful, pretty in a country-casual kind of way, and savvy.

Fiona wore no makeup and didn't even dye her graying hair. She was tall and showed no sign she tried to hide her age. The day he walked into her office and announced he was here to claim his granddaughter, she glanced up from her computer screen, and Nigel received the most heartwarming smile he'd experienced since his first wife had died. That smile burned in his memory.

He could see she was cautious, but in her line of work, family members of displaced minors who were "good citizens" were rare. She grilled him for an hour before even discussing the child. She'd done her preliminary research, and he could see she had used the local New Zealand agency to investigate him as a potential caregiver for Maddison.

Finding a safe, loving home for this remarkable child was Fiona's only goal when Nigel walked into her office. Her investigation centered on his history as a parent. Why had he lost contact with his daughter?

Not all parents of wayward children were to blame for their child's behavior. Fiona had finally kicked her drug-addicted son to the curb after he refused to attend Narcotics Anonymous. Still, if she took all the families who found themselves in her office, most would be classified as dysfunctional.

Fiona saw Nigel sitting on a bar stool. She waved and pointed to a booth. He picked up his schooner and waved to the waitress to show he was moving. The waitress nodded, finished taking an order, and then approached Fiona and Nigel.

"Hi, Fi. You certainly get around these days. What number is this guy?" The waitress couldn't keep from laughing.

"Kelly, if you don't tell this bloke—" Fiona paused. "What's your name? Where did we meet? Anyway, tell him you're joking, or he'll leave, and I'll have to pay for the drinks."

Nigel got the joke. "The question is, what's your name? And in case you've forgotten, we met when I bailed you out of jail three years ago, and you ran out on me with the judge."

"Fi, he got you there. Apparently, he has a sense of humor, so this one might be worth the investment. You want the usual?"

"No. Just a diet tonic."

"As if. G and T?"

"Minus the G. He's a client, and I need to keep it professional."

The waitress turned to Nigel, who put his hand over his beer. "I'm trying to make a good impression, but how about a menu?"

"I've eaten, but the key lime pie is to die for." Fiona smiled again. "How's the patient?"

"Remarkable. Maddy is one lucky kid. She has two grandfathers who have talents that every child could use."

"Oh yeah? What's yours?" Fiona took a sip of the tonic.

"Well, according to the said child, not much." Nigel recounted his scalding-bathwater story.

"You two men have no hope. This kid has you both wrapped around her finger." Fiona took another sip. "Let's talk about you. We should keep this away from work. What do you do in your spare time?" She glanced up and saw Nigel consider this.

"Ladies first."

"Pottery." She glanced at Nigel shyly. "I know. It's kinda lame, but it makes me happy."

Nigel cocked his head. "What's lame about it?"

"I rarely complete anything. I just like to place the clay on a table and work it with my hands. I like the feel of the wet clay bending and taking shape. So, what do you do?"

"Until recently, I rarely took time off. I was headed out to fish the day I received your letter about Maddy. I love to fly-fish. Now that I'm not lecturing, I'd planned to go to the Northern Hemisphere this year to fish in the Rockies. Do you have children?"

"Hey, listen, if you plan to lecture me about yet another woman without children and without first-hand knowledge—" But she was cut off.

"No, it was just a question. I'd like to know more about you. That's all. So far, I think you're doing a wonderful job."

Fiona glanced again at the man. Geez, Louise, he's so bloody good-looking and so smart. Fiona had done a check through the New Zealand counterpart of her agency, and Nigel was a respected colleague with no criminal record. That was rare in her business. Then, to find Maddison's other grandfather with a similar profile was like Christmas.

"I'm sorry. One son, but we're estranged. I had a few problems and had to abandon subsequent family plans when I removed the incubator. I'm guessing you would know more than I do about it. Can we change the subject?"

Nigel was relieved. "How about a walk on the jetty? I promise not to ask anything else controversial. Labor or Liberal?"

Fiona and Nigel laughed, knowing that was almost as controversial a question as one could ask in Australia.

"Thank God. At least you didn't ask for my footy team." Fiona knew that could lead to a full-on domestic.

"Seriously, don't you follow rugby?" Nigel shook his head. He looked at his wrist, pretending to check his watch.

"Boy, is it that late? I don't want you breaking curfew. We'd better go back."

Fiona looked up into the darkening sky. "Let's see. I'm trying to remember who won the Trans-Tasman cricket last year. Hmm."

"Okay, you win. I'm not officially divorced, but no one's around. May I kiss you?"

"Not a chance in hell, Kiwi." Fiona desperately wanted to kiss this man but not enough to lose her job. "We can revisit that question after we sort out your precocious grandchild. That's if you're still talking to me. Any specific funeral requests from Ben?"

Fiona mentioned she thought it would only be a minister, the immediate family, and one or two people from the agency who attended Daniel's funeral. The Yarran family had left for the APY Lands and would not be attending. Daniel's ashes would be given to Ben, who would place them in the cemetery alongside his mother.

Chapter 22

Eavesdropping

Nigel returned to the beach house and read some papers his students were publishing. It was still early, and Ben walked down to the beach before retiring. He was still adjusting to the time zone. "Hey, old man. How'd it go? Can you take over so I can go down to the beach?"

"No prob. It was okay," Nigel lied. He was trying to get his hormones under control. Oxytocin and prostaglandins were one thing, but his catecholamines were causing his stomach to do abdominal somersaults.

Ben loved walking on the beach at night. There were no waves, and the warm water lapped as it rose and fell on the sand. It was cooler than daytime. Many people walked on North Beach at night. With no wind or crashing waves, conversations could be easily overheard.

Something caught his attention. Three women were walking toward him from the town end of the beach. He was sure he heard them say, "Maddison." He turned to the ocean and pretended to watch the lights from the ships anchored a few miles out in the gulf.

"I hear her mother is back in town, and she's coming to get her daughter back finally." The woman sounded very annoyed.

"Oh, really? Well, I heard the mother's been dead for years, and the little girl's father killed her and buried her in one of the opal shafts up in Coober Pedy."

A third one huffed and told the two women they did not know the entire story. "You're only guessing. Neither of you would have a clue. My hubby drank at the pub where the bloke poured beers, and he knew him. My hubby said he used to talk about his wife like she was alive. Apparently, she left them to go to Thailand with a movie star. She never returned. The poor kid is homeless. She's living with abos in an old farmhouse between here and Moonta. Can you imagine? She's white as white."

"Margie, you can't say 'abo' anymore. It's not right. I hear they're a nice family."

"Whatever." Margie sounded annoyed. "I hear she has family from overseas. I reckon they're staying in the area. She's such a pretty child. I think the funeral is tomorrow or the next day. I might attend. Anyone want to join me?"

"I'm working, but you could go with Betty and see if the little girl's mother shows up." The three women moved on, and Ben could no longer hear their conversation.

Ben returned to the house, where he found Maddison sleeping on the floor next to the dog. Tag wagged his tail, but as Ben leaned down to pick the sleeping child up, he growled.

Ben hesitated and patted the dog's head. He slowly picked Maddison up, took her to the bedroom, and placed her on the bed. Maddison didn't wake, and Ben bent down to kiss her forehead.

Maddison swatted him. "Daddy, go to bed. I'm fine. I've got school, and I need to sleep. Mrs. Donovan left scones on the table."

Ben realized the child was sleeping. He covered her with a sheet, went to the porch, and checked his phone. There was a message from Janet and Doug. "See you at the funeral. We're bringing food."

Chapter 23

Rest in Peace

"Grandpa, it's time to get up. It's only an hour until my father's funeral. Here's your coffee." Maddison set the coffee on the table and returned with a plate of scones. "Pop's in the shower. We need to leave soon." She turned and asked Ben to zip up the dress she wore.

Ben fumbled with the zipper. He had tears in his eyes. His only son was to be memorialized in a few hours. There would be no internment. Would he be bringing his granddaughter?

Ben had prepared a brief speech describing Daniel for the service—at least the Daniel he knew. The minister planned a formal ceremony, and then the public could talk about the deceased. Ben knew he would be the only one to speak. They placed Tag in the bathroom in case he wanted to stand or had to relieve himself. Maddison patted his head and told him she would be back soon. "Don't embarrass me, Tag. I won't be long. Stay put, or else."

Nigel, Ben, and Maddison arrived at the church a few minutes before the service began. Maddison wore her new sleeveless white smock summer dress with tiny blue bows. She turned to her grandfathers and took a hand from each. She glanced at Ben and squeezed his hand. "It's okay to be sad, Grandpa. I'm here, and if you need to cry, that's okay."

Nigel looked around and shook his head. "What's with all the cars?" There had to be twenty cars. He thought this would only be them and the social workers. "Maybe there's another function?"

They walked up the stairs of the simple stone church. The arched stained windows made the small room seem bigger than Nigel imagined from the exterior. There were ten to twelve pews on either side of the center aisle. It would be a lovely place for a small wedding. The thought made him smile. He admonished himself for having such thoughts at a time like this.

The church was almost overflowing. Ben and Nigel were surprised at the number of people sitting in the pews. They recognized everyone from the social services, the veterinary clinic, and the neighbors, Doug and Janet, but most were strangers.

Maddison pulled away and ran up to the second pew. She threw her arms around the beautiful lady sitting with a well-dressed man in a suit. Maddison cried and hugged her. Nigel and Ben glanced at one another and shrugged as they made their way to the front pew.

They turned before sitting while waiting for an explanation. The man stood and extended his hand. "Jim Donovan, and this is my wife, Laura."

Ben was the first to shake Jim's hand. "Pleasure to meet you. Can we talk after the service?"

Jim Donovan nodded. Both Nigel and Ben were in awe of the couple. Laura Donovan was the woman who had taken the time to instruct Maddison. She started their grandchild on her educational journey.

Mrs. Donovan leaned toward Maddison and whispered to her. Maddison gazed at the woman and then reluctantly walked around the pew to sit between her grandfathers as the minister entered the room. The minister performed a traditional Anglican service. He then asked Ben to come up and speak to the mourners.

Ben went up to the podium and stared out at the people who attended. "My granddaughter, Maddison, her grandfather, Dr. Nigel Buckby, and I would like to thank you for attending the service today honoring my son. I don't think many of you knew him, and if the truth is told, I didn't know my son as an adult. I want to speak to the son I raised. Daniel was a beautiful boy. He was intelligent and curious. Daniel had autism, and just so you know, there are different spectrums of the disorder. Daniel barely graduated from high school. He was ridiculed and bullied at school. It was a tough gig for a child who would not accept comfort from others. While he could function and live independently, he could not put his arms around his mother and cry. I'm guessing you know people with this disorder. Please show grace to them and especially their family."

Ben regained his composure. "Danny had his issues. One was relating to others, but I can see he set aside any reluctance to distance himself from his beautiful daughter, Maddison." Ben gazed down at his granddaughter and smiled.

"By all accounts, he was a good father, and it shows in this child sitting in the front pew. Nigel and I are the lucky ones who can continue to watch Daniel's beautiful daughter grow and become a person who her father will look down on from heaven with pride. That is all I have to say, and thank you for coming to celebrate my son's life, even if your main reason was the food."

There was a murmur from the congregation. Then Jim Donovan stood and went to the podium. "My name is Jim Donovan, and I employed Dan for three years. Dan and his daughter, Maddy, came to our station in Western Australia looking for work. I was dubious about Dan and reluctant to hire him, but he had a one-year-old kelpie and a small child. We're seven hours from Kalgoorlie, and my wife insisted we allow them to spend the night. We were crutching lambs, and Dan offered to help to pay for a night's lodging.

"He sent his pup to work the sheep, and once shown the crutching technique, he could perform the procedure in half the time of my experienced shepherds. I asked him where he'd learned to work so fast. He mentioned his dad was a vet and had watched him do surgeries. Once in a while, he cut sutures for his father."

Jim Donovan gazed down at Ben, who wiped tears. "But the pup sold me on the need to employ this young man. That dog was one in a million. He answered only to Dan and Maddy, and the rest of us might as well have been sheep. I've never seen a dog so focused on responding to Dan's commands.

"When I entered the house that evening, I was informed I would sleep in the jackaroos' quarters unless I hired this man and his daughter. Laura was in love with Maddy and wouldn't let her go for anything. Anyway, we enjoyed several wonderful years with them and only sent them packing when we realized Maddy needed an education we couldn't provide, even with the School of the Air. It killed us to let the dog leave our station."

Jim paused and glanced down at his wife. "I'm gonna pay for that. Make room in the jackaroos' shed. It killed us to lose that beautiful child and her father. Sometimes you have to sacrifice for your children. We sent our two boys to boarding school, knowing they would never choose to come back. Life on the land is tough. Maddy is different. She will find joy and happiness wherever she goes. She's very much like her father. Daniel Monroe, or as we now know, Taylor, was an intelligent, hard-working, honest man. He will be missed." Jim returned to his seat. His wife placed her arm in his and kissed him.

The service was concluded, and everyone went outside, where food and drinks sat on tables. Many people came out and shook Ben's hand and told him how sorry they were for his loss. Ben recognized one of the voices from his walk on the beach. He wanted to say something, but this was Maddy's moment, and he pretended the woman was there with good intentions.

Maddy went to the Donovans and talked to them. Nigel went to join them. Finally, one of the women from the beach last night came up to him. "That was a very nice service, Mr. Taylor. Oh, I guess it's Dr. Taylor?"

"Yes, thank you for coming. I think we have something in common." He smiled and offered her a cup.

"Oh, what's that?" She beamed broadly, and Ben poured some punch into her cup.

"If I'm not mistaken, I think we both like to walk on North Beach after the sun goes down."

She was startled. She didn't respond for a moment. She then smiled through pursed lips. "Maybe we do." The woman blushed and walked over to her companion. He watched her whisper to the other woman.

"Hey, Ben. How's the patient?" Lindy Smart had observed the interaction and appeared amused. "You never know who you'll meet on the beach."

"Or overhear. I'm supposed to cheer you up. How can I do that, Dr. Smart?"

"Ah, the out-laws are at it again. It's your turn today. I'm supposed to cheer you and Maddy up today, though. We can work on me another day."

Ben cocked his head. "I've been studying the Yorke Peninsula. I hear there's a place called Innes National Park. Any chance you would go with us and show us around?"

"That can be arranged. How about next week after we know Tag's a little better? I think Janet plans to have us all over for dinner tonight. Did you know they know the Donovans, and they're staying with them tonight?"

"Small country." Ben took his second piece of Janet's banana cake.

"Incestuously small." Lindy smiled as she gazed at the group. "I hate standing under these trees. You never know when one is gonna drop a branch. Have you heard of the term 'widowmaker'?"

Ben glanced up and realized he was safe, but Maddison was with the Donovans directly under a large limb of a gum tree. "Let's see. Along with snakes, sharks, and dingoes, do I now need to add eucalyptus trees? It's surprising there's anyone left on this continent."

"That's how I felt when I moved here. You get over it and take precautions. I thought I was escaping the violence of the American inner cities and guns, but I had a client murdered here. You adjust. There're dangers you can avoid, and then there are the others."

Ben studied Lindy's face. Gray hair aside, she appeared to be youthful and athletic. "Do you regret moving to Australia?"

Lindy appeared to consider this. If she'd put her foot down and demanded she and her husband stay in America, he would have stayed. "No. Not in a fit. Best career move I could make. I've had a glorious life here. The pressure is infinitesimal compared to my life in the States."

Lindy and Ben observed Nigel, who was staring at a car that had pulled up to the church. They observed a leggy woman with long blonde dyed hair step out of the car. Nigel immediately put a protective hand on Maddison's shoulder. Everyone turned and stared at the woman.

The woman was dressed in jeans and a tie-dyed shirt with holes that revealed her bra straps. The lady stood surveying the crowd. She finally recognized what must be her daughter. Nigel was shocked to see his daughter and wished she had better clothes.

Isla Buckby watched her father standing next to Maddison, and she noted a protective hand on Maddy's shoulder. "Showtime." She turned to the man who had driven the ute. She whispered, "I don't think the natives are friendly."

He replied, "Yeah, but let's get it over with. I didn't come all this way to walk away."

Nigel had a sharp intake of breath. He felt Maddison's body tense. Nigel had discovered the only picture that Maddison kept hidden in a book was of her mother. It was probably taken before Maddison was born. He knew she had recognized her mother.

Isla Buckby, or was it Taylor, walked straight over to Maddison and kneeled down to eye level. The crowd had stopped talking and watched the interaction. "Hello, darling. I'm your mother."

Chapter 24

Unexpected Guest

Maddison stared and leaned back into Nigel's leg. She reached up and took her grandfather's hand and, gripping it, she tentatively said a quiet, "Hello" in return. The Donovans stood ready.

Maddison glanced furtively at her mother. Finding her mother had been a dream come true. What Maddison had long imagined as a warm reunion unraveled into a living nightmare. Her mother was nothing like the kind, beautiful woman she'd held onto in her dreams. Instead, this woman was disheveled, erratic, and glassy-eyed. This was not the mother she'd dreamed of, and not the woman in the picture she'd hidden and examined so often. Maddison was terrorized. *I won't go with her. They can't make me.*

Fiona walked over to Isla Buckby. Extending her hand, she introduced herself. "I'm Fiona Harding. I'm Maddison's caseworker."

Isla didn't respond and ignored the extended hand. She stood and surveyed the gathering. "I guess I'll take my daughter."

Fiona was prepared for something like this. "I'm sorry, Mrs. Taylor. Are you Isla Taylor? Maddison is under my supervision until we can determine what is in her interest. Would you like to come to my office where we can discuss this?"

Isla was not ready for any obstruction to her plans. "Maddy and I have some catching up to do. We need to chat. I think that's the first order, and then I'll discuss the arrangements for a transfer. As her mother, I have a right to my daughter. I don't think anyone has a legal right to her that usurps mine. After all, I'm her mother." This was stated in a non-emotional, demanding tone.

Isla bent down again. "Darling, you want to come with your mother, don't you?"

Maddison was frightened. She understood her mother would most likely be her future legal guardian. Oh, how she had dreamed of the day she might see her mother again, but she could see her mother was under the influence of something.

"I'm sorry, Mum. I can't go with you now. My dog is sick, so I need to stay with him. I can't."

Nigel had seen enough. "Isla, I." Nigel was in shock. "Well, we were sure you were dead. I'm sorry. Your mother passed many years ago. Can we talk privately? I'm so glad to see you're alive. I want to help you. Perhaps we could meet at Ms. Harding's office."

Ben watched the entire reunion and was alarmed. "Excuse me, Isla?" He had walked over and stood beside Maddison. "I'm Daniel's father and Maddison's grandfather. You're as beautiful as Maddison has described you. We're so happy you and Maddy have found one another. How about I take Maddy back to her dog and you and Nigel can discuss things?" Ben wanted to avoid violent and emotional conflicts for his granddaughter.

"I want my goddamn daughter, and you can't keep her from me." Isla turned, tripped on the root of the tree, and fell.

Ben and Nigel both rushed to her and helped her stand. Her companion was waiting beside their car. He appeared to be as drug-affected as Isla. Ben observed Nigel, who appeared distraught. Ben whispered in Nigel's ear, "I'm going back to the house. Why don't you go back to Fiona's office? Call me after you've discussed this with Fiona."

Nigel was close to tears. Confirmation that his daughter was alive was one thing, but he could see she hadn't changed her ways. She always hid her drug use when she was still living at home. Now he was seeing the devastation that her substance abuse had done to his beautiful, smart child. His heart ached, but he wanted to hide it from Maddison. He would protect her with his life.

The Donovans offered to take Maddison and Ben back to the beach house. This left Nigel with his rental car. Nigel bent down and kissed Maddison on the forehead. "I'll see you and Tag back at the house, darling. You have nothing to fear."

Maddison stared at the car, which was entering the main road back to Kadina. She appeared to be shocked. Ben held her hand as they walked to the Donovans' car. She said nothing on the way back to the beach house. She leaned into Mrs. Donovans where they sat together in the back seat. Maddison's silence spoke volumes.

When they arrived at the Smart's beach house, Maddison immediately ran next door. Tag had remained where he was left. Maddison and Ben helped the dog onto the grass, where he relieved himself and then walked a few feet to the edge of the grass and lay down in a small area of shade.

Maddison brought him his water bowl and some meat treats. Tag's appetite was improving. Ben observed this and knew this dog would survive. He felt such relief. So much was on the line with this dog. His granddaughter didn't have any obvious need for a cuddle toy or blanket. This dog was her sole source of emotional support.

After a few minutes, Maddison went into the house and returned wearing a tee shirt and shorts. She went over to the neighbors and knocked on the sliding glass door. "Would you like to see Tag? He's out on the lawn."

The Donovans walked over and saw the poor creature. They were greeted with a wag and a successful attempt to stand without help. Jim bent to scratch Tag behind the ear. "You poor bastard. You've been through it, for sure, mate." He glanced at Ben, who'd returned from the house with a beer.

In all the drama, everyone forgot Ben had just attended his only child's funeral. Laura considered the man's plight.

"Where are our manners, Ben? How are you? What can we do for you?"

Ben was feeling the swing of the emotional pendulum from today's events. His son was now eulogized and, to most people, forgotten. There was a threat to his granddaughter's well-being with the arrival of Maddison's mother. And then the almost hopeless injuries to the dog appeared to be resolving. But he was a man, and he had responsibilities. "I'm fine."

The Donovans knew better. Laura came over and sat down next to him and took his hand. "I can't thank you enough for what you and Nigel are doing for Maddy and for Tag. You're obviously a gifted surgeon."

Ben deflected the praise. "No, I just helped Dr. Hancock. It was a team effort. The actual hero is Nigel. He's footing the bill."

Chapter 25

Wake

Nigel drove with Fiona to her office. Both she and Terri took him into a private room. Fiona stared at Nigel. "Can we get you some tea?"

"More like a stiff drink. I don't know what to say." Nigel stared at a poster on the wall. "Bombshell? I guess that would be the only way I can describe the events." He paused and sipped his tea. "If Isla had been anything but drugged to the hilt, Maddy would have done everything to go with her." Nigel rubbed hi thigh. "I'm glad she's alive, but Isla's not fit to take on a child. I'm guessing there'll be a negotiation, and she'll ask for money to relinquish custody. She hasn't changed. I'm glad Isla's mother wasn't there to see that performance."

Terri handed Nigel a cup of tea. "This is more like what we're used to with our cases. We can deal with it, Nigel.

You have no worries. We're sworn to protect the child. The question is, how will this play on poor little Maddy? Before you arrived, we had a talk with her, and she was adamant she would go live with her mother if we could find her. I guess you can blame us. We did a search, and we're probably to blame for finding her."

Terri sat back in her chair. "At least you know she's alive. We all live hoping we can fix our children's problems. There are some good options for addicts these days."

Nigel shook his head. "I suppose I'm like all parents. Where there's life, there's hope. We took Isla to rehab in New Zealand. She lasted a week before she went back to her dealer boyfriend. We tried one more time, but she left the facility, and we never saw her again. I'm so glad my wife didn't see her today. It would have killed her." He looked up and realized the irony of talking about his deceased wife to his new love interest. Still, Nigel would do anything to get his pre-teen daughter back.

Fiona placed her hand on his. "We all have family members who have disappointed us. We try, but sometimes the desire to change must come from them. Hopefully, she'll come and see us today or tomorrow."

"I'd better go back to the beach house. Thanks. I need to know you won't let Maddison go with her if she's..." Nigel faltered. He was in shock. "You saw it."

Terri and Fiona stood and assured Nigel that they would not allow Isla to take his granddaughter unless there was a change in her circumstances. "We'll call you if she comes here. Go home and comfort your granddaughter. That's the best you can do."

Nigel returned to the beach house. Ben was alone in the kitchen. "Hey, Nige. How about a beer? Everyone's out back."

"Shit of a day, Ben. A beer will hardly suffice."

"I'm not sure which of us saw the worst of it. I guess there's always hope she'll get some help." Ben was divided. His parental journey was over, but poor Nigel still had the issues and guilt that came from raising a less-than-ideal child.

"Yeah mate. You're the one we should be comforting. Sorry. What can I do?" Nigel sighed.

"Go out and calm the kid. We have serious competition with our guests." Ben handed Nigel a beer, picked up a tray with cheese and crackers, and left Nigel.

Maddison was in shock. Since she moved from the station, her secret goal was to find her mother. She never thought her dream reunion would have scared her like it did. Her mother reminded her of the times when Maddison sat outside the hotel in the outback when her father had told her to wait for a minute while he got them drinks. She and Tag sat on a bench and waited for hours while men would come and go, and her father would not leave until he was kicked out.

Men would come and sit with her and tell her stories and try to get her to sit on their laps. The hotel owner would chase the men away and then throw her father out. Daniel would be incapable of driving back to the station, and they would sleep in the truck until morning.

This was worse. Her mother frightened her. Maddison sensed this woman was so affected that she was scary. Maddison wondered if she could help her. In the last year, Maddison thought she'd kept her father sober. Could she do it with her mother? She'd encountered drugged-out men and women at the caravan park. They could not stay once their behavior was detected. Cleaning the rooms following their departure was one of the worst jobs Daniel had to do.

If the Donovans hadn't shown up, this would have been the worst day of her life. She asked Mrs. Donovan to walk on the beach. She thought Mrs. Donovan would say something to ease her mind.

Mrs. Donovan agreed, and the two held hands as they walked down the path along the cliff face, through a sizable accumulation of seaweed and finally onto the pristine beach where families and teenagers played and swam in the shallow waters.

Laura Donovan didn't waste time. "Rough day, Maddy?"

"Yep." Maddy picked up a shell and handed it to her companion.

"I like your grandfathers." Laura Donovan tried to help Maddison find the good in the day.

"Yeah?" Maddison paused. "I miss the station. I wish I could go back."

"Maddison, we sold the station. We don't live there anymore." Mrs. Donovan stroked Maddison's hair.

Maddison was surprised and disappointed. She turned to Mrs. Donovan and, for the first time today, she cried, "Why?" She gulped as she asked it.

"Well, we had several reasons. One is we're getting older. It's getting harder for us. We want to see the world, and we want to be closer to our grandchildren. We haven't seen them for over a year, and we want to be part of their lives." She put her arm around Maddison's shoulder. "You know, you have two wonderful grandfathers. I can see they love you. You're a lucky little girl."

"But they're old. And they live in other countries. I'll have to leave Australia. It's my home."

"Maddy, I don't know how old your grandfathers are, but I know Mr. Donovan and I are older. If we were younger, we'd fight the devil to keep you ourselves. Buck up, old girl. My guess is you'll have a wonderful life, and I wish I could be there for all of it, but we both know that won't happen. I know nothing's been decided. Have you got a favorite? You don't have to tell me. Just keep an open mind—it's early days. If you still want to be a veterinarian, I think either of your grandfathers would be keen to help you reach your goal."

Maddison didn't answer. She considered this. It was like when she found out she was leaving the Donovans. When would the losses stop? When would she know where she and Tag would live and with whom?

"How's Nanna? I miss her stories about the old days." Nanna was an Aboriginal elder. She'd lived on the Donovans' station for over fifty years and well before the Donovans had bought the Coonana Station. She had passed several months ago.

Mrs. Donovan didn't want to burden Maddison any more today. "Oh, her stories are wonderful. Shouldn't we get back?"

"I suppose. Are you still going on your trip to Ireland? When do you leave? I'd like to see where Mr. Donovan's family lived." Maddison had several dreams about Nanna. Nanna came and told her stories about those dreams. She suspected Nanna had passed. It was too much to add to her troubles today. She looked up at the cliff face and saw Pop waving to them.

Mrs. Donovan waved back. "Dinner must be ready."

When they climbed the path to the grass verge and crossed to the veranda, Dr. Smart had arrived. She was helping her mother-in-law with the food preparation. She saw Maddison and smiled. Maddison returned the greeting. Dr. Smart was living proof a woman could be a vet.

After dinner and when everyone was sure Maddison was asleep, the conversation turned to the problems facing her and her grandfathers. Ben was sixty-eight and Nigel was four years younger. Both men were healthy and had only recently retired. Neither had any intention of raising a six-year-old—well until they met her. Neither had any significant obligations in their respective countries. What was stopping them?

Both men considered the prospect of relocation. Working together or nearby and sharing the parenting duties was an unmentioned possibility. Would either man be considered a suitable long-term parent by the agency?

Laura Donovan was the first to broach the topic. "Anyone want to discuss the elephant in the room?"

Everyone smiled and acknowledged the topic. Both Nigel and Ben stared at one another. Nigel spoke first.

"Ben, no one will think less of you if you feel it's too much for an old man."

"Ditto, my friend." Ben had switched to sipping on a port that the Smarts had offered him.

Nigel abstained. "Ever think of living in New Zealand? I could teach you to fly fish."

Ben nodded. "How about you move to the States? You can fish year-round, and I could teach you the proper use of an AK-47. Of course, there are the earthquakes to consider."

"But you don't live in California." Nigel knew he was kidding.

"Uh, no. I was thinking of your little rock and rolling island. I must admit, Charleston is sitting on a large fault. The town was almost destroyed in the 1800s."

The Donovans found the topic amusing, but then remembered Maddison. Jim Donovan observed the interactions of the two grandfathers. "The YP seems pretty nice. Any chance of a compromise?"

"It's a consideration." Nigel thought of Fiona and smiled. As a citizen of both the UK and New Zealand, he didn't fuss about the idea of moving.

Ben realized he was in a corner. The beach was nice, but the Yorke Peninsula was rather stark. Then there was Maddison's education. At some stage, she would have to attend a school catering to exceptional students. The YP was only a temporary solution. Still, he would think about it. Maybe they could co-parent Maddison. How would that work?

Doggie duties were performed, thank-yous given to the Donovans and Smarts, dishes washed, and one more beer each was consumed without comment. Each man had something to consider. Nigel picked up the sleeping child from the living room and carried her to her room. She swatted him when he kissed her but was asleep a second later.

Nigel returned to the living room. "Your thoughts, mate?"

Ben was emotionally exhausted. "Let's give it a day or two. I want to get through the holidays. This poor kid deserves a Christmas."

Chapter 26

Isla

Isla knew she had made a mistake by crashing Dan's funeral. Her new boyfriend had insisted they take the child. He referred to the child as a meal ticket. He'd researched Daniel Taylor, and while he didn't suspect there was any money in the estate, he thought Isla's father would pay them to drop any custody demands.

Isla was past any interest in the money. She was consumed by guilt for abandoning her daughter and Daniel. She'd never wanted to be saddled with a child. When she found out she was pregnant, she wasn't even sure who the father was. Of all the men she'd slept with, Daniel was the only one who would take responsibility. In all likelihood, he was the father, so Isla never told him about the others.

She remained clean and sober during the pregnancy, but shortly after Maddison was born, she went back to her old ways. She and Dan fought, and one day, she walked away. She'd met an older man who'd given her anything she wanted until his demands for "compensation" became too bizarre, and she left with a friend for Thailand.

Isla knew she was walking a tightrope, so periodically she would check into a rehab facility, which was usually funded by whomever she was living with at the time. She returned to Australia, and in Queensland, she assumed a new identity. There may have been an issue with a rather large hotel bill in New South Wales, so she stayed away from her old haunts.

In Queensland, she hooked up with a group of religious families. For several months, she was once again clean and sober, but eventually, she was asked to leave the commune when it was discovered she was shoplifting to meet her needs, which had once again returned.

As a beautiful woman, Isla never lacked companionship. She went through men and relationships regularly. She saw many of her companions die from overdoses, and she was smart enough to use reliable sources for her needs. One man after another would use and abuse her and then kick her out.

It was a chance encounter with a mutual friend of Daniel's who informed her he was using a new name. She still was unable to track him down until she was told he might live in South Australia. She had no priors in the state and could go there without fear of being arrested. Her new boyfriend had nothing better to do, and he suggested they might go there and see if they could get money from Daniel with a promise that she would never try to take the child.

Shortly before they left Queensland, Isla went to the library to try once again to locate where Daniel and Maddison lived. It was by pure chance that she found the article about the accident and Daniel's death. Damn, Isla wasn't in any position to parent the child. Her boyfriend did further research and realized Isla's family, or possibly Daniel's family, would assume custody.

The boyfriend encouraged Isla to take advantage of the situation, as this might be an opportunity to get a large payout to walk away and leave the child with her grandfather. He had a friend who was a lawyer in Adelaide. Through the lawyer, he received information about Daniel. He quietly encouraged Isla to get control of her daughter and any assets that might go to the child.

Chapter 27

Swimming Lessons

Maddison woke early and went straight to Tag. He wagged his tail and stood on his own. Maddison whispered, "Hey, Taggie, stay for a minute. Let me start some coffee."

Maddison was still thinking about her mother. She wanted to remember her mother in the picture she had, not the woman she'd met yesterday. She was frightened her mother would take her away. She didn't want to go with her. She was sure her mother was on drugs. She'd seen people like that before, and her father had cautioned her to stay away from anyone who acted like that. Mrs. Donovan was the mother she really wanted.

She set up the small coffee maker as she had for her father and then placed a towel under Tag's abdomen to help him walk out to the grass to relieve himself. Maddison considered yesterday's events. If yesterday wasn't bad enough, her beloved adopted family was leaving. She'd hoped the Donovans would ask her to go with them to Ireland, but she knew that wouldn't happen. She had to stay and care for Tag.

Maddison heard the beep indicating the coffee was perked and waiting. She wished one or the other of her grandfathers would be up soon. She stood and gazed down at the beach. There were several people walking on the water's edge. The sea was like glass, and she wished she could go swimming. Her father had not taught her to swim. She could tread water, so the surf didn't scare her. She wondered if either of her grandfathers would continue the lessons.

Maddison wanted to cry when she remembered meeting her mother. Her hopes for a reunion and possible new family were crushed yesterday. Now she had a fresh fear. What if they made her live with her mother? She'd run away.

She overheard the caseworkers saying she would not get a proper education here. She loved her last teacher, but she knew she wasn't learning as much as she did with Mrs. Donovan. Miss Osbourne said she was so smart that she would be ready for uni next year.

She considered her grandfathers. They were kind and smart and, so far, didn't get drunk. Her mother's father was humorous. She didn't understand most of his jokes, but she knew they were funny. Her other grandfather looked like her father. She wished they could have met him. Maddison wondered what would happen today. She dreaded seeing her mother again.

Tag lay down on the grass, and Maddison went into the house to prepare her dog's breakfast. She knew he needed antibiotics, but she'd been told her grandfather was in charge of the medication. Her grandfather emerged from his room and patted Maddison as he headed to the bathroom. "Maddy, let me give Tag his medicine before you feed him."

Her grandfather came out to the porch with the pills and opened Tag's mouth, placed the pills at the back of his throat, then nodded to Maddison. "You're the good carer, and I'm the bad guy. Tag will always love you."

"Tag loves you too, you know." Maddy didn't look at her grandfather as she commented. She wanted to say she was so grateful for her grandfather's help but didn't want to say she loved him. She liked him, and she was grateful, but she felt if she said it out loud, her grandfather might leave. She was happy with things as they were.

"Maddy, after Tag eats, why don't you get your swimsuit on, and we can go down to the beach? I'd like to see how you swim. We're having breakfast with the Donovans, so it will have to be a quick swim."

Maddison wanted to be cautious. "What about Pop? You know I can't play favorites." Maddison turned away and helped Tag stand.

"Let's let him sleep for a while. He had a rough day yesterday." Ben felt bad. He knew his son was dead, but Nigel had hoped his daughter would be found and be the kind, caring mother she should have been all along. Ben knew Nigel's, and probably Maddison's, hopes had dissolved.

Down at the beach, Maddison tentatively stepped into the water. It felt cool, but the waves were small. Her grandfather took her hand, and they walked farther into the clear, calm surf. They had to walk a distance from the shore to reach an area deep enough to swim in. Maddison's father usually picked her up and then threw her into the deeper water, forcing her to dog paddle back to him. She waited, but her grandfather only walked farther until Maddison rose with the water. She kicked and used her free arm to stay afloat.

"I've got you. You're safe with me, Maddy. I won't let go until you tell me it's okay." The words surprised her. They were foreign. She sputtered and let go. She'd played in the water at the caravan park, but the pool was shallow, and she could always stand up. No one noticed she didn't know the basic strokes of swimming.

Maddison let go for a second and then grabbed his arm and clung to her grandfather. She let go again and then moved her arms to stay afloat. She went back and forth, treading water and holding on to her grandfather.

He never pushed her, and he slowly had her using her arms to perform the freestyle stroke that he'd learned as a child. He held her waist as she eventually used both her arms and kicked with her legs. After a few minutes, he let her go, and she performed a few strokes, and then she stood as the tide retreated, and the level of the water decreased.

The two spent several more minutes before Nigel joined them. They walked to a deeper area, and soon Maddison was swimming from one grandfather to another. Maddison didn't want it to end, but she knew there were things that had to be done today—hard things.

Both grandfathers took her hands and lifted her over the clumps of seaweed as they returned to the house. She didn't let go of either hand as they walked up the path to the cliff top overlooking the beach.

Nigel glanced at Ben and smiled as Ben stared at the path ahead. Both men were fit, but the path was steep. Nigel suggested they shower quickly and get ready for a quick breakfast with the Donovans. Maddison said she didn't need a shower. She had sand and flecks of seaweed clinging to her legs.

"The shower or the outside hose. Your choice, my dear." Nigel was firm.

"Grandpa?" Maddison stared at her other grandfather.

"Maddy, I'm guessing you might want me to side with you on that. Sorry, darling. Not gonna happen." As they approached the house, Ben grabbed Maddison and put her in a headlock while Nigel got the hose and attempted to remove the residue from her suit and body. Mrs. Donovan emerged as the two men attempted to rid Maddison of the last of the sand.

She shook her head and pointed to the two men. "I saw you all swimming. Maddy, you're becoming a wonderful swimmer."

Maddison grinned and ran to the woman. "They're abusing me, ma'am. Can you take me away?"

Mrs. Donovan didn't reply. She pointed to the door that led to the laundry. "Get, before I take a switch to you."

Maddison turned to the men. "You don't want to disobey Mrs. Donovan. That could be painful." She rubbed her bottom. Ben suspected the whole interaction was for show. He took Tag out once again onto the grass while Nigel showered.

They carried leftover scones from the funeral to the Smarts for a quick breakfast. Maddison hugged and said goodbye to the Donovans, who piled into the old truck. Maddison was grieving once again with yet another loss. Nigel could see Maddison's sorrow. He knew this had been a pattern all this poor child's life. He was determined to stop his granddaughter's losses.

Chapter 28

Daniel's Gift

Maddison, Nigel, and Ben arrived at the social services offices and were asked to wait while both Fiona and Terri were taking a call. Maddison sat between them and had a magazine. Nigel looked down and saw the magazine was for women and opened to a page about how to rekindle a relationship, including pictures of men and women in compromising poses. He immediately took it out of her hands and replaced it with a children's comic book.

"Hey. I was reading that." Maddison immediately reached over to exchange the comic book for the magazine. Nigel took her hand and firmly stopped the exchange.

"You can't read that, anyway." Nigel then took the magazine and opened it to a page about Princess Diana and Prince Charles. He then looked at the date. It was a couple of months old. Don't these people ever stop trying to use the poor woman to sell their sleaze?

Ben was absorbed in reading a message on his phone. Lindy Smart asked him if Maddison wanted to spend the day with her in the truck. She was going down to Minlaton to see a couple of horses for the Butlers. She could come by and pick up Maddison so they could get some things done without "little ears."

Ben texted her: Can you come to Fiona's office before she and Nigel come to blows?

Lindy: ??

Ben: It's not little ears. It's little eyes.

Lindy: :) O-M-W.

Ben had to think about O-M-W. On my way? He answered: Thanks? I think?

Ben turned to Maddison. "Darling, would you like to ride with Dr. Smart on a call?"

Maddison stood up and fist pumped. "Yes, yes, yes. When?"

"I think she'll be here in a few minutes."

"I don't have my work clothes. I need my boots." Maddison was ready to cry.

"Where are they?" Neither Nigel nor Ben knew of any work clothes for Maddison.

"I can't go in these clothes," Maddison wailed.

"Ben, do we have time to get her some boots?"

Maddison stared out the window and saw Lindy pull up in front of the building. Maddison was beside herself. "How am I gonna work without my proper clothing?"

Both Ben and Nigel were about to see this precocious child have a meltdown. She was a child after all.

Lindy Smart walked in with a bag of clothes. "Mrs. Yarran left these with me when they brought in Tag. Is there somewhere you can change?"

Nigel took Maddison to the bathroom. Seconds later, Maddison returned wearing her old clothes and boots with holes in the soles. Maddison advised them not to wait up for her. "It'll be a long day. Leave a key under the mat, and I'll let myself in."

Both Ben and Nigel high-fived each other. Ben grinned. "Nige, this is great. First, we know she's human. Second, we know her limits—she has typical fashion expectations. And we also know we don't need to live forever. She'll let herself in, and our presence is only a temporary need until she can drive."

Fiona entered the waiting room and observed Nigel and Ben laughing hysterically. "Must be hilarious. You gentlemen ready?" She dreaded the next conversation.

Nigel was given tea, and Ben asked for coffee. They both could see this would not be a fun discussion.

"Ben, we found a will. Your son left all his assets to Maddy. We assumed it would be his personal possessions, and of course, the vehicle was written off. We were wrong. While he worked for the Donovans, they had helped Daniel set up a trust fund for Maddy. Jim Donovan had a broker who guided them both, and Jim gave him his initial startup money in return for Tag's services. We were given the trust account information from the Donovans. They're the executors. Did they mention that yesterday?"

The two men shook their heads and shrugged. Terri sat back and continued, "We were able to order a copy of the trust, and this arrived late yesterday. We didn't open it until we received a call from Isla."

Both Ben and Nigel were unaware of a will or trust. "It's news to me?" Ben was pleased his son had done this much to protect his daughter.

"Here's the problem. Well, it's a pleasant problem, but it is a problem. Did you know Daniel was active in the stock market? Looking at the portfolio, he apparently was a bit of a savant in trading shares and equities. I'd kind of say he was a Warren Buffett, but his work might eclipse Berkshire Hathaway."

Ben was handed some paperwork, and Nigel watched as Ben scanned the document. Ben was shocked at what he was reading. The assets were close to a million dollars, and Maddison was almost set for life. The implications for Ben were overwhelming. His son was not a total failure. Daniel had channeled his autism disorder tendencies into managing a program that had accumulated assets that Ben would have paid money to learn.

Ben was so amazed and sad at once. If he could have only known his son, he could have told him how proud he was to be his father. Ben excused himself and left the room. He went to the bathroom and took several minutes to compose himself. When he returned, he asked how this would affect the decision to care for Maddison. No one answered for what seemed like forever.

Finally, Fiona began the discussion. "We have a problem. We aren't the only ones who have a copy of the trust papers.

It turns out Isla's friend knows a lawyer. He found a copy of the papers, and the two of them have filed a petition to seek immediate custody of the child and get access to the funds, so they can care for Maddison until a formal hearing will decide who will raise her."

Both Ben and Nigel gazed at Fiona and Terri. Ben spoke first. "I guess you know what I'm thinking."

Nigel answered, "Does it begin with an F?"

"We need a high-powered attorney. Do either of you know one?" Ben searched their faces.

"We have to remain impartial and not be seen to take sides. You may want to call our friend who had a legal problem and found a legal eagle. He's not cheap, and this isn't his specialty, but he's the guy in South Australia who gets the job done. We didn't tell you this. Ask Lindy. She knows the situation."

"Okay? Was it a custody issue?" Nigel put his hand on his forehead. But it wasn't okay. Nothing was okay. It was going from bad to worse. He and Ben knew the courts would often side with the parents despite evidence that the parent was an abuser. At least, that was how things worked in New Zealand.

Terri hated herself for times like this. She knew how drugs affected Isla was yesterday. She could see the toll this woman's long-standing drug abuse took on her body and mind. Sometimes Terri wanted to quit. "Actually, it was a murder."

Ben stood. "I'm stepping outside. I need to phone a friend about a horse."

Ben had Lindy's number on his phone. He prayed she would answer. She didn't. He left a voice message. "Hey, Dr. Smart. It's me, Ben. I need a favor ASAP. Can you call me back? It's urgent regarding your new vet nurse." He hung up and sat outside the social services office.

After several minutes, Nigel joined him in the car. Ben was staring at his phone. "No answer. How can we find out who this person is and get the contact number?"

Nigel opened his phone. He Googled murder cases in South Australia and found several. He was surprised considering that the country had banned firearms. Most were knives, but there were still several gun related murders. He scrolled, looking for something that would give them a clue. Then he saw it.

"Bingo. I'll bet five this is the case. It's a vet who was accused of murder." He read the news reports about the case and then went back to read more.

"Jesus, Dr. Carly Langley was accused of murdering her neighbor. She supposedly drugged her with phenobarbital. She planned to murder the old lady for the inheritance."

Ben's phone rang. "Hey, it's me. What's up?" Ben was relieved to hear from Lindy.

"Houston, we have a problem. Is this on speaker?"

"No. I had a feeling this was not for little ears. How can I help?"

"Do you know a vet named?" Ben turned to Nigel, who whispered the name. "Do you know Carly Langley?"

"Yep. She's one of my best friends. She's a horse vet who used to work up north but now lives outside of Gawler. Why?"

"Do you know the lawyer who helped her? We need legal help. Maddy's mom is petitioning to take custody. It's a long story."

"You're kidding me?" Lindy was shocked.

"I wish I were." Ben and Nigel were on speaker and could hear the conversation.

Nigel gave Ben a hurry-up motion with his hand. "We need the lawyer's number, Lindy. Do you know his name?"

"Give me two minutes. I'll text you Carly's number." She hung up, and the men went to Nigel's car and waited. It was another hot day, and they sat inside the car with the doors wide-open.

Ben received a text with Carly's personal number and a good-luck four-leaf clover. Lindy sent a second message to text her if they needed anything else. They received a third text saying one of Carly's children was sick, and she may not respond right away.

Ben dialed the number, which went to voicemail. He quickly explained he was a vet from the States and needed some advice regarding a legal issue, and Lindy Smart had recommended a lawyer who had helped her in the past. He needed the lawyer's number, and it was urgent.

They went back to the beach house and waited. When they returned, Ben saw Tag had moved from his mat in the laundry to an area on the carpet near the porch. Ben opened the door, and Tag limped out on his own to the grass verge and relieved himself. Ben petted the dog. He thought about how important this dog was to Maddison, and he knew if Nigel's daughter got custody, there was no chance she would take on the dog as well.

Ben would never abandon Tag. He was in love with him as much as his granddaughter was. He knew Nigel would do the same. Once Tag was settled back in the house, Ben joined Nigel and his laptop, perusing the news articles about the case and the lawyer. Luke Sullivan did not do family law. He apparently helped the vet beat the false charges of murder. How was this guy going to help? Maybe it's another lawyer who they were all remembering. It was over four years ago.

Ben's phone rang. "Hello? This is Carly. May I speak to Dr. Taylor?"

Ben couldn't speak fast enough and fumbled with the phone. "Dr. Langley, hi I'm Ben Taylor. I'm over on the Yorke Peninsula, and I need a family law lawyer regarding my granddaughter. Lindy Smart and some people from the child protection agency said you know someone who maybe knows someone who can help me. It may be urgent. I'm so sorry to bother you. I understand you have a sick child."

"Thanks. Yeah, I thought being accused of murder was the low point in my life. I was mistaken. I'll text you my friend's number. She's a reporter who's the partner of the barrister who saved my butt. He changes his number all the time, but her name is Kate Kilroy. She'll be able to direct you. They're both friends. Let me call her first and give her a heads-up. I need to go. Good luck and say hi to Lindy for me."

Chapter 29

We Need a Solicitor

Kate Kilroy's number came through as a text from Dr. Langley several minutes later. Immediately, a silent number flashed on Ben's phone. He answered with a hello.

"Hi. This is Kate Kilroy. I'm sorry, I don't know who you are. Are you a friend of Carly's?" Her voice was all business.

"Ms. Kilroy, I'm Ben Taylor. I'm a friend of a friend of Dr. Langley. We have a bit of an emergency regarding the custody of my six-year-old granddaughter. I need a..." Ben paused. "Well, frankly, I need a ball-buster lawyer. I understand your partner helped Carly. I'm an American vet too. We need a recommendation, is all. We know Mr. Sullivan doesn't do family law, but we've been told he knows people who may be able to help us."

There was a long silence. Ben shrugged as both he and Nigel waited. Finally, a man's voice came on the line. "This is Luke Sullivan. So, do you know Carly?"

"Uh, not directly. Well, really, not at all. We're out on the Yorke Peninsula, and we've become friends with a vet friend of hers. I'm a vet too. My son was killed in an automobile accident out near Kadina, and I came over to see about his daughter. At the same time, her maternal grandfather, Dr. Nigel Buckby, came out for the same purpose. We're both on a speakerphone. We didn't know we had a granddaughter, and we only found out our granddaughter's mother was alive yesterday. It's complicated, but we don't want to waste your time. We simply need a lawyer who can perform miracles."

Nigel nodded. "Mr. Sullivan, I'm Nigel and the other grandfather. I'm from New Zealand, and we just want the best for our granddaughter. Can you give us a contact number? We're sorry to take up your time. We heard about you, and we're desperate."

Luke Sullivan had such a cultured voice. "May I call you back? I'll need to make some enquiries. Is this a good number?"

"Yes. We think we may need an urgent application for the court regarding temporary custody. My daughter has drug issues, and to be honest, until yesterday, we didn't even know she was alive. She showed up at Ben's son's funeral and fell in front of everyone. The agency said she's seeking a temporary injunction to take Maddy. So you see, it's urgent. Thank you for your help. We're quite capable of paying anything to ensure our granddaughter's safety and future."

"Got it. I'll call you back within the hour. What is your granddaughter's full name? Do you have a case number? And did you say you're in Kadina?"

Nigel reached over for the papers and gave Luke Sullivan the details. He closed the phone. "I'm sorry, Ben. I should have done better in raising Isla. I regret so many things about all this. Should I have mentioned the inheritance?"

"Nige, we all have regrets. We can explain all the details when we talk to whoever takes the case. What's the story about the vet accused of murder?"

"From what I've read, she was accused, but in the end, it was possibly COVID that killed the old lady. It seems Carly Langley was the target of a plot to murder the woman by a mad lawyer and the vet's husband. They planted evidence to blame the vet. Her husband was having marital affairs and wanted to put her in prison. It sounds convoluted. Apparently, it was on television as one of those news documentaries." Nigel realized it was close to lunchtime.

The phone rang again. Ben answered it. "Hi, Grandpa. How's Tag?"

"Hey, honey. I'm putting you on speaker. Tag's fine. Are you having a good time?"

"Hi, Maddy, are you ever going to come back? We miss you." Nigel turned from Ben, and Ben could see him wipe his eyes.

"Of course, I'm coming back. I'm out with Mr. Butler. He has draft horses. He and I are riding out toward a herd of cattle. We're bringing them into the corral. Mr. Butler's uncle was a famous pilot, and there's a museum with his plane at the museum. Dr. Smart and I are going there to have lunch in town, and there's a chocolate shop, too. We have another call now, and I wanted to tell you I'll be late. This is so much fun. I helped with a castration and repaired a hole in the belly. So, I'd better hand the phone back. Don't wait up for me."

Lindy got on the phone. "Or as a translation, we're having a serious vet-girl day, and we'll stop by Mickey D's on the way home, but we'll be there before dark. All's good. She's brilliant company. Thanks for letting me take her. Hope everything works out?"

"Yeah, thanks for the referral. We're waiting on a call from the legal eagle. We talked to him already. Thanks again. Take care."

Ben appreciated Lindy's involvement. Maybe her connection with Maddison might help her overcome her grief? It was ridiculous to use a verb like overcome. He knew he would probably never get over his personal heartache for his losses. He wished Tania could have met her granddaughter. Maddison didn't resemble his side of the family, but she had that take-no-prisoner attitude Tania showed, even toward the end of her life when she put her foot down and told everyone she was not spending another cent or minute fighting the inevitable. She told the doctors and Ben they could all go to hell. Maddison was Tania's granddaughter, for sure.

The men made sandwiches but decided against the beer. They took Tag out to the porch, and while he rested on his elevated bed, they ate cheese sandwiches and drank lemonade. Neither man spoke.

Nigel considered his options. If he could have Maddison come and live with him, he would be happy to move to South Australia. He'd visited the wine country and the Barossa with Bette when Nigel had come for reproductive conferences. He also liked the McLaren Vale area south of Adelaide. He could easily nip over to New Zealand and indulge his need to fly fish. He would love to teach his granddaughter to fish.

Nigel tipped his head back. He craved sleep. Last night was rough. He kept reliving the funeral and the unexpected entrance of his poor daughter. He shuddered at seeing her trip on the tree roots that rose above the ground. He hated to think she was living in such a state of deprivation.

Ben used his phone to reply to a few emails from home. The clinic was thriving, and the neighbor picked up his mail. They'd had a light dusting of snow in Charleston. He couldn't believe he was wearing shorts and swimming in the ocean, but had he gone on his Caribbean scuba diving trip, he would be in a similar environment. He considered how his life had changed in the last few days. In a million years...

An hour later, his phone rang. It was another silent number. "Hello?" He clicked on the speaker.

"Hi, Ben. It's Luke. Do you want the good news or the bad news?"

"We only want good news, Mr. Sullivan."

"It's Luke, and you're going to get all the news. First of all, the solicitor I wanted, and by the way, we call most lawyers solicitors or barristers here, can't take the case. He's accepted the case for the little girl's mother. He's the ball-buster you required, but that won't happen. You know it's almost Christmas, and trying to find a decent lawyer in Adelaide is nigh on impossible, so you're going to have to deal with me. I'm so out of my depth on this, but I did a little research, so I know more about the case. I feel if we work quickly, we'll have a chance of sorting this out for the benefit of your granddaughter. I need to ask one important question. I need a straight answer before I agree to take on the case."

Both Ben and Nigel nodded. Nigel answered. "Yes. Of course, is it the money?"

Luke Sullivan laughed. "No, much worse than that. If your granddaughter could be in a safe and loving home that was not yours, could you be happy and abide by the court's decision?"

Ben answered, "If we knew she was safe, and she could reach her full potential, and she was loved, I think both Nigel and I would be thrilled." Ben glanced over at Nigel, who shrugged and nodded.

"Okay, how fast can one of you come over? Mr. Buckby, I'm guessing you would be the best one to come. Does one of you need to stay home with Maddison?"

"She's not here right now, but I think Ben can stay when she returns, and I can meet you wherever you'd like. I'll start driving as soon as we hang up. Where do you want to meet?"

Chapter 30

Legal Eagle

A few minutes later, Nigel was on his way to Luke Sullivan's home in Glenelg. It would be a two-hour trip each way. Nigel hedged his bets and took an overnight bag. He had a to-do list for Ben. Ben would call the minister and anyone else he could find and get witness statements from Isla's appearance at the funeral. Mr. and Mrs. Smart were happy to provide a statement about what they saw.

The Donovans had flown to Sydney and were spending a day visiting their son and daughter before flying to Europe. They will download a statutory declaration form and detail their observations. They gave Ben their contact numbers and email address in case there were any problems.

The minister said his back was turned, and he saw nothing. He felt it was improper for him to take sides, but he had heard from some of the attendees that it didn't look good. He talked about the family unit and how it was his goal to reunite families in conflict. This guy has no clue. Ben and Nigel suspected the minister thought women who were abused should stay in the matrimonial home—so disappointing.

Ben wondered if the women he overheard at the beach, who had attended the funeral, would support him or be one of those stand-by-your-man kind of women. He had to be home when Maddison returned. It was a long shot, but maybe he might see one or the other on the beach. He put Tag in the house and shut the door and walked down to the beach.

Ben walked for an hour up and down the shore and didn't see anyone he recognized. There was a woman with a Kelpie who he knew was staying down along the row of houses along the cliff face. She usually had on earphones and may have been listening to music or maybe an audiobook. He noticed the dog had a wry nose. The nose turned to one side. The dog was not young and was red and tan. Tag was black and tan. This dog loved to chase a ball and would run in and out of the surf as its owner threw or kicked the ball. He waved, and she smiled and returned the wave but did not talk. Ben returned to the house, medicated and fed Tag, then waited for a report from Nigel and Maddison's return.

Nigel didn't waste his driving time brooding about what he had to do. As he drove toward Adelaide and the adjacent suburb of Glenelg, he called his neighbor and fishing partner. "Hey, Jock, it's me. Don't tell me how the fish are biting. I don't want to know."

"You've missed little, bro. It's been raining, and the water isn't fishable. How's it going over there? How's your granddaughter? Any word on Isla?"

"Yeah, that's what I'm calling about. Do you still have a key to my house?" Nigel hesitated.

"Yep. By the way, you're getting low on the Glenfiddich and the Penfolds, but the rest of the stuff isn't worth the walk from my house. What can I do for ya?"

Nigel laughed. This was the first time he'd laughed all day. "You're worth your weight in gold, mate. God, I need something to laugh about."

"You know humor is a sign of intelligence, and something tells my intelligent mind this isn't a social call. What can I do to save your sorry arse again? Don't ask for bail money." Jock never missed a chance to kid Nigel.

Nigel laughed again. "Yeah, damn, well, I'll be seeing ya."

"Wait, old man. Seriously, what can I do for you?" Jock's voice told Nigel he understood the call was serious.

"I need some papers sent to me here in Oz. I need them tomorrow. Are you home? I think you have time to get them to Fed-Ex."

"Oh, that's all? Damn, I thought you wanted me to mow the lawn."

"Yeah, that too. I hadn't thought about the lawn."

"Bro, do you think I'm letting the neighborhood go to hell? Your lawn is mowed. Where're the papers, and where do you want them sent?"

Nigel explained he had a folder on Isla in a file cabinet in his den. He needed the entire folder sent to him. He would call with an address in a few minutes, but if Jock could get it going, Nigel would supply the details. "There's money in the jar next to the Glenfiddich unless you already dipped into that for the lawn service."

"No, but good to know, bro. I'm headed there as we speak. Of course, I'll need details for Tui. You know she loves you." Tui was Jock's wife. She'd been struggling with renal failure for years and had started dialysis two years ago. She'd been an incredible support to Nigel when his first wife passed.

"Thanks. I want to hear about her renal situation. Has she moved up on the transplant list? If I can get these papers, I'll be eternally grateful."

"I'm already in the house. If I can't find it, I'll call you back."

Nigel immediately called Luke Sullivan and received an address to send the documents. If they hurried, the files would arrive tomorrow. Nigel called back and gave his neighbor the address.

Jock was already on his way to FedEx. "I've got you covered—all good. Now tell me what's going on? Tui is the same, and she's still doing dialysis as we speak. There's no change in her status."

The men chatted for a minute, and then Jock announced he was at FedEx and would text him the tracking number, but he needed to get home and get into the grog. "Tui will expect an update in a day or two. Don't disappoint her."

Nigel had all Isla's arrest information and court papers until she moved out. He'd paid her legal bills, and his only requirement was to have a copy of any documents. When Isla moved out at eighteen, she asked for bail money a time or two, but he didn't provide it and was then shut out of her life.

He secretly knew his wife had given her any money needed for bail, but then Isla left the country, and neither he nor Bette ever heard from her again.

At least he'd kept the documents from her youth. He hated to do this to his only child, but he had to think of his granddaughter's safety. He shook his head, wondering how Maddison had survived living with Ben's son. The kid is a survivor. No doubt, she was safe when she lived with the Donovans. Thank God for the Donovans.

Nigel arrived at the address on Adelphi Terrace facing the Patawalonga River, where it entered the St. Vincent Gulf. It was a large apartment complex with views of the river. Across the street was a grass verge that bordered the waterway. Families threw frisbees and played cricket. Nigel was jealous.

Nigel remembered his youth and his prowess at cricket. He'd been a star and was even scouted for future fame and glory playing for England, but then he found medicine, and he only played for his med school team. Nigel was the captain, but as he progressed in school, he was offered paid research assistant positions and tore his Achilles ligament, ending his cricket dreams.

Nigel coached Isla's team when she was young, but she opted for netball after a few years. He took Isla to cricket matches when England played the Kiwis, but she showed little interest in the games. She did fish with him in the early days, but while Nigel was happy to hook even one trout on a day of fishing, Isla found it boring.

Isla loved her dad and wanted to be with him, but when puberty hit and she had her first crush, she abandoned her parents, using them only for a place to eat and sleep. Both Bette and Nigel were engrossed in their work and hadn't noticed Isla's decline. If Nigel could return to that time, he would have sacrificed his career. It was his greatest regret.

Nigel ascended the steps to the apartment, pressed the doorbell, and waited. A smart, well-dressed woman in a tailored pantsuit answered the door. "Mr. Buckby? I'm Kate Kilroy. Please come in."

Chapter 31

Lindy's Sidekick

Lindy was in heaven. She didn't remember having such a fun day in God knew how long. It took her about ten minutes to realize she had a precocious six going on thirty-year-old riding with her. Maddison was not shy and had a head full of interesting questions and comments. Who is this person, and why is she hiding in the body of a kid?

"Dr. Smart, thank you for allowing me to ride with you today. You know, I lived on a station, and I know quite a lot about vet stuff. So, if you have any questions, I might know the answers."

Lindy could hardly contain her mirth. If it had been any other child, she might have been annoyed, but there was something about this self-composed, inquisitive girl that struck her as a genuine intellectual in the making.

Maddison knew enough not to pretend to know it all. "I have some questions. I don't want you to think I know everything. I know there's lots to learn. Is it okay if I ask questions?"

Lindy was sipping coffee. They'd gone straight from the department office to McDonalds to get supplies. "Shoot, oh learned one."

Maddison was perplexed. Didn't she just say she had a lot to learn? Wasn't Dr. Smart listening to her? "Uh, well. This isn't about vet stuff. I'm wondering about something else. Mrs. Donovan would say this is a question about matters of the heart. I know what she means, but it isn't the heart. It's in your brain."

"I like heart better. I'm with Mrs. Donovan's take." O-M-G, who is this kid?

"Well, never mind where it comes from. I was wondering if you liked my grandpa. I know you're kinda young for him, but I'm sure you could catch up, and I've been watching you watch him. You have a lot in common, and if you got married, then I could live part time with you two and part time with my pop. I could tell the judge I'm going to live with you and my grandpa, and then Pop could marry Ms. Harding. Then the judge would know I'm going to be living my best life and be safe. I kinda think my mother wants me to live with her, but I don't feel I'd be safe. I don't think she'd let me have Tag either."

Maddison stared straight ahead and waited for a response from Dr. Smart. "You don't have to answer now. There're roos in the paddock. You better keep an eye out. If you killed me, I'd think your marriage prospects might be limited."

Marriage prospects? Lindy was trying to hold back the laughter, but that was it. She burst out laughing. This made Maddison laugh, and soon, the two were feeding off each other. One would laugh and look at the other, and then the other would laugh. It was like that all day.

Lindy was finally able to speak without laughing and said she would consider it. "You know, oh wise one, there are some people who have a once in a lifetime love of their life. That is all they need, and any further searching to get the lost love back is unnecessary."

"Well, sometimes there is a second person who could fill your needs, and maybe they aren't the love of your life, but they can do the laundry or make the bed."

This started Lindy off on a second round of paroxysmal laughing. Oh, Jamie. I wish you could have met this kid.

Chapter 32

Legal Turkey

Nigel was ushered to the living room, where Luke sat watching cricket. It was the Ashes. Nigel was aware the game was on. England and Australia were playing in Adelaide at the moment. He'd thought about taking Ben and Maddison, but after the funeral, there was no more thought about the long rivalry match series between the two teams.

An Adonis of a man in casual clothes turned to Nigel and stood briefly. "Luke Sullivan, call me Luke, and you're Nigel? Do you follow cricket?" Luke offered Nigel a beer.

"Uh, I guess." Nigel wanted to get right to work, but he didn't want to seem ungrateful. "Yeah, I follow it."

"So, who are you barracking for today?" Luke settled back down on the couch.

"That's tough. I'm guessing if I say anything but Australia, I may be shown the door? I was short-listed to play for

Lancashire, but my education and an injury got in the way. I was raised in the UK, but I'm a Kiwi through and through. Between England and Australia, I'd go for the Aussies."

"You're lying, but I'll accept it." Luke went to the kitchen and returned with a beer.

"No, I really did." They tipped their beer bottles to each other.

"I meant you're lying about who you barrack for."

"Yeah. I'm kind of desperate." Nigel pulled out a picture of Maddison and then another taken after the funeral with Ben, Maddison, Tag, and him.

Luke set the beer down. He put the television on silent. Kate had excused herself. "Mate, you've got a hill to climb. I shouldn't even be talking to you anymore. You don't have a lot of time. When I informed the court that I would act in this matter, I was told there would be a hearing tomorrow to decide on an interim application for the mother to take the child until after the holidays, and the regular Family Court would see cases again in the new year."

"You're kidding. If I hadn't found you, how would I have known?" Nigel was astounded.

"The Child Protection Department will be in attendance and have representation. They told you, didn't they?"

"Yes, but..." Nigel was reeling from the unfairness of the situation.

"Well, here's the deal. I can't represent you now. Something more important has come up. In fact, I can't even discuss the case with you anymore. You need to leave after the game is over. Let's not be crazy here. I'm representing someone else at the hearing tomorrow. The only good news about this is you guys no longer need to rob a bank."

Nigel stared at Luke and shook his head. How would he get legal representation?

"Can you recommend someone?" Nigel wanted to hit the man.

"Sorry, mate. Not at this late time. You'll have to show up and represent yourself."

"Luke, I'm frankly disappointed in you. I drove all this way, and I have important documents coming to you tomorrow. If you don't mind. Since you're representing the other party now, do you mind not opening them, and I'll pick them up?"

"The court meets at 1:45 p.m. tomorrow afternoon. If the papers get here before I leave for court, I'll bring them without opening them. I won't look at them. You have my word."

Nigel wondered what his "word" was worth. "I better leave then. I guess I have some work to do." Nigel stood up and walked to the door.

Kate Kilroy met him in the foyer. "I'm sorry, Dr. Buckby. I did some research on your granddaughter's story. I wish we could have helped. I can see how disappointed you must be. Luke is a man of principle, and I've never been able to influence his actions. Good luck."

Nigel went to his vehicle and opened the door. It was hot, and he sat in the driver's seat with the door open, the engine running, and the AC turned on. He cried for the second time this week. The last time he cried before yesterday was when he returned from Bette's funeral. How would he tell Ben? He didn't have to.

Ben received a call from Fiona. "I'm trying to reach Lindy, and she isn't answering. I know she's down near Minlaton with Maddy. Have you heard from them?"

"Yes, they called an hour or so ago. Are you sure you have the right number—ending in 92?"

"Yeah, I guess I'll keep trying. There've been some developments in your case. Because you're now a plaintiff, and there's an interim court date tomorrow, I can no longer discuss the case with either you or Nigel. I hate this, but it's policy. We only want what's best for your granddaughter. You must believe us. Sorry about sending you on a wild goose chase."

"I'm not following you." Ben didn't understand what Fiona was alluding to.

"The barrister I suggested isn't available."

What the hell? He was thinking of a more graphic word. "Does Nigel know this? The hearing's tomorrow? Why the hell are we hearing this now?"

Ben didn't even say goodbye. He immediately called Nigel. He was blunt. "Are we screwed?"

Nigel was checking into a nearby hotel. He was lucky to get a room. The tourist spot was always booked out during the holidays. The people living inland came to the beaches to get away from the heat of summer and enjoy the Christmas festivities. This usually meant sand, surf, and cricket.

"I have a room for the night. It doesn't have AC, but I have Wi-Fi, thank God. Let me call you back when I'm in the room."

Ben ran next door to the Smart's patio and knocked on the door. Janet opened the sliding glass door. "Hi, Ben. Doug's watching cricket. Would you like to join him?"

"No, I'm having some issues. Fiona from the Child Protection Department is trying to get a hold of Lindy. Lindy's working farther down the peninsula and hasn't answered. Do you know if she has a second phone?"

"No, I don't. Did you try the clinic?"

"Great idea. Thanks."

"Is there a problem, Ben?" Janet stepped out onto the veranda, away from the noise of the cricket game.

"I'm not sure. We may lose Maddy." Ben choked when he said it.

Janet put her hand to her mouth and shook her head. She then hugged Ben. "Is there anything we can do?"

"I don't know. I'll know more in a few minutes."

Nigel finally called Ben. "I don't usually swear, but we're fucked, mate. The legal eagle has gone to the dark side. I don't know when it happened, but he didn't even have the courtesy to call us. I went to his house. He offered me a beer, asked me about the cricket game, and then told me he'd already sided with the other side."

"Is that legal? I mean, we had an agreement. This is bullshit."

"Tell me about it. There's a hearing tomorrow at 1:45 at the Family Court. Hell, I don't even know where that is. Isla's asking for an interim order to get temporary custody of Maddy."

"Can she do that? Did Sullivan give you any suggestions for someone to represent us?"

"Ben, I'm going to get online and see what I can find out. The bloody place is in holiday mode. It's common down here, and it's the same in New Zealand. Give me an hour."

"Should I head down? Maddy's still with Lindy. She won't be back for at least an hour. Fiona's trying to get a hold of Lindy. I think the court may want to interview Maddison. She's a six-year-old, for God's sake. She shouldn't be asked to choose."

"No. You stay with her tonight. Let me do some research. I'll call you later. Get Maddy to bed early. She'll be exhausted from her day with Lindy. We can talk after she's asleep."

Ben hung up and went back over to Janet and Doug's. He explained what he knew and asked them to be on standby in case he needed them to write a new witness statement or to babysit. He returned to the house and helped Tag out to the grass. With dog duties done, Ben checked his watch. It was after six, and there was no sign of Lindy or Maddy.

Ben opened his laptop and began researching the Family Law Courts of South Australia. There were several men's websites with helplines and complaints about how men were shut out of their children's lives by court decisions.

What the hell. He dialed one and then another. He didn't want to leave a message when no one answered. He went back to the official website of the court. It was clear Luke Sullivan must have written the application for Maddison to spend the Christmas holidays with her mother.

The info from the men's groups was that orders preceding a long holiday were often sustained as the child had settled into a routine and might even have been enrolled in a school. The parent who did not have custody was then placed at a disadvantage and, not surprisingly, regained no traction with their application for custody.

He phoned Nigel. "Maddy needs her own lawyer. I see there's a provision for that. The other thing I see is, if they give Isla temporary custody over the holidays, we might as well pack our bags and go home."

"Yeah, I saw that. I talked to someone in the parents' group. We need to ask the court to ensure Isla has a clean drug test before we hand over custody. The woman who suggested it also said it was a long shot to get an order like that, but we should clarify we want the best for the child. We're happy to reunite her with her mother, but for the sake of the child, we ask that Isla have weekly tests during the holiday period. She also suggested anyone living in the house has to be drug tested." Nigel said he'd already had the submission written and would print it off down in the motel lobby.

"That seems reasonable. In fact, it seems like we really want to help Isla. Do you think it'll work?"

"Luke Sullivan is a cocky bastard, and he doesn't seem to take this seriously. He's much more interested in cricket. But I also did some research on him. Sullivan seems to always be for the underdog, and he's very successful. I think we have our work cut out for us. I'm guessing we're underestimating him. Any word from Maddy?"

"No, but she's due any time." Ben paused. "Hey, I hear Lindy's truck. I'll get Maddy to bed and call you back."

Ben went to the door near the driveway. He went out and found Lindy attempting to wake the sleeping child. Ben smiled and opened the door, scooped her up, and carried her into the house.

Tag realized his master was back and stood, whined, and wagged his tail. Ben placed Maddison on the bed, removed her boots and manure covered pants and shirt. With the help of Lindy, he put on a clean nightgown and tucked her in. She woke for a second, stroked Tag's head and was gone. Ben moved Tag's bed into Maddison's room. "Sweet dreams, little one." He kissed her, and this time, she didn't bat him away. He closed the door, leaving a small crack so Tag could come out if the need arose.

Ben turned to Lindy. "Want a drink?"

Chapter 33

Lindy

Lindy and Ben settled down on the porch, facing the ocean. It was still hot outside, and the sun was setting. He texted Nigel that Maddison was home and asleep. He had a beer, but Lindy only had a soft drink. She recounted the day, minus the talk about matters of the heart. She said she hadn't laughed so much in several years.

"That kid is a riot. Where the hell did she come from? My kids were smart, but she's off the scale. How will you ever be able to provide the nourishment she needs to reach her potential?"

"The question is, will I get a chance? Did Fiona get ahold of you? She was trying to call."

"Yeah. It wasn't me. It was Maddy she wanted to talk to. I don't know what she wanted as Maddy only answered yes or no and didn't want to talk about the conversation."

Ben was surprised the authorities would even talk to a six-year-old about such matters. "My guess is it's about the hearing tomorrow. Maddy's mother has an urgent application to the Family Court seeking immediate custody. That's why I needed to talk to your friend about her case, and the bastard lawyer who helped her."

"Bastard lawyer? That's harsh."

"He invited us down to see him in Glenelg. Then when Nigel showed up, the lawyer offered him a beer and then told him he couldn't act for us anymore because he was representing another party with no actual explanation. I think that fits the bastard moniker."

"Yeah, pretty much. Carly said he was her patron saint. She's still friends with his partner, the television presenter, and they take her kids to the Crows' footy games."

The sun was setting, and the sky was alight with the reflection of the orange sun rays. Lindy stood up and walked over to her in-law's house. She turned to watch her shadow against the white wall. The shadow was blue. She pointed to it. "Ever seen a blue shadow?"

Ben walked over and blinked. "It's an illusion."

"Of course it is. When Jamie and I were first married, we would come and stay here for the weekend. We took pictures of our shadows. I have some horrendous ones from when I was full term. Jamie called them the 'blue whale' pictures." Lindy stopped and was having a moment.

Ben knew she'd gone to a dark place. He'd spent time in there and waited for her to come out. He went inside and checked on Maddy and looked for any emails about tomorrow's events.

Lindy came in as well and said she needed to go. "Do you want me to keep Maddy for you tomorrow while you go to court? The outlaws will watch her if you want me to come and give evidence."

"Would you mind watching her again? I'm wondering if we need to bring her to town. If they make us give her to Nigel's daughter, I'd hope there would be an order to say she needs to be out here on the YP."

Lindy noticed he used the local nickname for the Yorke Peninsula. She wondered if he'd even explored the area. "Have you been down to Innes yet?"

"No, we'd planned to go, but you know things have gone downhill since the funeral."

Lindy saw Ben was in a different space at the moment. Ben was headed to the dark side as well. It was hard burying your only child, but finding out about his son's life, death, and granddaughter in the same message was gut-wrenching. Then, in a flash, he could lose his only grandchild. If Isla gained custody tomorrow, Lindy knew Ben would never see the child again.

He and Lindy hugged. It was a brief hug, and he felt no attraction, but maybe she could be the sister he never had.

Lindy stepped away and laughed to herself, remembering her conversation with Maddison. There was no physical attraction, but she thought she'd ask. "Ben, how are you at doing the dishes and laundry?"

"Not something I aspire to, but necessity is a great inspiration. My staff came for the first few months when Tania became ill and then died. But eventually, they told me to suck it up and learn to dance with the vacuum cleaner. Why?"

"Oh, just testing your skill set for future reference. Maddy would love to get us together. She seemed to think that, even if I didn't love you, you still might be a suitable house cleaner."

"What? I'm sorry if she made you uncomfortable or tried to entice you to Team-Maddy, but I'm pretty happy living with the memories of my past marriage. I'll talk to her. It won't happen again."

"Ben, what I told you was in confidence. I had one of the funniest days since I lost Jamie. Don't ask her to stop. I love her innocence and spontaneity. The day was pure magic. Colin Butler's one of my favorite clients. He's fallen in love with her as well. She's advising him with some sheep he has, and they plan to go riding as soon as she's allowed." Lindy walked to her truck. As she opened the door, she stopped. "If she stays in South Australia, you're going to have to move here permanently. You realize that? You'll have to learn to clean houses, too." Lindy laughed and slipped into her truck. "Good luck, and let me know."

Chapter 34

Carly Langley

Lindy immediately called Fiona. "Hey, girlfriend, do you want me to babysit the kid tomorrow?"

"Yeah, maybe. Sorry for chasing you today. I needed to ask the munchkin some questions. Some days I hate my job."

"I don't envy you. If parents would only behave like parents. I know not to ask, but I'm going to put in my two cents. The kiddo is worth saving. That she's so unaffected by her upbringing is a wonder. By the way, if no one agrees, I'd be willing to take her."

"Get in line, sister. The hearing isn't until the afternoon. What have you got going on? I expect Ben thinks he'll have to have her at the court, but that won't be the case. Maybe pick Maddison up before ten so Ben can get down to support Nigel."

Lindy turned her truck onto the main road to her home. "Speaking of which, how are things between you and Dr. Delish?"

"You mean before or after I told Nigel I could not support him in court? You didn't hear me say that. By the way."

Lindy grimaced. "Oh, geez. Never mind."

Lindy immediately called Ben. "Have Maddy dressed in her finest work clothes and ready to tango by eight and tell her to prepare to work. Oh, and pack her swimsuit."

"Okaaay? By the way, I found a great Instagram page on housecleaning."

"Liar." Lindy immediately hung up and called Carly Langley. She had not caught up with Carly since the last South Australia vet meeting.

"Carly, is it a good time to discuss men?" Lindy laughed.

"The emasculators are in the autoclave as we speak. How's things at the edge of civilization? Ready to join me?"

"Nah. Too much drama over here. Then there's that funny thing about clients who never call you at night. You have your people, and I have mine. The good news is this is not a referral. Apparently, you failed me today. What's with your Superman lawyer buddy?"

"No idea. What are you talking about?" Lindy was perplexed.

"Esquires-R-Us invited my buddies over to his place, including a two-hour drive, and then refused to act for them after promising to help them with their custody case." explained Lindy.

"I don't think Luke Sullivan does family law. The guy whom he referred me to for my divorce moved to the UK.

That's all I know. Luke and Kate never discuss their work. Sorry, Mom. No clue."

Lindy laughed at the "mom" reference. Yes, she was older, but not by much. "Enough of that kind of talk, oh-young-one."

"Listen, oh ancient one, Lukalicious never, ever, ever, turned down a good guy who was down on his luck. You might want to reconsider the friends you keep. Is this about the young girl whose father was killed, and everyone thought she was an orphan?" Carly grinned, remembering how Luke Sullivan had helped her when she was accused of murder.

"Maybe." Lindy hesitated. "So, how's things for you?"

"Never better. We're starting Georgie on a new chemo round. My intern bailed on me, but Rich is on his way back." Carly was always so positive in her son's battle with his brain tumor.

"What about your med school student au pair?" Fiona had met her and was in awe of her ability to care for children.

"She's doing placement in the APY Lands. She'll be gone until mid-Feb."

"I can't believe you let Rich leave. He was a godsend when you lent him to me, when Jamie was..." Lindy stopped. "Well, you know."

Rich Hamilton worked with Carly when she was accused of murder. He was younger than her and had a crush on Carly, who was in the process of divorcing her two-timing bastard of a husband. Carly was exonerated on the murder charge and moved from the mid-north to Gawler. In all this, she had two daughters and twins on the way. Rich stayed and worked for her for four years. Carly sent him packing when she was sure she would never give him the children she knew he wanted. In the meantime, one of her twin boys was diagnosed with a brain tumor.

"The parting of fools." Lindy sighed.

"Yeah. Well, all is not lost. Rich is on his way back to help while I take Georgie back and forth for the chemo. He's starting the day after tomorrow."

Carly's ex had lost his medical license when he was complicit in framing Carly for the murder of the old lady and family babysitter. He'd spent a few months in jail but was back out practicing as an emergency doctor. He'd started another family and, by all accounts, was involved with a new woman. Lindy had heard the story when Rich came to work for her while she was dealing with Jamie.

"So, one of the grandfathers is a vet, and he's an orthopedic specialist? What's with the other guy?" Carly asked, thinking of how she could use his skills.

"The bone doctor does the smallies. He's of no good to you. The other is a human reproductive specialist from Kiwiland. Both are super nice and super smart. Neither was aware their kids had survived and reproduced. The father was autistic but high functioning, and the mother was, or should I say, is a druggy."

"And the kid's normal?"

"Not at all. She spent the day with me, and I can say for sure she probably has an IQ in the genius range. I don't remember ever laughing so much in my life. I wish you could meet her. I'd adopt her in a heartbeat."

"Mom, Mom, Mom. Do not, I repeat, do not get involved."

"Oh, thanks for your advice. I should send Maddy over to you for a day and see if you say the same thing. Pulling into the Ponderosa, gotta go, kid. I got horses, chickens, and two lambs that need me."

As American-born vets, both knew the term was from the Bonanza television series. Carly grinned. "Stay safe, old wise one."

"You too. If Rich stays, can I borrow him?"

"Nope. I'm a little slow, but I think I finally see the light."

Chapter 35

Flying Blind

Nigel called Ben one more time. "I hope you trust me. I've written out depositions and now have them printed. I received one from the Donovans and one from Doug and Janet. By the way, in their stat declaration, the Smarts said we could have the place as long as we wanted."

"I don't trust you. I'm coming as well. Lindy's going to take Maddy again tomorrow, and then I'll drive down to Adelaide. I should be there at noon, so find a place for us to eat before our execution."

"Good news. There're great restaurants down here. I'm staying on the esplanade at Glenelg, and we can take the tram into the city. I won't be good company when this is over. Prepare yourself."

"That'll be two of us, mate."

"At least you're talking like one of us." Nigel gave Ben the motel's address and rehearsed what he intended to say.

It wasn't pretty. Outlining his child's fall from grace was the last thing he wanted to do, but he could not stand by and allow Isla to ruin his granddaughter's life. If it came to a crunch, he would offer Isla all his savings and the deed to his house to have her sign off on any custodial aspirations.

Nigel woke up at dawn and walked down to the esplanade. There were mostly older people with dogs walking up and down the beach. He saw occasional joggers and a few people swimming near the jetty. It was a cloudless morning, and the day promised to be hot. Nigel was worried. He'd been in court with Isla before and wasn't allowed to talk. He hoped he wouldn't be told he would be prevented from speaking because of some procedural technicality.

Nigel returned to the motel room and showered. He went to get coffee and a bagel. As he walked into the coffee shop, he saw his former colleague from his early days when he came to New Zealand. "Karan, how are you?" Karan turned and waved. She was ahead of Nigel in a long line. She signaled for him to come up and join her, but he knew this would anger the people in the line ahead of him. He waved her off. She went to the counter and ordered two cups of tea and bagels and lox. As she turned from the counter, she handed him the bag of bagels and gave him a signal to follow her.

There was a small table on the sidewalk. She handed him a cup of tea, and they each took a bagel. "Nigel, how long? Ten or fifteen years? I can't believe it's you. Where's Bette?"

He gazed at her face. Karan was ageless. She probably only saw the sun on the weekend. She was a researcher who spent her life in the lab. He owed her an explanation. He noticed she stared at him, and he felt uncomfortable.

"Bette died several years ago. And you? Are you still married to Larry? How are the girls? Did Cheryl finish her PhD?"

Karan smiled. "I retired last year. Cheryl moved to Perth. She teaches over there. She has twins. Jill is still here and preparing to care for me in my old age. She's gay. They've adopted a boy. How's your daughter? She was such a stunner."

Nigel thought about how much he wanted to say. "Let's say that hasn't gone well. She has a daughter who looks like her mum. I'm over here trying to sort out a few things."

Karan stared at him for a second, and a vague look came over her face. "How's Bette?"

Nigel realized Karan had some memory issues. She knew him from the past, but he suspected she would not remember this conversation tomorrow. "Bette died, and I'm on my own now." There was no point in telling her about his pending divorce. Karan was younger, but despite her appearance, she showed cognitive issues that alarmed Nigel. He knew he had to stay mentally fit to care for such a young, smart child. He pretended to ignore Karan's decline.

"Nigel, I may need your help. Can you help me find my car?"

Nigel never lost a second. He could see she was confused and worried. He asked to see her driver's license and then called an Uber to take her home. He hated leaving her, but he needed to get back to prepare for court. He took her phone and added her phone number to his and said he would call her in a few minutes to make sure she got home safely. He also copied her daughter's number. He dialed it as soon as the Uber left. Jill answered right away. She was interstate, and she explained her mother had early stages of Alzheimer's and was coping, but they were adding a granny unit behind her house for her to transition into soon.

Nigel asked about Karan and driving. Jill said she didn't have a car and used public transportation. "It's kind of a nightmare some days, but when she's having a good day, we can't keep up."

"Is your father still around?" Nigel had always enjoyed Karan's husband. They fished together a few times.

"Dad died last year. My parents divorced several years ago. Mum doesn't even talk about it. So far, there are more good days than bad, but it's early. I dread what's coming."

"Jill, I may move here, so if I can be of any help, you have my number now." Nigel hung up and thought about his inability to recall simple words or where he'd set his keys. God, please give me ten more years at least.

Nigel returned to his motel room and went over his submissions and speech. He prayed the judge or magistrate would allow him to present his side of the story. His phone rang. It was Fiona. He wanted to talk to her at length, but he knew this had to be all business.

"Hi Fiona, will you be in court today?"

"Yes, I just wanted to wish you luck, but you know I'm here for your granddaughter. We only want the best for all parties. Do you know where to go?"

"I think so. I guess I'll see you there then?"

"Both Terri and I'll be there. Good luck."

Good luck? Nigel thought about the irony of luck playing any role in his granddaughter's fate. His feelings toward Fiona were confusing. He wondered if it was her perfume triggering his primal connection. It was the same one Bette had worn. He laughed, thinking of his interest in pheromones and the short, ill-fated research project that had led him to study ovulation, and the chemical signals leading men to seek women when they were close to ovulation.

Nigel understood men were attracted to women who were ovulating, but the grad student who conducted the research was found to be having an affair with two of the women at the same time, and the project was abandoned. The grad student was dismissed, and a year's worth of data was lost. *Jesus, I need to be thinking about the task at hand, not failed research projects.*

Ben called to say he was downstairs, and he needed the room number. When he came through the open door, he saw Nigel had his laptop open to a family court webpage. They shook hands and then awkwardly hugged. "Shall we head downtown? I saw the court is in the CBD. We can get a bite to eat, and then we can walk to the court if that's okay?"

Nigel was surprised at how well Ben had researched the area. "Yeah, the place will swarm with holiday shoppers. We need to think about some gifts for Maddy. It's less than ten days before the jolly fat guy arrives."

Ben didn't answer. He'd spent many Christmases alone or with staff or neighbors. He'd hated Christmas ever since Daniel had gone missing. Now he was probably going to be deprived of yet another family Christmas.

"Man, it's hot, isn't it?" Ben had stopped at a mall and bought a sports jacket that fit him and, surprisingly, looked good.

Nigel had a suit and tie. "Let's go to the mall and get you a tie, mate." They climbed onto a crowded tram with the well-dressed riders and people who appeared homeless. The body odors were eye watering.

There was a young pregnant woman who had a small boy in tow. She appeared to be close to delivery, and Nigel laughed to himself, thinking of her having the baby while on the tram. Your Honor, the reason I'm late is that I had to deliver a baby on the way to court. The idea of him delivering a baby was absurd. His research was primarily in vitro fertilization and capacitation of sperm—one pheromone study aside. He'd help deliver Isla as the obstetrician mistakenly thought he was a practicing doctor and not a researcher who never saw patients. He laughed as Bette had protested, and the OBGYN ignored her.

There was a scream, and they glanced over at the pregnant woman whose water had just broken. There were several people who appeared to be competent to handle the situation, but no one stepped forward. Ben immediately went to the woman's side and asked her how he could help. He turned to Nigel. "Nige, you go on ahead. I'll be there as soon as I can." A distinguished middle-aged man suggested she be taken to the Ashford Hospital. They had just passed the complex. The woman didn't have a scheduled hospital.

She was terrified. She kept repeating, "It's coming. I can feel it." She quickly explained her husband was a pilot and out of town. She was new to Adelaide and had no place for her small son. The three men helped her off the tram. The middle-aged man summoned an Uber. He apologized for not taking her himself. He had to be in court in an hour.

"Nigel, you better get there as fast as you can, and I'll do my best, but this woman needs help." The little boy was crying, and Ben picked him up and placed him in the car for the short ride to the hospital. He laid his sports coat down on the seat so the seat would be protected. The other man gave the driver fifty dollars and told him to keep it in case he had to stop and get the car cleaned and would lose fares.

Ben and the woman left, and Nigel and the older man went to the tram stop to wait for the next ride. The middle-aged man held out his hand. "I'm Trevor. Nice of you chaps to help her. I hope it turns out okay."

"Nigel and Ben, yeah, us too. Thanks for your help." The two men shook hands.

"Nice of you two to stop what you're doing. I hated to leave her. I have a pregnant daughter, but I'm due in court."

"She'll be fine, mate. I'll text my friend and ask her to name the baby after you. When is yours due?"

"Two weeks, if she holds on. She lives in Sydney. My wife and I are going over after the birth. It's our first, but we've been told to wait. How about you? Any grandchildren?"

Nigel remembered his obligations and began thinking about what he was going to say. "Yeah, just one. He showed Trevor a picture of Maddison and then one of the three of them. My friend is Maddison's other grandfather. That's her dog. Tag is the most important thing in her life. Ben just saved his life. He's a vet and fixed the dog's broken bones." The middle-aged man glanced at his watch. "You know, I'm going to be late. I think I'll grab another Uber. Have a great day, Nigel."

"Yeah, good luck with your case." Nigel assumed he was a solicitor and wondered what his case was about. If Trevor only knew about his case, maybe he could represent them. He should have asked for a card.

When the tram arrived at Rundle Mall. He called Ben but received no answer. He went to a food court and had sushi and a soft drink. He searched around the mall, but it was almost time for his case. His heart rate was increasing, and his palms were tingling. He tried Ben again, but again there was no answer. He turned his phone to silent as he entered the building. He took the elevator to the third floor.

He'd already gone through one metal detector but had to go through a second when he walked through the corridor of the courtrooms. He saw Fiona and Terri sitting together in front of the room assigned to their case. He waved but didn't sit near them. He searched for Isla, but she wasn't there. He was disappointed. He hoped they could talk. He could make his offer with no one knowing. He'd trade his entire cumulative wealth for custody of Maddison.

He watched the court officers at the metal detectors, hoping to see someone he knew come through. No one he knew entered. Then he saw Luke Sullivan dressed in his robes. He went into an area where the clients could converse privately with their legal representatives.

He watched as Fiona and Terri were summoned into the same room. What's that about? How come they aren't asking me to join them? This case is rigged. I'll bet Isla's already won and doesn't even have to appear. Nigel was furious.

No, he was apoplectic. Where the hell is Ben? Several people emerged from the courtroom, and an officer called their case number. As Nigel entered the courtroom, he checked his phone one more time. He'd received a message from Ben.

"It's a girl. Good luck and thank you."

Chapter 36

Family Court

A court clerk approached and asked Nigel who he was and what was his interest in the proceedings. Nigel reported he was the grandfather and currently taking care of the child in question. He was told to sit in the area behind the barrier.

Fiona and Terri sat at a table in the front. A young man in a gown was seated at the table across from the women. Nigel expected his daughter would arrive at any moment. He went up to the court clerk and explained he was representing himself in the matter and shouldn't he be up in front?

The clerk looked at his docket papers. "I'm sorry, sir. You aren't listed. I can ask the judge. Do you have any documents or submissions?"

Nigel handed him his submissions and the statutory declarations he'd collected. He glanced around, but Luke Sullivan wasn't in the courtroom. Where was his packet from New Zealand?

"I doubt the judge will allow a late filing, but we're delayed as one party is missing. I'll ask the judge." The clerk knocked on the door near the front of the room. Nigel saw him bow as he entered the room.

The clerk returned and told Nigel that he was sorry, but Nigel was unable to submit any documents. Nigel was heartbroken. He felt he'd been duped by all concerned. There was no time to prepare or get legal help. This was so unfair.

He sat for several minutes while the clerk went out into the hall. Nigel heard the clerk call Isla's name. If she doesn't show, the game may be up. It was all he could hope for.

Luke Sullivan strode into the courtroom, and he observed the people sitting below the judge's bench roll their eyes. Was this a good thing or a bad thing? But then Nigel turned to watch Luke Sullivan walk up to the bench and sit with Fiona and Terri. Nigel didn't understand. None of them would look his way.

Finally, the clerk asked everyone to rise. "The Honorable Judge Trevor Hutchinson presiding."

Nigel's mouth opened, and he felt he had a sliver of hope. This was the man who stopped to help the pregnant woman, along with Ben and himself. At least Trevor was shown a picture of Ben, Maddison, and him all together. That would be his submission.

"Please be seated. I understand one of the plaintiffs is still not here. In the meantime, in the interest of full disclosure. On the way to the court, I met one of the interested parties on the tram quite by accident. We shared a moment as we both helped a woman who was in labor. If I need to recuse myself, then let's decide now, and we can recommence in January."

Luke Sullivan spoke first. "Your honor, Luke Sullivan, acting on behalf of the child through the Department for Child Protection. We're willing to wait if my learned friend is willing, and since his party is late, perhaps a January date would be the best option? As far as your participation today, we are grateful for your acknowledgment, and we are sure you will not let it influence any decisions on your part."

"Your honor, Michael Fitzpatrick, acting on behalf of the mother. I'm sorry, Your Honor. I would like to proceed, but as you can see, my client must be unavoidably detained. I have no problem with your continuing in this case, but perhaps we could give my client another few minutes?"

The judge glanced at his watch. "We only have twenty minutes left, and then I'm scheduled for another urgent application. I would suggest we recommence next month when we can all be prepared. How does that suit you, Mr. Fitzpatrick?"

There was no mistaking the judge's preference and directions. The young man appeared defeated. "Yes, your honor. That will be fine."

The judge wasted no time in dismissing the case. Nigel looked away from everyone. He was going to cry for the third time in a week. After everyone left the courtroom, he turned to leave. Fiona approached Nigel as he covered his face with his hands. "Sorry, Nigel. It was too important to leave it to the usual legal personnel on our staff. We felt

Luke would serve Maddy's needs and desires better than yours. You can hate me forever for doing that, but I needed to play my best card. There was too much at stake." They walked out together, and Luke was standing next to Terri.

"Bloody pom. Thought you could lie to me about the Ashes?" He smiled and walked away. He turned and said, "It's not over, mate. I may be your worst enemy. I'll be expecting a report that Maddison had the best Christmas ever." Luke raised his hand and pointed his finger as he walked toward the lift.

The clerk came up to Nigel as he and Fiona joined Terri outside of the courtroom. The two women high-fived one another.

The clerk whispered to Nigel, "Sir, may I speak to you privately?"

Nigel stepped away from the women. "Sure, mate. Or should I say, sir?"

"Definitely a mate question. How is the young lady? The judge wants to know if she made it to the hospital."

Nigel smiled. He pulled out his phone and saw several messages from Ben. "My friend's still at the hospital with the woman's son. The woman's family won't arrive until tomorrow, and her husband was flying back from San Francisco. Oh, it's a girl. I don't have any more details other than that."

Nigel was close to tears again. This place was growing on him. "I can give you my number if he wants to know more." And he did.

Chapter 37

Space to Breathe

As Nigel rejoined Terri and Fiona, his phone rang. "Nige, what the hell's going on? Is it over?"

"We have a reprieve. So much to tell you and so little time, mate. How's the family?"

"Vivian, little Kit, and the unnamed are all doing well. Do you know they let the mothers stay overnight after a routine birth? The problem is Kit and I've bonded, and it looks like I'm stepping in until a suitable relative can be found."

Nigel briefly explained that, sad and true to form, Isla was a no-show. "Then the judge admitted he had a conflict of interest, and so the case is postponed and will be reset for trial next month. And by the way, that bastard Luke has officially gone back into our good books. He clearly barracks for the wrong team in cricket, but he was batting for Maddy in court today. She's in excellent hands with

Terri and Fiona. I'll come down and join you as soon as I can get there. O-M-G, mate. We really dodged a cannonball today."

"Before you go, what was the conflict?"

Nigel grinned. "You. More later. Do you mind if I have a quick drink with Fi and Terri?"

"Mate, you drink to your heart's content, but don't forget, we have a little girl waiting for us back home." It reminded Ben that he still hadn't remembered why Nigel's voice was so familiar. He was determined to figure it out without asking.

Nigel planned to head back as soon as he could. "I'll be home by six at the latest. Do you want me to relieve you at the hospital?"

"No, leave the key to your hotel room with me so I can crash if I can get away from the hospital. Vivian was amazing. Two pushes and it was out. I was right there. Kit got to see his sister being born. Between you and me, there have been several suggestions from the little boy that they all go home and leave the baby at the hospital."

Nigel called Doug and Janet Smart. He told them the case was delayed, giving no details. Doug said they were home all day and had let Tag out and back in several times. They said they'd be happy to care for Maddison if the men were late. They would call Lindy and update her. "Congratulations to all concerned. We're looking forward to a wonderful Christmas."

Nigel had a quick celebratory drink with Fiona and Terri. They were on the wagon, so it was tea and scones. They were driving back to the YP as well. Nigel asked them if they had talked to Maddison about her wishes. They both shook their heads. "We did, but you understand that's confidential." Terri pursed her lips, stifling a smirk. "Dr. Buckby, I'll say you're being observed by very insightful women, and we'll be speaking often to our client. Your parental scorecard is a topic of regular discussion."

Nigel said he better find Ben and excused himself. He caught a ride on the tram and walked from the nearest station to the hospital. He found Ben sleeping and holding the little boy, who was drooling on Ben's shirt lapel. Nigel took a quick shot and waved to the mother. The newborn was sleeping on the cot next to the bed. Nigel nodded and put his finger to his lips.

He sat in a chair next to the door. A large vase of bright flowers and a balloon were brought into the room. He still didn't speak. He was beyond exhausted. The last twenty-four hours were torture. His need for sleep overwhelmed his desire to experience this beautiful moment. Isla had been the perfect child. She'd slept in between feedings and rarely fussed. She was never fussy. Nope, she'd saved it all for her teen years.

Ben was awakened when Trevor Hutchinson and a woman who was probably his wife entered the room. She pointed to the flowers and smiled when she noticed Ben and the sleeping toddler. Nigel nodded and pointed to the baby.

Ben wanted to thank the judge for his role today but thought any mention of the proceedings was probably best left unspoken. He tried to convey his gratitude without speaking and only nodded and smiled.

The couple stood over the plastic crib and marveled at the tiny girl. The mother recognized the man as one of her benefactors. She tried to reach for her purse, but Trevor shook his head.

Vivian whispered, "The Uber driver gave me back the money."

Mrs. Hutchinson said, "Use it to get yourself home."

"Ma'am, I'm not poor. I was just foolish. You shouldn't reward foolishness. We were trying to go see Santa and the Magic Cave. I'm not due for several days."

Mrs. Hutchinson remarked, "Well, we can't let a trip to see Santa be denied. I'm Marilyn, and this is Trev. We'd love to take your son to see Santa. I know you don't know us, but I'm an upstanding citizen, and so is my husband, occasionally."

Ben gazed down at his sleeping charge. He didn't want to wake him. The boy eventually woke, and there was a rush to get him to the bathroom in time. Ben picked him up, and the two disappeared and returned with an upturned thumb.

Ben shook Trevor's hand. "Thanks for your help today. I don't know how she would have made it without your quick thinking. I'm Ben Taylor."

"My pleasure. I can see you sacrificed a lot for this woman. After today, I never want to see you and your partner in court again. Marilyn and I are about to have our first grandchild, and we can only hope she will be fortunate to find such kind men as yourselves. Now leave so we can help Vivian and learn something about caring for a grandchild."

As Ben and Nigel left, Kit ran to Ben and flung himself at Ben's leg. Ben pulled the boy's hands off his leg. "Hey, soldier, it's your turn to be the man of the house and take care of your mom and sister. If you're good and help your mom, I'll bet Santa will reward you."

The temporary bond was not lost on Trevor. He said nothing. He'd probably have to turn the case over to a colleague if it came back to court. He wanted to tell the men good luck with their case, but he knew he would have to recuse himself for sure if he acknowledged the connection.

Ben and Nigel caught an Uber back to the motel. Nigel hadn't slept in days. They had the room for the night, so Ben drove back to North Beach and the YP, and Nigel fell in a heap on the bed. He'd get up early and return. "Great day, Ben. I never want to have another twenty-four like that again."

As Ben walked out, Nigel warned him. "It's only temporary, mate. We got lucky, but we may have a nuclear explosion coming our way after Christmas."

Chapter 38

Revision

Ben checked his phone for messages after he refueled. There was an email from Sarah back at his veterinary clinic.

Hey Boss-man.

We're missing you. Any chance you want to come out of retirement? BTW, someone is asking about you and all your priors. Seriously, it seems Interpol, or someone purporting to be Interpol, called the clinic. I asked them to give me their credentials, and they seemed legit. What are you up to over there? How's your granddaughter? When are you coming back?

Delay any reply at your peril.

Sarah

His reply was brief.

Sarah?

Who are you? Having a great time and loving my new life. Can you send a copy of my birth certificate? I may apply for citizenship.

BT

Ben thought that would make Sarah sit up. He'd always planned to consult and maybe even do a few days back at the clinic here and there. He'd kept his veterinary license for that purpose. His small stint in helping with Tag's surgery made him want to do more, but he knew getting a license in Australia would be difficult. Nope, I'm done. But how long could I hope to hang on for Maddy's sake?

Ben's mother died at ninety-two. Nigel was younger than Ben by four years, but he said he didn't have longevity in his family. Nigel mentioned his parents both drank and smoked excessively. Nigel never smoked and only drank in social situations.

Maddison was used to being "the adult" and caring for her father. She was mentally and emotionally so much older than her six years of age. If they could get custody and be in her life until she turned eighteen, Ben was sure Maddison could have a wonderful and full life. She'd be in vet school. She had the resources to pay for tuition and maybe even do an internship and residency in the States, or, God forbid, the UK.

But what were her prospects if both he and Nigel died in the next few years? Were they really the best option? The court must be taking this into consideration. Should we be searching for better options?

Did Ben really want to move to either Australia or New Zealand? Was there any chance Nigel would move to America? That was a long shot. Ben was enjoying his time in Australia, but only because he knew it was temporary and more like a vacation.

This reminded him that the national park at the end of the peninsula was still to be explored. Then Christmas was coming. When he was home, he'd talk to the neighbors about the rental agreement. He felt that winter at North Beach might be cold and windy. He'd also heard sharks were a consideration, thinking of his new retirement hobby of skin diving.

There was so much to consider and plan. Ben made a mental list. He would talk to the Smarts about extending the lease for two months. He'd take Maddison down to Innes National Park. Ben would investigate the school and see if it was appropriate for Maddy. A Christmas tree needed to be sourced, and he wanted to buy presents for his granddaughter and for Nigel. Ben wondered about becoming a temporary citizen and maybe explore other areas of Australia.

When he pulled into the driveway, he'd planned his course and would write everything he'd considered. But then, as he opened the door to the back entry, Maddison ran to him and hugged him. Tag followed behind her. He walked out to the living room and kitchen, and both Janet and Doug Smart sat at the dining room table with Monopoly opened and piles of money sitting at the empty spot.

"Good thing you're here, Ben. I'm about to go down. This kid is a real estate mogul. She plays for blood." Doug stood. "Want a beer? I'll go get one from our fridge."

"That sounds so good. I haven't eaten, but it's way past someone's bedtime. I need to medicate Tag, and then maybe we can sit on the porch."

Janet went to the house to fix a plate for Ben, while Doug took Tag outside. "Let me know when you're ready, mate."

Ben skipped Maddison's bath. He helped her change into pajamas and sat by her bed. "What did you learn today?"

"Well, we went on four calls in the morning. We saw a horse that's losing weight. Dr. Smart thought the teeth might be bad. Did you know a horse's teeth keep growing and get sharp, and you can file them off? Dr. Smart said if the horse wasn't better, she would take blood and see if the liver was sick. There're lots of plants that horses eat that cause liver disease. Then we saw a horse with a bowed tendon.

"Grandpa, no one would tell me about what you and Pop were doing. Mrs. Harding called me and asked me some questions about how I felt. I told her I was hot, but she meant if I was happy. I told her the truth. Do we have to go on the lam? Do you know what that means? It's not a baby sheep."

"Yes, I do, and no, we don't. We can stay here. What do you think 'going on the lam' means, Maddy?"

"It means to hide out, like Dad and I did to hide from Mum."

"Did you want to hide from your mother?"

"No, well, I mean yes. I wanted to see my mother, but Dad said she only wanted me to meet her boyfriends. I don't know what he meant. I didn't want to live with her.

I just wanted to see her. I'd never have left my father. Who would take care of him if I weren't there?"

But that was the end of the conversation. Alarm bells were ringing—meeting her boyfriends? Maddison was asleep. Ben bent over to tuck her in and kiss her goodnight. She swatted him, as was her usual. He petted Tag. Tag's bed was now permanently moved into Maddison's room. Unlike Maddison, Tag wanted more petting and scratching. Ben watched Tag and thought of his role in Maddison's life. And how long are you going to be here for the precious girl?

Ben sent a quick thank-you text to Lindy and knocked on the neighbor's door. Doug came out with two beers. Janet followed with a plate of leftovers and moved the sprinklers, watering the small garden and grass. It was another cloudless sunset that promised to bring temporary relief from the heat. They all stood and watched the sun dip into the ocean and slide away.

"It's not a terrible life here, mate." Doug returned to the patio and his beer. "Course, life on the land was pretty sweet, too." He turned to Janet, who rolled her eyes.

"Yeah, drought, flies, floods, dust, a seven hours drive to town, and the only electricity was from a generator. Hard to leave all that." She leaned over and kissed Doug.

Ben had a moment of jealousy. He would love to have reached over and kissed his wife tonight as well. He couldn't share his elation over today's outcome.

Ben nodded. "Yeah, you're not joking." He hadn't experienced regular company since his wife's death. After Tania's passing, Ben had women bringing him food and trying to cheer him up. Ben knew they had aspirations of being the next Mrs. Taylor. He was still good-looking, had all his teeth and health, a good income, and was lonely. He was the perfect target. But he'd finally made them all realize he was not interested, and the uninvited guests eventually stopped coming.

Ben explained what had happened in court with his limited knowledge. He described the pregnant woman on the tram and the unexpected birth. He mentioned the judge and Luke Sullivan's switch from Nigel and Ben to the government's social services.

Janet sat down after moving the sprinkler. "You two have an angel following you. I can't believe your luck."

This made Ben remember his wife. When she first died, he dreamed of her most nights. They had conversations usually centered on the daily chores he now did and then their son, Daniel. Eventually, the dreams became less frequent. He dreamed of her a few nights ago when she told him to take care of her grandchild or die trying.

"Yes, maybe there's more than one angel helping us."

Chapter 39

Almost Famous

Nigel rose early. He needed some time to decompress. He'd been to the edge of hell and back. He walked on Glenelg Beach one more time before returning home. He saw a message from Ben asking him to consider doing Christmas shopping for Maddison while he was in the "big smoke." He remembered the term from a visit to New York City with two American graduate students. Adelaide was hardly that big, but then again, it's all relative.

He'd researched the Rundle Mall and the Magic Cave. He thought it would be fun to take Maddison to see Santa. They wouldn't want to shop with her, and if he could get a few things, it might be a quick way to knock out Christmas.

Nigel wanted to get home, but it made sense. He got breakfast near the Glenelg jetty and walked down to see if they were catching anything. He went to a small bakery and ordered a bacon and egg sandwich and tea. He walked out onto the jetty, and he noticed a couple staring and pointing in his direction. He glanced behind himself, thinking it couldn't be him. Nope, it was him they were acknowledging. Nigel smiled and waved. Well, that's interesting.

He continued and felt his phone vibrating. He realized it was his former associate, Karan. "Hi, Karan."

There was a moment of hesitation. "Is this Nigel Buckby?"

"It sure is. How are you today?" It was strange, since they'd found each other only yesterday.

"I know I'm a voice out of the past, but this is Karan. I saw your picture in the paper and realized you must be in Adelaide. Maybe you don't remember, but we used to work together in New Zealand. I think it's great what you did. I called and told the newspaper who you were. It sure was nice of you to stop and help the lady having the baby."

"Huh?" Nigel then remembered Karan was having memory issues. He didn't want to upset her. "Oh, hi, Karan. I'm so glad you called. Of course, I remember you. How could I forget all those late nights in the lab? What are you saying about my picture? I'm not following you."

Nigel noticed a woman with two children staring at him. "Hey, Karan, are you all right?"

"Well, it's been such a long time since we've seen one another. After I saw your picture in the Advertiser, I only wanted to say hello and tell you what a delightful surprise it was for me to find out I know a hero."

"Yes, it's great talking to you too. Thanks for calling. We must catch up soon." Nigel was sick. He'd had such a pleasant meetup yesterday. Her memory issues didn't appear to be too advanced then, but she must experience good and bad days. He wondered if this was going to be his problem soon. He had to stay healthy for Maddison's sake. He'd talk to Ben tonight about their ability to care for their granddaughter in the coming years.

A young couple approached him as he returned from his jetty walk. "May we have a picture with you?"

"Why?" Nigel knew he was not up to speed.

The man was holding up his phone, prepared to snap a picture. His partner was pregnant. "Haven't you seen the paper? You're famous. It was you who helped a lady giving birth on the tram, wasn't it?"

"I'm not sure what you're talking about."

"You're on the front page. You and two other men were photographed helping a lady when she went into labor on a Glenelg tram."

"Sorry, mate. A picture?"

The young man pulled out his phone and scrolled until he found the picture of the woman in anguish and the judge, Ben, and him, leaning over to help the woman. None of the men were identified.

He went to the news agency and bought a paper. There it was, a picture with the caption, Unnamed Good Samaritans Save the Day. Nigel's face reddened. He was hardly a hero. His phone rang. He didn't recognize the number. "Hello?"

"Dr. Buckby, Kate Kilroy. Can I have a minute of your time?"

"Should we be talking? Aren't you and Luke together? I don't want to do anything to jeopardize our custody case."

The couple waited for Nigel to finish his conversation. "May I call you back?"

Kate Kilroy responded. "Sure, I'll text you a good number. Thanks."

The woman wanting the picture walked closer and stood next to Nigel. "I'm pregnant, and we thought it would be cute to have a picture of you for our baby Instagram account."

"If you don't use my name, it's probably okay."

Nigel posed for the picture and dialed Kate Kilroy back. "Hi, Kate. Are you sure it's okay for us to be talking?"

"Luke is recusing himself from the case. He's convinced his friend with family court experience to come back and handle the case. I wanted to interview you. Adelaide needs a good news story, and frankly, so do I."

"But what about the judge? We'd love to have him again if we go back to court."

"Oh, with the picture in the paper, he's out for sure. There's nothing pending, so that's all sorted for the time being. The solicitor who was acting for Isla said she's done a runner, and he has no authority to act for her. I'd like to write a quick story about the tram incident and then explain why you're here. Luke said it would be fine, and it can't hurt your case to have the public behind you."

"I don't know. You know Isla is my daughter, and her issues are painful to me. If Maddison understood, it would be painful to her as well."

"Okay, I understand. How about we have a quick interview with you about the tram part?"

"I'd have to check with Ben. Maybe you could interview Trevor Hutchinson and his role? Or maybe the mother?"

Kate was still eager to do the story. "Can I get back to you on this? Will you discuss this with Ben? It could be a kind of pay it forward story. I understand the tram was crowded, and no one let her sit down?"

"Yeah, but I don't think sitting would have changed the outcome."

"Nigel, Luke has asked me to tell you he has tickets to the cricket game on Saturday if Australia hasn't already won."

"Tempting. I haven't kept up with it. I've been occupied with a few matters." Nigel did laugh. "I'll let you know by lunchtime."

"I could come out to Wallaroo if that would help." Kate was pulling out all the stops.

"I'll call Ben and call you back. Thanks, Kate. I'm sure you're trying to help. I'm not sure publicity is a good thing right now."

Nigel immediately called Ben. "You will not believe this."

Chapter 40

Christmas or Bust

Ben and Maddison were up and out on the porch. It was going to be a scorcher, and Maddison wanted to swim again. Tag was not cooperating. He was sniffing around. There'd been an incursion, and the residual smells and feces from another dog were present. He finally re-marked his boundaries and performed his morning rituals. He was ready for a nap.

Ben laughed when he heard about the picture. "The joys of a small town. I was never on the front page of my newspaper back home. So, they don't know who we are?"

"I think they do now. Long story, but I was recognized this morning down here, and Kate Kilroy wants to do a good news story. I suggested she talk to the mother or the judge. She even offered us tickets to the cricket game on Saturday."

"I watched the highlights last night. I kinda think it's not my cup of tea—no offense intended. How about my suggestion?"

Nigel understood Maddison must be nearby. "I'll get on that as soon as the stores open. How is she?"

"She misses you," Ben lied.

"Tell her I miss her, too. I'm going to the big mall. Any suggestions?"

"I'll text you—little ears."

Nigel heard Maddison. "I heard that. Hurry, Grandpa."

"Nige, the sea calls. Take your time. Maddy and I'll get some food, and maybe we could find a tree and some ornaments."

After a swim in the bay, Ben and Maddison went to Kadina. Maddison was keen to find a tree. Most of the Australian trees were made from synthetic material. They ranged from tacky to really tacky from Ben's perspective. Maddison saw a pink one that she wanted. Not gonna happen.

"Oh, really? I think your pop and I are more traditional. Any chance you'd consider a green one that looks close to real?"

"I've never had a tree. Mrs. Donovan had a wattle bush that we decorated. It was outside. She let me help her decorate it with tinsel and baubles. Santa came and left me a present every year. I tried to wait up, but I fell asleep and never saw the bloke. Some of the kids at school said there was no such thing as Santa. I feel sorry for them. I guess Santa only brings things for kids who have trees. Last year, Daddy didn't get a tree, and we didn't get a present, so maybe if we have a pink one, he'll see it better and leave us a present."

"Do you remember what present Santa left you when you lived with Mrs. Donovan?" Ben wanted to cry. His life had been so easy, and Daniel had received presents every year. Why couldn't the simple task of giving his daughter a present from Santa be beyond his abilities? He managed a portfolio that amassed a fortune, for God's sake.

"Books. Lots of books. Santa knows me so well. He knows I love books."

"Where are your books?" Maddison had a small library of about five books.

"I left them for the other kids on the station. Mrs. Donovan thought that was the best thing for me to do. She said I could get all the books I wanted when I lived near town and the library. We had the school library, but it had little for me."

"What kind of books do you like to read?" Ben knew this was a perfect way to get present ideas, giving nothing away.

"I like books about dogs and horses and vet stuff. I don't like books with cartoons. I kinda liked Harry Potter, but it was scary, so we stopped reading it. I read Black Beauty. It was okay, but sad too."

"Did your father read you these books?" Ben hoped for the right answer.

"No, Mrs. Donovan did. Now I read them. Do you think there's a library here?"

"Let's find out. I need to send a message to your pop. Why don't you go down the next aisle and pick out some ornaments?"

Ben texted Nigel: Heads up, get some horse and dog books. Probably at the high school or university level. He inserted a wry face.

Ben joined Maddison as she went through the various ornaments. "Grandpa, could we go to another store first? I think these are too expensive."

Ben smiled. "Atta girl. No doubt you're a Taylor. The thing is, this is probably as inexpensive as we are going to see today. I think we're going into Adelaide in a few days, so if you want to wait, we can. How about we find the library?"

Ben hoped she would forget about the pink tree. The library was closed for renovations. They had lunch and saw Fiona walking briskly down the sidewalk.

Ben didn't even realize Maddison had run out to join her. He was staring at his menu and only realized Maddison had slipped away when she failed to answer his question. He saw them out on the street and stood and waved her in. Fiona said she only had a minute but would have a salad with them. She had business and was meeting clients in an hour.

"Ben, you have no clue how difficult this job can be." She appeared to be distraught. "Never mind. It's people like you who make the bad days tolerable. By the way, I saw the picture of you and your rescue team in the paper. Nigel didn't mention it. All he said was that you were on your way to court and were held up."

"Isn't life funny? You never know sometimes. I looked at the picture, but it was on my phone. Was the little boy in the picture?"

This piqued Maddison's attention. "What little boy?"

Ben went to the counter. There was the Adelaide Advertiser for sale. He turned it over and was told he would have to buy it if he wanted to read it. Ben saw the picture and bought the newspaper. On the front page was the picture of the judge, Nigel, a distraught woman lifting her crying son into Ben's arms. Someone on the tram must have taken the picture.

Maddison came over and stared at the picture. Ben put his arm around Maddison's waist as she read the headlines. Maddison asked about the little boy. "How come you're holding him, Grandpa?"

"Maddy, his mother was about to give birth, and she was in pain, and she was crying. It scared him, so I picked him up and comforted him when we transported them all to the hospital. He was so cute. They were on their way to see Santa in the Magic Cave, and her water broke. Once the baby was born, he asked if he and his mother could go home and leave the baby."

Maddison appeared shocked. "Well, that little sh-brat. I'd love to have a baby sister or brother." Both Ben and Fiona stared at one another.

"Good thing you didn't swear. And I suppose it's a good thing I'm not a spanker." Ben gave his granddaughter a warning look.

Fiona stifled a laugh. "Duty calls." She picked up her food and waved goodbye. "The good with the bad."

Ben thought her duty might involve a child who was being mistreated. He didn't ask. He still had the task of finding a Christmas tree. They walked down the sidewalk and saw several trees at the lumber store. Thankfully, there were no pink ones.

"Maddy, why don't you look inside and pick one out? I know Santa never missed my house, and I always had a green one."

"If you think so." She was dubious, but she wanted to get back to the house and Tag.

"I can guarantee it."

"Well, you can't really. It's not up to you. I've been good all year. Maybe once I was bad, but he deserved it. I know Santa would say so too."

Ben tried to keep a straight face. "What was the transgression?"

"Huh?" She seemed perplexed.

"What did you do Santa might not like?"

"A boy called my father stupid. I socked him. He deserved it. My dad was different, but he was smart. I was sent to the principal's office. I had to say I was sorry. I wasn't, but my dad made me do it."

Ben had to turn away. When he could talk, he agreed. "I think Santa would be proud. Would you rather have the pink tree?"

"Naw, but can we have pink tinsel?"

Chapter 41

Pink Tinsel

Nigel returned in the afternoon. The presents were wrapped and hidden in the Smart's garage before he entered their house. He hugged Maddison and picked her up. "I missed you, darling." Maddison clung to him.

"I missed you too. Did you see the little boy who Grandpa was holding?"

"Yes, but only for a short time. How's Tag? Did you get a tree?"

"We did. It's green, but we have ormanents and pink tinsel. Grandpa said we had to be together when we decorate it." She pointed to the tree next to the television set.

"Yeah, well, thanks for waiting. I'd love to help with the ormanents." Nigel didn't correct her pronunciation. It was rare she mispronounced words, but it was endearing. "What's for dinner?"

"The Smarts are having us for dinner, and Dr. Smart is coming too," Maddison whispered in Nigel's ear. "We need to let Grandpa and Dr. Smart sit next to one another. I'm working on a plan."

Nigel nodded and leaned down where he'd sat with Maddison on the couch. He whispered, "What's the plan?"

Maddison smirked and put her finger to her lips. "You know." She cupped her face, turned from Ben, and pursed her lips in a kissing motion.

Nigel gave her the thumbs up. "Yeah, I'll be in that too."

Maddison shook her head. "No. You can't."

This made Nigel grin. "Oh, I get it."

Nigel showered and asked Maddison if she wanted to walk with him on the beach. She jumped up, and the two left for a walk. Tag wanted to go with her, but Ben stayed with him in the house. He went up to his room and sat on the deck with a beer. A buzz from his phone showed a new email had arrived.

I'm not sending your damn birth certificate. Come home, you crazy bastard.

Love,

Sarah

Ben missed his "other family," but there was no comparison to his granddaughter. He kept thinking about how she defended her father and was reminded of all the times he'd done the same. He'd reply to Sarah tomorrow. He made a mental list of presents he wanted to buy for the various people he now knew here in Australia. This reminded him to call Lindy Smart when he was alone.

Lindy answered right away. "Hi, Ben. Great pic in the Tiser. Can I have your autograph?"

Ben figured the locals must call the newspaper the Tiser for short. "Only if I can get some ideas from you."

"I owe you. Your granddaughter is the best thing that's happened to me in years. She can ride with me anytime."

"Chip off the old block. Does that go for her grandfather?" Ben was so pleased to hear one of his progeny was valued. He'd never heard this about Daniel. They could never leave him with anyone, anyway. It was gut-wrenching to think Tania had never experienced this small joy.

"Nope, just Maddy. What can I do for you?" Ben could hear her stifling a laugh.

"I'm trying to get some presents for Maddy. She said she wants books on horses and dogs. Any suggestions?"

"I'd have to think about it. She picked up and read a magazine every time we came back to the clinic. It's called The Horse. A subscription would be a suitable present. I'll make a list and give it to you tonight. I haven't heard anything, but it sounds like you may have scored a small win at court?"

"It's only temporary. Maddy's mom was a no-show. The judge was compromised, though, and he won't be presiding next time. He's the one in the picture with us helping the woman."

"Damn. That was your judge?"

"Yeah. Any good vet cases you need help with?" Ben was already missing his life's work.

"I'll check with Gaz. He's always got something going."

"See you soon, and thanks for your help with Kid Taylor. She means the world to Nigel and me."

"She's a charmer. Yeah, later, gator."

Ben got online and ordered a subscription to The Horse magazine. He knew his stay in this house would be temporary, but he wondered if Maddison wanted to put up some pictures. Where were Daniel's belongings? He'd ask tomorrow. Maybe Nigel already had them.

Maddison and Nigel returned from the beach to dress for dinner. She went over to the Smart's house well before dinner was ready. She said she wanted to learn how to cook from Mrs. Smart.

"You don't have to do that, Maddy. Your pop is more than happy to do the cooking." Ben glanced at Nigel, who'd emerged from the shower.

"Uh, I'd hurry if I were you. You can always store the info for later." Nigel gave her the thumbs up. Maddison returned the gesture, knowing he was referring to her plans to unite her other grandfather and Dr. Smart. He wouldn't mind some help in that department. He hoped to see Fiona for something other than her work.

As soon as she left, Nigel popped a beer and sat down in a chair across from Ben. "Pink tinsel? Mate, what were you thinking?"

"Don't ask. She's got me wrapped around her little finger. I almost agreed to a pink tree as well. Never let her go shopping with me if you want sensible purchases. I'm weak."

"I guess. So, let me tell you what I bought." Nigel outlined a few books, clothes, and games. "I hope she likes them."

"Sounds good to me. It seems like she didn't have a Christmas last year. I don't think we should try to make up for her previous life with meaningless presents." Ben knew Nigel would agree.

He went to the liquor cabinet. There was whiskey and a few reds. He knew little about Australian wine—another future addition to his Australian education. "What shall we bring to dinner?"

Nigel surveyed the wine bottles and picked out a red to go with the steaks. "Nice selection, mate."

"Hey, Nige, did you hear anything about Daniel and Maddy's belongings when you first arrived?"

"No, mate. We can ring Fiona. There must be something. He must have a computer at least. How else would he do his trading? I'm still sleep deprived. Give me thirty, and I'll be ready for tonight."

Ben remembered his lunch. "I saw Fiona in town. She was having a bad day. She didn't say what it was about, but I suspect it might have been a child who was in a bad way."

Nigel paused. "Should I call her?"

Ben shrugged. "Tough one to say. Not sure, but why don't you wait until tomorrow? It looked like she had her hands full."

Nigel didn't call. He was exhausted from yesterday's events and the emotional rollercoaster from it all. "Give me five." He closed the door to his room. He had an hour before they would be expected. He emerged five minutes before it was time to leave. "I needed that. Thanks for letting me sleep."

"Benny, how are you doing? It's been a hell of a few days, mate."

"I was fine until you called me Benny. That's what my sister called me when she was about to rat me out for something. You know this was the second worst time in my life, and then there was our rebound of luck or fate. Do you know how many times I've cried in the last few days? Nige, I'm not a crier."

"Yeah, neither am I. It must be old age. We're both losing our filters. My dad cried in the last few years of his life."

Ben nodded. "Mine too."

Both men gazed at the window at the sun, which was just peeking down from the veranda shade. They each quietly wondered how this would end, but dared not reveal their concerns. Despite their initial resolve to sort out a place for Maddison and return to their respective homes, they knew each would stay here at all costs if it meant keeping this adult-like child.

Maddison was still next door. Ben took Tag out and gave him the last of his antibiotics. Tag would continue with a decreasing pain medication. He exceeded Ben's expectations in all respects. The men both checked themselves in the mirror and walked over with the wine.

"Hello, hello." Janet greeted them and announced they were in for an extraordinary dinner prepared by the new Julia Child of Wallaroo. Maddison beamed and stepped into the living room, bringing crackers and cheese.

Along with crackers and cheese were stuffed mushrooms and shrimp with sweet chili sauce. Nigel tasted one of each. "She takes after my side of the family, for sure." Then he remembered the implications, including his daughter, who almost disrupted their lives.

Ben countered, "I think she gets it from both sides. Her grandmother could put on a dinner fit for a king."

Lindy Smart entered the kitchen through the laundry door. She immediately came over and put her arm around Maddison, who was still holding the platter. "Who's your favorite vet? And when do you want to go on calls with me again? I'd suggest you and I have a private moment on the veranda with this spread." She directed Maddison toward the door when Doug reached over and took the platter.

"Not gonna happen, Doc. She's mine now. You all can go to hell and back."

Janet suggested Doug serve some drinks. Both Nigel and Doug started with beers. Lindy even had a gin and tonic. Maddison asked to sip Lindy's drink, but Lindy covered her glass. "No sips until you're seven or twenty-one—whichever comes last."

They were all called to the table. There were name tags for everyone. Lindy and Ben were seated next to one another. It was no surprise to the rest of the guests. Lindy blushed, but Ben was gracious. How could he tell everyone he was still in love with his wife? He sensed Lindy had similar thoughts. Throughout the meal, both watched Maddison glancing from one to another and then occasionally toward Nigel with an exasperated shake of her head.

Maddison and Janet asked everyone to go out on the porch to watch the sunset while she and Maddison cleared the table and prepared for the dessert. The pair joined them out on the veranda, and just after the sun faded from view, they announced the dessert would be served. Everyone returned to the table.

Maddison carried a beautiful small chocolate cake with Happy Birthday Lindy written in red letters, obviously done by Maddison. She placed it in front of Lindy and sang happy birthday, along with the rest.

Ben and Nigel gazed at the cake and then at one another and both shrugged. When the song finished and the hip-hip-hoorays were shouted, Doug sang an unfamiliar tune about why she was born so beautiful, as Janet shushed him.

Lindy was as surprised as anyone. "I think you have my birthday mixed up. I don't have birthdays anymore." Her phone rang, and there was a call from her son, followed by a second from her other son. "Did you get our cards?"

"Not yet. I hope you didn't break with tradition and send one this year?"

"Uh, no. But maybe we might come over. How does that sound, Mum?"

"You know I'd love to see you, but I know how hard it is. Please don't make a fuss."

"Okay. Well, we all just wanted to say..." The phone went dead.

Ben saw the disappointment on Lindy's face. He put his arm around her and turned when he heard the sliding glass door rattle. Several people were standing on the veranda.

Her colleague Gaz, two nurses, and the receptionist followed by others Ben didn't recognize.

"What the hell?" was all Lindy could say. She turned and pointed to Doug and Janet. "So much trouble."

Janet opened the door, and the vet crew poured into the living room, holding another cake. Lindy stood and went over to hug them. They all acknowledged Maddison and even brought a small scrub top with the Copper Coast logo and Maddy embroidered below the logo.

"Well, who's managing the clinic?" Lindy knew they were sharing a call with the YP Vets tonight. "You all ought to be hung."

Ben could see how much Lindy meant to her staff and the few clients who were invited. Only Janet and Doug were in on the surprise. Lindy hugged them both. "So much trouble" was all she could say.

Ben thought it was getting late and suggested he take Maddison and prepare her for bed. Janet said there was no way she was leaving. If Maddison gets tired, she could sleep on the couch in the living room. She introduced Ben to Colin Butler and a few more clients. They were all out on the grass.

Ben walked next door and allowed Tag out. Colin was particularly interested in Tag. He asked about his breeding. There were no papers, but Maddison knew his sire and the mother and where her father bought the pup. The Donovans could verify this when they returned from their trip.

"I might be interested in using him with two of my bitches. Maddy and I need to be better friends."

Nigel joined the conversation. "I'm Maddy's agent. Any negotiations must go through me. Any chance you know someone who would take us fishing?"

"That can be arranged." Colin explained he had several friends who had fishing boats.

Colin was about to expand when he was interrupted. Several people entered from the front of the house. "Happy birthday, Mum."

Two young men and what must be their wives with two small children emerged from the laundry and went directly to Lindy. Doug and Janet high beamed at one another as the children shyly smiled. "Grandma, these are your great grandsons, Arthur and Kade."

Lindy was standing next to Ben, and without thinking, Ben put his arm around her waist to steady her until her sons took her away. She turned to Ben, who shrugged. The only people who knew about the surprise were Doug and Janet.

Lindy's two grandsons were younger than Maddison. Both stared at her and smiled shyly. Nigel put his arm around his granddaughter and whispered, "Did you know?"

Maddison shook her head. Nigel could see she was taken aback and confused. She gazed up at Nigel, who hugged her shoulder with his hands and reassured her she was part of his family.

Tag came to her and sat awkwardly next to her. His pelvic fracture was healing, and the pain appeared to be decreasing, but he was far from over the injury. Maddison knew

Tag felt threatened by all the new intruders. He needed to protect Maddison.

Ben stood back and glanced at the two standing awkwardly by themselves. He nodded to Nigel and checked his watch—time for bed. He received the nod, and Ben walked over to Janet and thanked her for a wonderful dinner and surprise. Maddison thanked Lindy and her staff for the scrub top and hugged Janet and Doug.

Nigel waved and pointed to their house. "If you need an extra room tonight, the second room upstairs is unoccupied. We'll leave the laundry door unlocked."

"No, mate. Did we tell you the house on the other side is ours too? We have it covered."

Maddison was tearful, which told the men how tired she was. They had left their phones in the house during dinner, and while Ben helped Maddison prepare for bed, Nigel noticed he'd missed a phone call from Fiona. It was too late to return the call. He would listen to the message after he said goodnight to his granddaughter.

Ben stayed with Maddison until she was asleep. He'd noticed her watching the interaction of the two little boys with their father. He suspected she was grieving her recent losses. Her lack of emotion was like her father's, and he wondered if she was also on the autism spectrum. As painful as it was to see her sad and upset, he was relieved to see her showing a normal reaction to loss.

Nigel asked Ben to look at his phone. "Is there a message from Fiona?" Ben also received a text message, urgently asking either of them to call her.

Chapter 42

A Favor

It was half past ten. Nigel glanced at his watch and then back at Ben, who shrugged. "I'd better call her."

Fiona answered on the first ring. "Oh, Nigel. Thank God. I have a favor—a huge favor. It's okay to say no. It's highly irregular, and I may get fired for this."

"Is it about Maddy?"

"No, thankfully." Fiona's voice was low. She was whispering.

Nigel understood Fiona was with someone. "Shoot." Nigel turned to Ben, who was sitting and trying to listen to the conversation.

"It's okay to say no, but I'm in a bind. I'm desperate—really desperate."

"How can we help?" Nigel was now over the alcohol-numbing effect. He was ready to get in the car and go save her life.

"It's temporary. Maybe only a day—not over two days." Fiona prayed for the answer she needed. "I have a mother and child who need accommodation for the night. It might be a day or two longer, but no more. It's a domestic violence case, and I need to hide this woman and her son until I can organize a safe place. I'm at the office, and I know her partner is sitting in a car outside the building. The police are there, but they say he's done nothing yet to warrant an arrest. I need you to come and get them while I distract him."

"I don't want to put Maddy in danger. How safe is it?"

"The police say they can keep him from following you, and you can park your car in the garage. No one will know. I normally have options and can deal with it, but he's a policeman, and he knows all our safe houses and most of the ones in Adelaide. According to his wife, he's gone off his meds. He has schizophrenia. She said the mental health docs say he refuses to medicate, and he wants to reconcile with his wife. He was a good guy until he wasn't. Can you come down and get them?"

Nigel cupped the phone and briefly explained the situation to Ben. "I won't if you say no."

"As long as we aren't in the newspaper this time." Ben nodded.

"Fi, I'm on my way."

Ben walked out and prepared to open and close the garage door. "Take care, buddy. I know you'll sacrifice yourself for Maddy. I'll get the other room ready."

"Maybe wait. We don't know how old the kid is, and we don't want him to fall off the balcony."

"There's a child lock at the top of the door. We can reassess tomorrow."

Nigel drove up to the office. There were three automobiles parked outside the building. A police car with flashing lights was parked across the street, where two officers and a man were arguing. Nigel knocked on the glass door. Fiona peeked out of her office. Realizing it was Nigel, Fiona ran to the door, unlocked it, and escorted him into her office.

A woman in her early thirties sat with a sleeping boy in her lap. He appeared to be around four years of age. She had a small bag stuffed with clothes. Nigel was introduced, and the situation was explained again. They only needed a few hours to defuse the conflict.

The plan was for Fiona to alert the cops, who would distract the man while Nigel drove to the back parking lot. The woman and child would be placed in the car, and while camouflaged, Nigel would drive them to the beach house, where they would spend the night. The police would make sure the father wasn't allowed to follow Nigel's vehicle.

"Call me when you're in the house. Take care." Fiona then kissed him. "Kinda unprofessional, but there you go."

"Very unprofessional, and I'll take it under advisement. Go home and get to bed." Nigel had a surge of pleasure.

When he arrived at the beach house, Ben was waiting with the garage door open. Casey Morgan had not spoken during the entire trip. Her son had fallen back asleep as soon as the car moved away from the office.

Ben opened the door, and Mrs. Morgan climbed out. Ben put his finger to his lips and picked up the sleeping child and carried him up to the bedroom. Nigel followed with a suitcase and a bag of clothes. Ben pointed to the upstairs bathroom, and the men left.

"Well, it took risking all our lives, but I got a kiss." Nigel poured himself a small sip of whiskey. Ben went around the house and made sure the doors were locked. Tag was in Maddison's room. He'd emerged when strangers entered the house and his hackles were up, but he promptly returned to his bed when Ben sternly said, "No more."

Ben announced he was no longer sleepy and said he would be up reading before retiring. He had written a novel about a horse vet who was dying. "How often do they write about vets these days, and the poor bastard is dying? Go figure."

"Thanks, mate. See you shortly." It was two in the morning, and Nigel was craving sleep.

"Don't call me shortly." Ben laughed at the old reply.

"How tall are you?"

"I peaked at six foot two, but I'm on a downward spiral." Ben looked up. "The ceiling is getting farther away by the day."

"Tell me about it. Oh, to be six feet again." Nigel gazed up the stairs.

Ben sat back and put his bare feet on the coffee table. "Better under six feet than six feet under. Nige, can you believe how our lives have changed?"

Nigel lay in bed recalling the last forty-eight hours. He'd gone from one end of the emotional spectrum to the other and back again. Fiona thanked him with a kiss on the cheek. It was not an I-love-you kiss, but it was better than he expected. He tried to stop thinking about her and calm down.

For God's sake, old man, remember your age—punching above your weight again, and you aren't even divorced. Nigel was reminded to sort out his marital status ASAP.

Tag and Maddison rose early. She saw her grandfather sleeping on the couch and quietly crept by him and out the door. She allowed Tag to wander over to the Smart's grass where he picked up a few bites of dropped food. Tag strolled around and then settled onto his outdoor raised bed. Maddison had on her scrub top. She was so pleased and planned to wear it all day.

Waiting for her family to wake was torture. Maddison knew Mrs. Donovan would not be impressed. She also knew the reason they rose early on the station was to beat the heat and to make use of the light. Maddison went back into the house and noticed her grandfather was still sleeping. After her grandfathers returned from Adelaide, they acted strangely. She wondered if they were afraid her mum would try to snatch her.

She had so much fun last night, and after dinner, she saw her grandfather put his arm around Dr. Smart. She noticed Dr. Smart seemed to like it. Maybe her plan would work. She'd discussed it with Mrs. Smart earlier when they prepared the dinner. Mrs. Smart cautioned Maddison not to interfere and to let nature take its course.

Mrs. Smart didn't realize human nature was different from natural nature. Maddison knew her grandfather and Dr. Smart were too old to have babies. She remembered when the ancient stallion on the station got too old to breed the mares. He still ran with the mares, and he always slept next to the oldest mare. Goldy was the boss. She was in her thirties, and she still liked to sidle up to Chester. Chester would make a half-hearted attempt to breed the mares, but he was too arthritic. Maddison missed watching the herd of horses that ran on the enormous station.

Maybe Grandpa's too stiff? Why are humans so shy in expressing their desires? It's not rocket science. Heck. Maddison laughed to herself, remembering how Mr. Donovan used that expression when teaching the young jackaroos how to fix fences.

Tag whimpered. Maddison stared into the living room and saw her grandpa sitting up. She returned to the kitchen and made a bowl of food for Tag, started the coffee, and went to lie down on the couch next to her grandfather. "Mrs. Donovan says sleeping in is one of the seven deadly sins."

"Really?" Ben stifled a laugh. "What are the other sins?"

"I don't remember for sure, but one is not cooling off your horse when you finish riding. Why did you sleep on the couch?" Maddison was now intently reading the book Ben had left on the table. "Is this book any good?"

"It's not for kids, but I like it." Ben wondered where this conversation was going. He didn't want to discourage her. This was a moment he'd never experienced with his son. He prayed they had a few more minutes to lie side by side and chat like a father and daughter.

"Is there too much sex?" Maddison casually turned the pages.

Whoa, who is this kid? "What do you know about sex?" Ben sat up.

"Nothing." But it was clear she was lying.

"Then why did you ask? You know, Maddy, it's okay for you to ask me any questions. There are no bad questions. Never. But most six-year-olds usually have other things on their minds. Is there something you want to tell or ask me?"

"No. I mean, I know about sex, Grandpa. I lived on a station. I read about it. Mammals are mammals, is all Mr. Donovan would say. I won't say any more until you're older."

I'm older? Ben could barely maintain his mirth. Still, had his granddaughter been exposed to something no six-year-old should know about?

Nigel came down the stairs and put his finger to his lips and pointed up. Maddison sat up abruptly. "Is someone up there?" Could it be a woman?

Ben took the lead. "We have a guest. It's a friend of Fiona's, and she needed a place to stay for the night. Shall we make some pancakes?"

Maddison and Nigel went into the kitchen while Ben showered and dressed. Nigel told Maddison that Mrs. Morgan and her son Liam would be with them for a day or so. He didn't want to elaborate about the circumstances. He was dubious about his ability to keep any sordid details from his savvy granddaughter, but he would try.

He and Maddison could hear noises upstairs. "Maddy, go up and knock on the door and tell Mrs. Morgan we have pancakes for her and her son. We need to get you into the bath this morning. Phew, you still smell like dinner last night."

She ran to the top of the stairs and yelled, "Breakfast, come and get it or we'll throw it to the hogs." She immediately ran back down.

Both Nigel and Ben stared at one another. Ben started a bath for her. "Just when you think your progeny is exceptional, they revert to the behavior of a six-year-old."

Maddison inhaled her pancake and gazed up at the two men with crossed arms staring at her. "What?"

Nigel pursed his lips. "Bath time." He pointed to the bathroom. *Please let me remember these moments when I'm in "the home" and drooling.*

Ben went to make more coffee and pancakes. *Please never let this end.*

Casey Morgan and her son Liam descended the stairs. Casey was dressed in jeans and a shirt that failed to hide her pregnancy. Her long, medium brown hair was tied in a band at the base of her neck. Liam had on shorts that were too small for his growing body. His shirt barely covered his belly. He sucked his thumb and hid behind his mother.

"Good morning. Nigel's in the bathroom with our granddaughter, and I'm in charge of breakfast. Would you like coffee or tea?"

"Coffee, thanks. I forgot your name. I'm Casey, and this is Liam."

"I'm Ben. Coming up. What would Liam like to drink for breakfast? Orange juice or milk? And what does he like on his pancakes?"

Liam sat picking at his pancake. Ben offered to cut it up. The little boy glowered at Ben. He then picked the pancake up with his hands and put it on his mother's plate.

She stared at him and then suggested Vegemite and toast. "It's been a little rough for him. He's normally a good boy."

"I'm sure. Vegemite and toast coming up." Ben put the bread in the toaster. Nigel and Maddison emerged when the toast was done.

Nigel saw the switch and took over. As he was spreading Vegemite, his phone vibrated. He saw it was Fiona. "Excuse me." He walked out to the patio to take the call. "No-tell hotel. How may I direct your call?"

Fiona laughed. "I'd like to speak to the management. I need to make an assessment. May I enter the facility? I'm out on the street."

Nigel replied, "You know we have strict standards."

Fiona checked the street. Thankfully, no one had followed her. She'd parked down the road and had walked up to Nigel's rental. The gate was locked, which pleased her.

Nigel met her at the gate, and he shyly glanced at Fiona. "Social or business?"

"Sadly, business. How about we talk?"

"Come in." Nigel opened the gate and door to the laundry. He escorted her into the kitchen, where Casey sat with her son.

Maddison had left the room, and Fiona searched for her. Ben pointed to the bathroom. "Hey. Bad night, Ms. Harding?"

"Not so different from the others, aside from no room at the inn." Fiona noticed Ben had turned on the kettle. He knew she drank tea. Nigel was preparing a cup. Fiona asked to speak privately with Casey.

"If you two want to go out on the patio, I'll bring the tea out." Nigel figured this conversation was not for little ears.

When Maddison emerged from the bathroom, she was asked to entertain Liam while the grownups talked. Liam was reluctant to leave his mother. "We can play in my room, mate. Come on." Maddison took his hand and headed toward her bedroom. She turned back and gave Fiona a smile.

Nigel brought two cups of tea out onto the porch where the women sat chatting. He turned to go, but Fiona asked him to get Ben, and when everyone was present, she explained she was still having issues with finding a safe place for Casey and little Liam.

"What I haven't told you was Casey's partner previously worked with the Department for Child Protection as part of his policing duties for several years and had gone off the rails. He's threatened to kill Casey and take his son. He knows all the safe-house locations. We're trying to get them interstate. I guess what I'm asking is, can I keep them here for a few more days?"

Nigel would do anything to help Fiona, but Ben wasn't sure. "How do we know we can keep Maddy safe?"

"We don't think he'd harm anyone else. He's been a copper for ten or more years. He just wants access to his son.

He took him on an access visit and didn't return him. He's never threatened to harm the boy."

Ben understood the problems with divorce and custody. Two of his nurses had gone through similar issues during their divorces. Then again, they had their own concerns with Maddison's mother.

Nigel understood they both had to agree. He turned to Ben and shrugged. "Your call, mate."

Ben wanted to say no, but he stared at the woman in tears. "I guess. Do they need to stay in the house and out of sight?"

Fiona nodded. "It's just this for a few days. I can stay with them tomorrow if that helps."

Nigel was all in. Ben wasn't sure. If Maddison was the target, how would he feel? The men glanced at the woman with tears and shrugged.

"What about our trip to the Magic Cave and Santa?" Ben was hoping to take Maddison for a fun day.

"You two go, and I'll stay here with Fiona." Nigel wanted to take his granddaughter, but he'd just spent a day in Adelaide, and he didn't want to make the trip so soon again, anyway.

"No." Ben was firm. "We both go or none. I'll take Maddy, and we may do some Christmas shopping and exploring."

The three adults returned to the living room. Ben knocked on Maddison's bedroom and opened the door. He found the two children on Maddison's bed, where she was reading a story to the boy.

"Hey, you two. What are you reading?"

He watched as Maddison glanced at her book. "The Merck Manual. Liam likes sheep, and I was teaching him how to treat," she stared into the book, "grass tetany." She turned the book toward her grandfather and pointed to the highlighted topic.

"Huh?" Ben knew this was a cover, but for what? "Never mind. Would you like to stay here for a few more days, Liam?"

"No. I want to go home to be with my dad. I hate you."

Maddison stared at Liam and shook her head. "I'll be here, mate. You can sleep in my bed if you want."

Liam seemed to consider this. "I want my daddy. Will you come with me if I go home?"

"I can't, so why don't you stay? We can have McDonald's." Maddison tried to put her arm over Liam's shoulder, but he ducked.

"I hate McDonald's. I want my daddy, and I want our cat."

Nigel heard the commotion and came into the room. "Maddy, you and your grandfather are going out. Brush your teeth and get ready."

"I promised Liam I'd stay with him." Maddy set down the manual and looked at Nigel with pleading eyes.

Nigel was firm. "You're going to have a wonderful day, so get ready. Get your swimsuit, too."

Liam turned to Maddison. "Don't go."

Maddison put her arm around Liam, and this time he allowed her. "Liam, you need to be brave. I'll be back, and then we can read some more. I promise."

Liam jumped from the bed and ran upstairs to his room. His mother followed him. "I'm so sorry about this. He's been through so much. I'll go talk to him."

Chapter 43

What if They're wrong?

Maddison sat in the back of Ben's rental car. She was not happy to leave Tag and her new friend. She'd been told she and Ben were going shopping. That was the last thing Maddison wanted to do. She wanted to stay with Liam. He needed a friend.

She'd cared for several children on the station. Many Aboriginal children came to a makeshift school and had daily lessons to learn to read and other basic skills. Maddison had started her schooling there. It wasn't long before Mrs. Donovan noticed Maddison's advanced intelligence and would often ask her to help with the younger children.

It was another hot day on the YP, and the AC was blasting. Ben could hardly hear Maddison ask him a question. He turned down the fan. "What?"

"Where are we going?"

"Down the road. Is that okay?" Ben turned onto the road leading to Pt. Hughes.

"Where down the road?" Maddison sat back and crossed her arms.

"I thought we'd go to your old home at the caravan park."

"Why?"

"I'll tell you when we get there. What did you think of Liam?"

"He's okay. He misses his father." Maddison saw the caravan park and remembered the pool. She wondered if they were going swimming there.

They drove up to the office, and Ben opened the door. "It's too hot to stay in the car. Come on. I want to speak to the manager. What's his name?"

"Harry, but he won't be awake yet."

"Let's see." Ben took her hand, and they walked up to the small building. The caravan park was quiet. The pool didn't open until nine, and only a few people were out walking dogs or returning from early morning beach strolls.

"Hi, Maddy!" Maddison turned and ran to an older man and hugged him. "Where's Tag?"

"He got run over, Mr. Grant. He's okay, though. My grandfather here is a vet, and he fixed him up, but he can't be moved." Maddison pointed to her grandfather. "Where's Cosmo?" Maddison fed the cat early in the morning before school.

"Sittin' on the counter in the office, runnin' the show, as usual. I sure miss you and your dad. I have to get up early and do the cleanin' and feed Cosmo. Geez, he gets ornery when he doesn't get his breakfast."

Ben extended his hand. "Ben Taylor. And I didn't save Tag. It was the Copper Coast Vets, but pleased to meet you. I'm Daniel's father. I was wondering if there was anything left behind after..." Ben didn't finish the sentence.

"I go by Harry. Ben, I'm sure sorry about your son. I wasn't able to come to the funeral. I have a few things. I put everything in boxes, and it's all in the shed where I keep the mower. Would you like to pull around to the back, and we can load it up?" Mr. Grant took Maddison's hand and led her around behind the office while Ben drove the car around to the shed.

There were three boxes with clothes and paperwork. There was another box with framed pictures and a fifth with books. "I saved all your books, Maddy. I did what you always asked. If anyone left a book in the cabins, I kept it for you." He turned to Ben. "I never seen anything like it. Your granddaughter sure can read good for her age. I think she may be a genius."

"No doubt, Mr. Grant. She takes after my wife." Ben laughed, thinking how it sure wasn't him who endowed her with extraordinary intelligence, and he'd never allow Nigel to think it came from his side. Ben had done an internet search on Nigel and found he'd authored many papers on reproduction. Nigel was a leader in his field. Ben even discovered Nigel had won an international award for his cumulative body of work last year. Nigel never mentioned it. Ben could see he was unusually modest.

Maddison and Ben thanked Harry and left the caravan park. Maddison pulled out one of her books and was flipping through the pages. "I think little Liam would like this book."

"Maddy, you don't have to give him your books. We can go buy one for him if you like. He's going through a hard time right now."

Maddison stared at the ocean. She was quieter than usual. Ben sensed something was on her mind. He regretted getting involved with Fiona's case and exposing Maddison to the trauma of a custody battle. "Cat got your tongue?"

"Huh? Oh, I know what you mean. I'm cogitating. Do you know what that means?" Maddison sat forward and reached up and tapped her grandfather's shoulder. "Can we go swimming?"

"Yeah. Great idea, Maddymeister."

"My name's Maddy."

"Maddymeister is a nickname. You're so smart. Take my phone and look up, meister."

Maddison found the word and read the entry after Ben spelled it. "Denoting a person regarded as skilled or prominent in a specified area of activity. Which activity?"

"Everything. You're a clever young woman. You can do whatever you want in life. Your daddy would be so proud." Ben turned toward the parking lot near a small beach with a sandy area.

"Maybe it came from my mother." Maddison undid her seatbelt. The sun was biting. They were alone, and she changed into her swimsuit with no sign of modesty.

"Maddy, don't say that. It would break my heart." Ben put his clenched fist over his heart. He laughed. "Well, I suppose you could consider her contribution to your genetic make-up. You sure got your looks from her."

The two walked out to the beach. Like many of the beaches along the eastern side of the peninsula, the water was shallow for a great distance and the waves were minimal. The two walked into the water a long way before it was deep enough to swim.

Maddison clung to Ben and reluctantly ventured farther away from him as she practiced her strokes. She could do a backstroke, breaststroke, and a partial freestyle. They swam for almost an hour when Ben noticed she was tired. "Okay, let's go back to shore and rest."

"I'm not tired." Maddison wanted to stay in the water.

"I am. Back to shore. We can sit in the water, but I need to rest." *This kid doesn't know her limits.*

They returned to a shallow area and sat in the water. "Crabs!" Ben saw a large blue crab. He thought about how to get some without getting pinched.

Maddison saw one as well and knew the pain from a crab pinch. She stood and sat on her grandfather's lap. Ben was surprised and delighted. He put his arms around his granddaughter. "You're safe with me, darling. I won't let the crabs get you."

They sat staring away from the shore. There was a large ship heading up the coast toward Wallaroo. "Grain ship. It's heading up to unload its cargo."

Maddison knew this, but she had other things on her mind. "Grandpa, how do you tell if someone's lying?"

"Ah, one of the mysteries of life. Why do you ask?"

"Just asking." Maddison sat, and Ben could feel the tension in her body.

"Maybe if you give me an example." He knew she wanted to talk. He sensed she was carrying a burden.

"Well, let's say your parents are getting a divorce, and one parent said the other parent was, say, bashing their boy, and the other says it's not true. Who do you believe?"

"That's a tough question, Maddy. It comes up all the time. The department where Ms. Harding works has to sort out the truth, and what is best for children. They try to figure out who is telling the truth, and they report to the court. It can be really hard sometimes."

"But what if they're wrong?" Her voice had a slight whine to it. Ben could feel her distress. He had an idea of where this was heading.

"It's true. They don't always get it right. But if there was information that, say, someone knew the truth, and they didn't say anything, then Ms. Harding couldn't help the child, could she?"

"No, I suppose not." Maddison shivered. She stood and turned around and sat down in Ben's lap again and hugged him.

Ben was in heaven. His son never had spontaneously hugged his father. This was a moment he would take to his grave. He rubbed her back, pretending to warm her, but he knew it was not the warmth she sought. He thought again about how he wished this could be Tania holding her grandchild. He had to stop thinking about what could never be. He waited. It was seconds, but it seemed like forever. He continued to rub her back. "You and Liam talked?"

"Yeah." Maddison rested her head on his chest. "Grandpa?"

"You can tell me anything, darling."

"Your chest hair is scratchy and going gray. How do you expect to get Dr. Smart to like you? Maybe you should shave."

Ben laughed. "I'll give it some thought, but I'm guessing there might be something else? Something on your mind?" Ben shifted as a small wave from the passing ship finally reached the shore.

"His mother is lying. She says it's Liam's father who hits him, but it's her. He hates her and wants to be with his father."

"And you believe him? He's only four. Maybe he's mixed up?" Ben had watched the interaction between the two. He remembered watching the mother and son. Observing the boy's behavior, Ben suspected something was wrong. He had dismissed these thoughts. Fiona was a pro. He had to believe in her ability to sort out the truth.

"Why would he lie to me? I'm only a kid, you know. We weren't reading about sheep when you came in. He was telling me about his mother. He kept saying he wanted to go home to his father, but no one asked him. She wouldn't let him take his cuddle toy when they left the house. Liam said his mother hated it. It was his daddy's when he was a boy."

"Maddy?" Ben knew he had to walk a fine line.

"Yeah?" She gazed at her grandfather.

"I think you're a very brave girl. I hope you'll always tell me the truth. Sometimes it's hard to talk about the bad things people do. You can always talk to me."

"Can I tell you something else?"

"Anytime, darling." He braced himself.

"I want to help my mother, but I know she's sick. Don't let her take me away. Can you promise?"

"No, I can't for sure, but Maddy, I'll die trying."

Nothing more was said. It was lunchtime. Ben lifted Maddison from his lap and stood. The tide was turning in more ways than one.

Chapter 44

Course Correction

After shopping for Christmas presents, Ben and Maddison returned to the beach house. Fiona had left, and Nigel was playing with the boy. He didn't have many toys. Nigel made do with an old Snakes and Ladders board game from among the guest amenities for renters.

"Hey, Maddy. Did you have a good day?"

Maddison only shrugged. She thought about the day. It was nice to see Harry, and the swimming was good, but the rest of the day was boring. She was glad to see Tag was inside and went to pet him and apologize for leaving him. Liam immediately stood and asked Maddison to play catch with the ball he brought. They went out onto the lawn. Ben watched them and turned to Nigel. "Where's Fiona?"

Nigel went to the fridge and pulled out some hamburger mince and two beers. "She had an emergency. Casey's upstairs on the balcony on her phone. She smokes. I had to ask her to take it outside."

The two men went out and sat on the veranda to watch the kids play and to make sure Liam was safe. Occasionally, strangers used the grass verge to walk up and down the row of beachfront houses. If Liam's father had any idea his son was out here, he might use the area to snatch the boy. Neither man would admit his similar fears for their granddaughter.

They sat quietly, sipping their beer. It wasn't long before Liam and Maddison returned to her room. "We're going to read about the sheep again."

Ben knew this was his cue to talk to Nigel. Ben was mulling over how to present this revelation to Nigel when he heard Casey's phone ring. He'd pulled out his phone and showed Nigel a picture of Maddison he'd taken at the beach. Thankfully, he'd said nothing. Nigel looked up as they quietly eavesdropped.

"Hi, baby. Two more days in this shithole, and we can be together." There was a pause. "Yep, I've got him. I wouldn't leave without him. Child support, here we come."

Ben glanced at Nigel and shook his head as they continued to listen to the details of Casey's travel plans.

"Hey, I gotta go. I've got another call coming in from the dumbass caseworker."

They heard her leave the upstairs patio.

Nigel sat up. "What the hell?"

"I think we may be played for fools. Maddy said Liam told her he wanted to go home to his father, and his mother was mean. My guess is that's what the kids are discussing right now."

Nigel bristled. "Fiona said she's a wonderful mother, and she's checked her out." He sat forward with his elbows on his knees and his hands cupping his face. He turned slightly toward Ben. "What do we do? You don't think this happened with Isla and Daniel? Is she just trying to recover her stolen child? God, what a crap job Fiona has."

"We always want to see the best in our kids. I'll let you figure that out regarding Isla. In the meantime, I think we need to report this."

Nigel pulled out his phone. "I'm going for a walk on the beach. I need to phone a friend. Mate, do you mind starting the dinner? The kids will be hungry. I planned on hamburgers and potato gems. "

"Huh?"

Nigel smiled. "Tater tots, mate. You better get used to the lingo if you think you might have a chance with Maddy."

Nigel went out, and Ben began the dinner preparations. Casey came down and went to the fridge without asking and took out a bottle of wine. "Do you mind?" After pouring a glass for herself, Casey went into the living room and turned on the television. She didn't ask about Liam.

"Should you?" Nigel stared at her enlarged abdomen. Casey ignored the comment and poured herself a glass.

The children entered through the sliding glass door. Ben noticed Casey didn't interact with her son as they went to Maddison's room. He divided up the hamburger into small and large patties and placed the tater tots on a tray. He would not succumb to all the Aussie jargon.

"Where's Nigel?" she yelled from the living room.

Oh, how Ben wanted to say he was on a call to Fiona, ratting her out. "He's down at the beach getting some fresh air."

"Is that a reference to my smoking?"

Ben had to hold his tongue and replied, "Smoking? Do you smoke?"

"Only when I'm stressed. When I get on the plane, I'm throwing the coffin nails into the bin."

"Suit yourself. I was a smoker. I know how it is. I guess you have to think about your children?" Ben smoked in his youth. Watching his mother attempting to cope with COPD was enough to convince him to stop.

"So, where are you heading? Have you got tickets yet?" Ben placed the tater tots in the oven.

"New Castle to be with my parents. I'm going to beauty school. My mum is going to watch Liam when I'm in school. I'm starting over."

"Good for you. I'll bet you'll be glad to get back to all your friends and family." Ben cut some carrots. He wanted to put the hamburgers on the grill, but he wanted to monitor the kids and Casey.

Also, Ben was eager to go through his son's boxes. He thought he might take a quick look before sharing it with Maddison. She seemed strangely disconnected from her father. Her emotional connections seemed stifled, and Ben considered this might be from having a father with little ability to express his feelings. He felt he had a breakthrough on the beach, and he wanted to ensure Maddison was free to express herself. Even a tantrum would assure Ben she was normal.

Ben put the hamburgers on the patio grill as Nigel returned. "Beer me, mate."

Nigel grinned. "Here to serve." He glanced inside and saw Casey watching a game show on the television. He quietly mumbled, "Don't you love helping the downtrodden?"

"Can't tell you how good it makes me feel, but a beer would be the icing on the cake."

"Fi is up to her ears. I didn't have time to tell her anything." Nigel returned with a beer. "What the hell are we doing here?"

"We're saving one kid from a life of hell. I don't think we're doing the other one any favors, though."

"She's on the phone now. Isn't she supposed to be lying low?" Nigel walked back into the house to set the table and check the oven.

Ben returned with the hamburgers and knocked on Maddison's door. "Dinner's ready."

The two children immediately emerged and sat by one another at the table and away from Casey. They appeared to be in good spirits. Ben served them a hamburger and asked each child how many tater tots they wanted.

Casey stared at Liam. "He'll have six. I don't want people thinking I'm starving him."

"No. I want the same as Maddy." He turned to Maddison, who said she was having five. "I want five too."

Casey pointed to the tray and said to put six on his plate. Nigel watched this interaction, trying to make sense of it all.

"He eats what I tell him to eat." They heard a "bing" from Casey's phone. She glanced down and announced she was going out. "I'll be back in an hour."

Before anyone could say anything, she stood, took a large purse, and walked out. Both Nigel and Ben gazed at Liam, who didn't miss a beat. He began eating his hamburger, which was difficult to hold. Ben took it and cut both of the children's burgers in half. He placed two glasses of milk on the table and sat down.

"Pop, Liam and I want to sleep together tonight. He promises not to fart."

Ben tried to stifle a laugh. "Sounds good to me, but don't expect him to hold on to that promise. A man's gotta do what a man's gotta do. We'll put you upstairs, and Liam's mom can sleep in your room tonight."

The children asked to walk on the beach. "Sorry, we can't tonight. We have to keep Liam inside for now, maybe tomorrow. Here's the good news. You're both going to have baths."

"Good. Liam smells." He did.

Nigel suspected he had not had a bath for days. "Maddy, you get ready for yours, and I'll go up and get Liam's pajamas." He turned to Ben. "I'll flip you for the honors, mate."

Ben waved his arms crossways. "I'll do Liam if you do Maddy."

"I had one this morning." Maddy crossed her arms.

"And you swam in the ocean, and my guess is you probably have sand between your toes." And probably a few other places where sand collects. "We won't do your hair."

The two children were bathed, and each had a bowl of ice cream. Ben went up and searched for Liam's toothbrush. He realized there was more in the boy's travel bag than a toothbrush. A pipe hid in the lining of his small suitcase. *Jesus, this woman is a piece of work.*

"Nige, we can't let this go on. Either you text Fiona or I will. If they leave tomorrow, that will probably be this boy's last chance for salvation."

Nigel didn't have to text her. His phone rang, and Fiona said the police arrested Casey and a friend at the pub for solicitation of an undercover officer. Nigel then told her what he'd overheard and what Liam had told Maddison. "I'll come and get him. Damn, what a hell of a night."

"Fi, how about you go home and get some rest? You can pick the boy up in the morning." Nigel felt for Fiona. He could see how hard this job was—especially when you get it wrong. "Get some sleep. Let's have a quick walk on the beach at seven, then breakfast, and then you can decide what to do."

Chapter 45

Searching for Evidence

When everyone was asleep, Ben went to the garage and retrieved the boxes that held Daniel's belongings. He started with one that had clothing. He was amazed at how few clothes his son owned. He suspected some had gone to Goodwill. He went through the pockets and found nothing. He then opened the second box, which had the books that Maddison had saved over her brief life.

Harry Potter, The Fault in Our Stars, Lemony Snicket, Little Women, and The Diary of a Young Girl by Anne Frank, along with others he didn't recognize. Thank you, Mrs. Donovan. At the bottom of the box was a diary, My Life by Maddison Monroe.

Ben opened it to find the handwriting of a very young girl. The first entry was printed in pencil.

Janry 1

I live on a catle and sheep station in Austraya. I live with my father and my dog. I have a very very good life. I get up and make my father get up to go to work. I eat Vegemite and toast and then I brush my teeth and go to the big house to help with the school. Mrs. Donovan makes me set out the work for the day in our school. I am the teching assisstent. I help the other children with their letters and numbers. I can count to one thousand, so I am pretty smart. Mrs. Donovan says so, so it must be tru.

Ben wondered how old she was when she wrote that. He thumbed through more and found her spelling, grammar and penmanship improved. The last entry was difficult.

April 3rd

I miss Mrs. Donovan and the station. Harry keeps yelling at Daddy to do more and says he will kick us out if we don't do more. Tag hates being locked up when I am in school. The kids at school tease me because I'm friends with an Aborigine. Jarlee is my friend, and I will not leave him. Those kids can go to hell. I don't care if I get in trouble by swearing. My dad said the Aborigines here are good people.

My teacher is Miss Osborne. She's beautiful. I wish my daddy would marry her and then she would stay. I wish so many things would happen. I wish my mother would come back. Daddy doesn't know I know what she looks like. I am always looking for her. She's beautiful. I wish she would come back somethin fierce.

Daddy is gone at night. Sometimes I get scared, but Tag makes me feel safe. But sometimes it is not good enough. I know what Mr. Grant thinks about me being alone. He says if anything happens to me, he will call the coppers, and

I will go to an orfanage. Every night, he knocks on my door and asks if I'm okay. I always say I am. Sometimes I'm not. If I left, who would take care of my daddy?

Ben wiped tears and placed the diary back in the box. That was enough for the night. He was such a failure as a father. Why didn't he see the torment his son experienced trying to fit into a world of—Ben paused, trying to remember the term. Ah yes, they called them typical—and Daniel was atypical. Maddy won't be put in a box if I'm alive. God, please give me time to help this beautiful child.

Maddison smelled a fart. She quietly rose from the bed and, thinking it was Tag's, took him out onto the veranda. The sun touched the ocean and the blue water. She wanted to go swimming. She enjoyed yesterday. It was nice to sit on her grandfather's lap. He was safe. She hadn't experienced such a feeling before. It was only a flashing feeling because she knew she had to tell someone about what she knew about little Liam.

She was sure Liam would leave with his mother. It was terrible he had to go with her. Liam said his mother was always going out, and when his father was away, she left him and told him to stay in his room until she returned. Maddison's father never left her alone—she always had Tag.

Maddison returned to the house, set the coffee maker up, fed Tag, and returned to her room where Liam was still sleeping. He snored, and she heard him fart. So, it wasn't Tag. She dressed in her swimsuit under a shirt and shorts. Her pop greeted her and opened his arms. She liked the fact that both her grandfathers wanted to hug her. She was not accustomed to anyone besides the Donovans hugging her. Her father never cuddled her. She knew he loved her, and she knew he was different. She missed Mrs. Donovan's hugs.

"Where's Liam's mother?" Nigel put his finger to his lips and pointed to the veranda. She opened the fridge and removed the butter so it could soften. She walked back outside where she'd left Tag. He was already sitting by the door, waiting for her.

Nigel followed her, and the two sat down on the chairs where they could see the ocean and the ships that neared the Wallaroo jetty to pick up grain from the YP farmers.

"Liam's mother isn't coming back. Mrs. Harding is coming to get him this morning."

"Why?" Maddison searched her grandfather's face.

"I don't know for sure, but I think they may suspect Liam's mother might not be the best person for him right now."

Maddison's face brightened. "Oh good. I guess they realized she's a drop-kick."

"What? Where did you hear that expression?" Nigel was trying to suppress a laugh.

"Well, my dad would say arsehole, but he suggested I shouldn't use that word until I'm older." Maddison stood and peered down at the beach. "Want to go swimming this morning?"

"I may have to help with Liam, but I'm sure your grandpa can take you. One thing's for sure. We're decorating the tree today. I'm getting ready for Santa."

"Can we get a sign so Santa knows to stop here? He missed me last year." Maddy wanted to make sure there were no mistakes this year.

"Maddy, we can get two. One for the road and one out here on the grass. What would you like Santa to bring you this year? Should you write a letter?"

"Isn't it too late?" Maddison shrugged.

"No, the postie is never late with Santa's letters." Oh, how Nigel was loving this conversation.

"A book. That's what he always brings me. What about you?" She knew what she was giving her pop.

"A book sounds good to me, too. No sense overworking Santa. He has so many children to attend to. I think we should get your other grandfather a present too. What do you think he would like?"

"I don't know. What do you think?"

Nigel looked up and appeared to be thinking. "Santa usually gets things for kids, but maybe a framed picture of you would be a nice present from you and me? What do you think?"

"I had some school pictures, but they must be in the boxes." Maddison noticed her grandfather had brought the boxes into the house. "Pop? When's your birthday?"

"It's a long way away. You know, I never asked. I know you're six, but when is yours?"

"My daddy told me it was the thirteenth of August. Mrs. Donovan thinks I might be older."

"You sure act older. We should get a copy of your birth certificate. Maybe it's in the boxes."

They heard a knock at the gate, and Nigel's phone pinged. "Oh, Ms. Harding's here." He stood to unlock the gate. When he went out to open it, he saw Fiona with a young man. "Hi, Nigel. This is Liam's father. It's a long story, but can we come in?"

Nigel stared at the man and wondered what had transpired since the previous evening. He held out his hand to the man. They shook hands, and the man introduced himself as Brad. He appeared to be in his mid-twenties, clean shaven and fit. "I came to take my boy." He looked past Nigel, and Liam saw him through the window. Liam opened the door and ran to the man, who picked him up.

Maddison watched the reunion of the little boy, who clearly loved his father, as he fiercely hugged the man's neck and cried. Nigel watched Maddison and knew she was thinking of her own father. There would never be an emotional reunion like Maddison had just witnessed—there'd probably never been such an intimate moment for his granddaughter. Maddison went over and hugged Tag, who wagged his tail. She didn't return to say goodbye to her potential little brother. Nigel knew his granddaughter was already grieving.

As Nigel escorted Fiona and the reunited family to their car, Ben sat on the couch and patted the seat beside him. Maddison shook her head. In reply, Ben tilted his head and patted the seat once more. Maddison stared at him and then went and sat next to him. She put her head in his lap and covered her face.

Ben knew Maddison had lost a chance for a sibling. He would never be able to provide her with the family she desired. While Ben watched his granddaughter's agony, he also knew she would experience more emotional pain, but she would also find the joy of love. Ben knew Daniel's condition had limited his ability to feel both the highs and lows of emotional connections.

Nigel stared at Ben. Both men knew what the other was thinking. Were they up to the challenge? Would there ever be a reunion with Maddy and Isla as poignant as Liam's with his father? One of the two men had to survive for another twelve years, at least. Each hoped it was them. Could they both live another decade or two?

Knowing the child protection agency had a near miss, Nigel realized the fallibility of outsiders deciding for families. Even with the best of intentions, they sometimes got it wrong. He was determined to ensure that didn't happen to his granddaughter.

Chapter 46

Father Christmas

Nigel returned to the living room and, before he noticed Maddison with her face buried in Ben's lap, announced they were going to decorate the tree and go see Santa after breakfast.

Maddison sat up. "It's not the real Santa. He's up at the ninetieth parallel north with the elves, who are probably dwarfs. You know it isn't proper to say dwarfs now. You have to say little people. Daddy said it is a great way for little people to earn extra money at Christmas. Santa picks them up at their homes and takes them up to his workshop. Mrs. Donovan said it was true."

Nigel and Ben stifled laughs. Ben knew the Santa myth had little chance of lasting more than another year, but he would hold on as long as he could. Nigel had similar thoughts, and both men gazed down at the little girl, who wiped her tears.

The two men stared at one another, wondering what childhood dreams this clever girl still believed. Ben shrugged and stood. "I'll get the decorations. Then let's head to the big smoke and see Santa."

"I want to put the tinsel on the tree." She stared at the men, daring them to challenge her.

Nigel's jaw tightened, but he nodded. "Maddy, it's your tree. I know we'll love it." Or not.

Three hours later, they pulled into the parking structure of Rundle Mall. It was a weekday, but there were children everywhere. Maddison was instructed to always hold hands. Both Ben and Nigel considered the remote chance of seeing Isla at the mall.

They stopped and had a quick lunch and were off to the Magic Cave and Santa. The line was long, and Maddison was tired from her night sleeping with a restless four-year-old and the dramatic events of the last two days. She'd slept on the trip from North Beach to Adelaide, but she still was anxious, and both men observed her watching the people. They suspected she was searching for her mother.

They finally were next in line. Nigel wrote Maddison's name on a sheet as they stood waiting. He saw Santa's helper whisper into a small microphone, and Santa nodded as Maddison approached Santa. They declined having a picture taken, but they took their own. Maddison confidently walked up to Santa and put out her hand. "This is my first time. I saw the other kids sitting on your lap. Am I supposed to do the same?"

Santa was a pro. "Only if you would like to. It's not required. Maddison, where should I deliver your presents?"

"I'm living at North Beach on the Yorke Peninsula. You missed me last year, but I've forgiven you. It was with my father, and he's dead." She pointed to Nigel and Ben. "Those are my grandfathers. I'm staying with them until I get a permanent home."

"I won't miss you this year, Maddison. May I give you something now?"

Maddison whispered in his ear, "I don't really need anything, Father Christmas. Do you have anything for my grandfathers? They are trying so hard to be nice."

Santa stared at the men and recognized them from their picture in the newspaper. He waved them up to his chair. "I know you two. You were in the news. May I have a picture with all of us for Mrs. Claus?"

Ben shrugged. "Please don't share it, but sure."

Santa smiled and pointed to his lap. Maddison was confused. "I don't think we'll all fit."

"Just you, darling." He suppressed a laugh as he lifted Maddison onto his lap while Ben and Nigel flanked the throne. "One for Santa and one for Mrs. Claus."

"And one for us." Nigel couldn't have asked for a better Christmas present. He would send it to his former secretary and neighbors.

"Can I talk to you by myself again?" Maddison turned to her grandfathers and cocked her head. Ben and Nigel stepped away while Maddison whispered into his ear, "I know you aren't the real Santa, but I'm guessing you can get a message to the real one for me."

"Of course." Santa leaned closer to Maddison. "What do I need to tell the boss?"

"Tell him there is a little boy on the Yorke Peninsula who was supposed to go away, but he didn't, and he needs a present from your boss." Maddison laughed as he referred to the real Santa as the boss. "I've been good all year — well, except for a couple of times at the school, but they had it coming. Anyway, I'd like a pair of cowboy boots. I'd ask for a horse, but I don't have anywhere to keep one now. And thanks for the talk. I hope you have lots of eggnog at Christmas and get a kiss from Mrs. Claus."

As they walked over to where the rocking horses were staged, an attendant ran to Ben and whispered, "Cowboy boots. Santa said to tell you."

They had five days until Christmas. Nigel was on to the suggestion and whispered to Ben, "Cowboy boots or bust."

Chapter 47

Tug of Love

Maddison was asleep when they arrived home. Tag was next door and sitting in the Smart's living room when Ben knocked on the door. Lindy and her family were there for dinner. She brought Tag out and said Tag was the perfect gentleman. Her grandchildren had fallen in love with him. "I may have to adopt him to entice the grandchildren back for a visit."

"Why don't you head over to the States to visit them? You should take time off. The wheels won't fall off the practice, you know. You can't keep doing this forever." Ben bent down and patted the dog, who had done his duty, and returned to Ben's side.

"Is that what you were told?"

Ben smiled. "Yeah, pretty much."

"Hell, Ben. Do you know how hard it is to get a vet to work with large animals, let alone in rural communities?

The clients here are not demanding. They're willing to let me have time off, and besides, what would I do?"

"Needlepoint, golf, quilting. You could think of something."

"What were your plans? Weren't you counting down the days when you found out about Maddy?"

"Skin diving, tropical isles, scantily clad Polynesian women, piña coladas. You know, the usual."

"Uh, no thanks on the skin diving. I saw Jaws."

"I learned to skin dive, and the rest just would come with the travel." Ben bent over to pull a weed poking through the grass. "Well, a guy can dream."

Lindy took Ben's arm. "Polynesian women are not my thing. I need to get back inside. The little ones should be in bed, and the card games will begin."

Ben leaned over and kissed Lindy on the cheek. "Thanks again for all you've done." He walked toward his house and then remembered. "Where can I get a pair of cowboy boots for Maddy?"

"Let me deal with it. I'm guessing that's what she told Santa she wanted?"

"Uh huh." Ben was hopeful. "We don't have much time."

"I think I know her size. I'll let you know if I can help tomorrow." Lindy walked toward her in-laws' house. She touched her cheek. She felt a warmth she had not felt in years.

"Thanks, Lindy. You make an old man feel young again."

"Happy to oblige. That twenty-year age gap is like the Grand Canyon. Isn't it?" Lindy turned to head back to her family.

Ben sighed. Ben knew she was kidding about the twenty-year gap, but there was a disparity in their ages that could not be denied.

"More like the distance of the Pacific Ocean." Ben knew his place. He thought she'd returned to her children.

"I sail, by the way." Lindy didn't look back as Ben watched her open the sliding glass door and enter the house. He wondered if the sailing reference was a hint that she might have more than a passing interest in him.

Ben returned to his house and retrieved the last box from his bedroom. Nigel joined him at the dining room table, where Ben retrieved piles of papers from his son's last box. He hoped he would find some documents that would be helpful in getting Maddison a passport. He handed Nigel a small laptop. "Want to see what's in here?"

Nigel plugged it into the power socket and attempted to retrieve any data. "Any ideas about a password?"

"Tag, Tania, Maddy, but I doubt any of these will work. He was a geek, if he was anything."

The paper documents were tax and pay receipts. There were no pictures or birth certificates. There was Daniel's expired passport, but nothing pertaining to Maddison. "Nigel, I can't even find a birth certificate."

They spent an hour trying various passwords on the computer. "Maybe Maddy knows the password? I'm beat, Ben. See you in the morning. What a day."

"Yeah, you know, last year at this time, I was sitting by myself studying pamphlets of Caribbean diving junkets. What were you doing?"

Nigel looked up. "Probably having an argument with my soon-to-be ex about how I need to be more attentive to her needs. I already knew she was having an affair with her boss. Oh, how I wanted to call her on it, but I tried so hard to make it work. I'm glad it's over. You know what they call custody battles here in Australia?"

"No, enlighten me."

"Tug of love. So, how is this going to end?"

"Well, either I take the child genius and return to the States, or you do and return to New Zealand, or we find a compromise."

"I don't know, Bennie Boy. What do you bring to the marriage? I cook and have fewer miles."

"Vet medicine, good looks, and a full head of hair."

Nigel rubbed his receding hairline. "You win. See you in the morning, darling."

"I don't know. The YP isn't so bad. How about we head down to the park they all talk about tomorrow? Lindy might have a source for the cowboy boots."

"God, Bennie, you're desperate. Would your interest be in a certain YP vet? You know Maddy needs to be in a school that caters to exceptional kids. I don't see it happening here."

"I'm way too old for the vet, and she made it clear tonight. Maybe there's a place we could consider that would make us all happy. Where would you like to live if you could live anywhere in the world?"

"I'll think about it. Get some sleep. You're driving tomorrow."

For a second, Ben was on the verge of remembering the actor with the accent, but he could not pull it out of his memory bank. As wide as the Grand Canyon? Ben had a jolt of reality. He needed to check himself. He sat out on the balcony watching the ocean. There were a few teenagers down at the beach playing music. He remembered his teens. Oh, how he had wished his son could have experienced any part of the joys and even pain of young love. He was determined his granddaughter would not miss out. He wondered if Daniel's relationship with Isla was a mutual attraction, or was it pure lust?

If Nigel won custody, Ben would move to New Zealand. He could find joy in any environment where Maddison would reside. He was a survivor. There was no way he would sacrifice her need for his comfort. This was his last chance at a legacy. This reminded him. He would need to change his will.

Nigel couldn't sleep. He thought about the upcoming trial, cowboy boots, his divorce, Fiona, and, of course, Maddison. He would do anything to protect his granddaughter from a life with a drug-affected mother. He felt confident with good legal representation. At least that was an easy hurdle. Please God, let that be true.

As for Fiona, the jury was out. Nigel wondered if Fiona would, or could, move her workplace. She was close to retirement. Would she be willing to move back closer to Adelaide so Maddison could attend a school where her intellect could be nurtured? He had so much to consider and how much he would sacrifice to care for his granddaughter.

He planned to call his solicitor in the morning. He needed to settle the divorce and rewrite his will. Isla had always been the recipient after his wife died, but no one could find his daughter after extensive searches. Now he would change the recipient to Maddison. She was set for life thanks to her father. *My contribution will be icing on the cake.*

Nigel shrugged, thinking of two old men living together in a house with a little girl for the rest of his life. He liked Ben, despite his movie-star good looks. *If I can live long enough to get her through high school, then I'll die a happy man.* He smiled again, realizing Maddison would probably be done with high school in a few years. *Not that big of an ask, really.*

Chapter 48

Innes National Park

Another hot day broke as Ben, Nigel, and Maddison left for Innes National Park at the bottom of the Yorke Peninsula. Nigel searched the internet and found several places in the park to explore. The lighthouse, Pondalowie Bay, Stenhouse Bay, and finally Dolphin Bay might be a good place to have lunch. Nigel and Ben packed chairs, a fishing rod from Doug Smart, and a cooler.

The Smarts were going to care for Tag for the day. His improvement was remarkable. Tomorrow, he would go to the vet clinic to have a radiograph to ensure the plates were holding, and the bones were knitting.

Once again, Maddison complained she should be in the front seat, and if they didn't allow her to sit up front, she would be carsick. Ben handed her a bucket and a towel—end of discussion.

They reached the park at the tip of the peninsula before noon. They stopped at Stenhouse Bay first, and Nigel showed Maddison how to toss a fishing line off the jetty. Ben kept referring to the jetty as a dock or a pier, but Maddison was firm. "Grandpa, if you think you're going to raise me, you better get used to calling things by their proper names."

Nigel shrugged. "From the mouth of babes."

"Pop, I'm not a baby either. I need to make you both understand I have my limits." She could have been rude, but it was said with no malice. Both men stared, daring each other to laugh.

"Maddy, where did you get that expression?" Ben was amused by this child's responses.

"Daddy used to say that. I think he got that from Mrs. Donovan."

"What happened if you went over the limit?" Neither man had ever hit his child.

"I got smacked or sent to my room." She looked away, remembering past times. Ben suspected she would take a thousand smacks to bring back her father.

They caught two fish and three crabs, which were put in the cooler. They saw the lighthouse and Pondalowie Bay, but they settled at Dolphin Bay for lunch. They had the beach to themselves until two young women arrived and shed their clothes and swam in the surf. Ben was sitting facing Nigel and Maddison. Behind them were the two women. Neither Nigel nor Maddison was aware of the two women's attire or the lack thereof...

"Great idea, Nige. How did you decide on this little oasis in the park?" He watched Maddison, who was completely unaware of the situation. "Is this a designated…" Ben paused, trying to think of a way to signal to Nigel without Maddison becoming aware. "Shall I say, clothing optional beach?"

Maddison replied, "You mean, is it optional to wear clothes? If you guys are thinking of taking your clothes off, I'm leaving. Old men with no clothes would scar me for life. I'd rather go into foster care."

Both Nigel and Maddison turned to view the women emerging from the water. The women were screaming and pointing to what might be a shark a short distance from the shore. Maddison's mouth opened, and she covered her eyes.

Ben watched the "shark" swim, and after his diving lessons, he knew it was a dolphin. "Nigel, get your phone ready. I'm taking Maddy out to swim with the dolphins." He picked her up and carried her to the water.

Maddison clung tightly to her grandfather. "Are you sure it's a dolphin?"

"There are three of them, and yes, darling. I know you said you would not kiss boys or have children, but I would never risk your genetic potential. Just hold on to me."

Ben walked out until he was waist deep. Maddison fiercely clung to his neck. Ben slapped the water with his free hand while holding Maddison high on his torso, so she was barely in the water. The dolphins cautiously swam closer and finally circled them as the waves rolled over them all. Ben waved to Nigel, who was filming the event. The two young women joined him and cheered Ben and Maddison along.

This went on for several minutes. Maddison relaxed and even slapped the water to encourage the dolphins to come close. She stroked one briefly as it swam past them. The dolphins finally moved away and headed for the deeper water.

Ben and Maddison returned to the shore. "Did you get it on your phone, Pop?"

"Sure did, Maddy. You were very brave out there." Nigel took Maddison and carried her to the blanket. The water down at the tip of the peninsula was much colder, and Maddison was shaking. She sat down on Nigel's lap and allowed him to rub her and attempt to warm her.

Ben returned to the water and swam for a few minutes before returning to shore. He thought about Tania once again, but strangely, he also thought about Lindy. He wondered if she ever had swum with dolphins. He had thought about her several times today. Wider than the Grand Canyon—check yourself, Bennie—she's out of your league.

Maddison fell asleep in Nigel's arms. The two women had one more frolic in the surf, sans clothing. Ben would occasionally turn to watch them. Nigel didn't care. He held his granddaughter, and that was all he needed. Maddison slept for several minutes. Ben took the time to walk the length of the beach and hunt for shells and anything that had washed up on the sand. He found nothing interesting. He returned and suggested it was time to head home. The drive would take two hours, and they still had to plan for the Christmas festivities and drinks with the neighbors tomorrow. Ben hoped Lindy was coming to join them.

"Do you mind driving, mate?" Ben was tired. He'd hit a wall. He'd fallen asleep on the couch and never really settled last night.

"When I hear you say mate, I know you want something, but sure, I was going to offer, anyway." For a second, Ben thought about Nigel's accent. Damn, who did he sound like?

They climbed up the stairs leading from the beach to the car park. At the landing, Ben asked them to stop so he could get a selfie with the three of them. He wanted to send it to his staff and brother-in-law. That might show the bastard that his sister was not a complete failure. Even though Tania was dead, she had a beautiful granddaughter.

Chapter 49

Life Interrupted

Ben reclined in the front seat as Nigel wound his way out of the national park. He was woken several times when Maddison saw emus and an echidna. He and Maddison finally fell asleep while Nigel continued up the peninsula.

Nigel thought about how nice the day was. He considered how compatible Ben was, and he thought about the different ways he and Ben could plan for their granddaughter's care. He knew he would stay in South Australia if he had to. He realized the three of them could be happy in New Zealand, but he had reasons to stay.

Nigel wanted to get to know Fiona. He planned to take it slow this time. There would have to be a compromise on everyone's part. He would not make any rushed decisions this time. Still, she was so beautiful and smart. He wondered if she could fall in love with an old man like him.

Then there was her mysterious son. How would he fit into their lives?

Isla was probably going to seek custody of Maddison. He still didn't know why she'd left her and what she'd been doing all these years. It was so painful to see her at the funeral. He inwardly winced. Thankfully, Bette was not there to see this. Her mother would be devastated to see her daughter in such a state.

Nigel watched the wheat fields become glowing gold as the sun was setting. It was so different from the green of New Zealand. The light sharpened the details of the stark landscape. He passed a tree where several sets of shoes hung from the branches. Was it where someone had died, or was it just a high school game?

The sun was low, and Nigel was glad when he turned north. But from a distance, he could see dust from a side road that would intersect with the paved road they traveled along. He knew they would meet and was concerned the vehicle was going so fast. Did Maddison's father go off the road to avoid another vehicle? He would never know.

Nigel slowed to avoid the dust from the oncoming vehicle, but a minute later, he failed to see another car coming from the east and he desperately braked. It was too late. Their car rolled.

Both Ben and Maddison reclined as they slept and did not feel Nigel break, but both heard his scream as a car shot through a yield sign and slammed into the driver's side of their vehicle. Their car spun, skidded, and rolled onto the driver's side. There was so much dust from the accident, Ben only glimpsed the second vehicle, which had pinwheeled and stopped only for a moment before fishtailing away.

The SUV lay on its side. Ben heard Maddison crying in the back seat. He turned with great difficulty and saw she was holding her head. He glanced at Nigel, who was not responding. Nigel was alive and breathing, but his forehead was bleeding. The front seat airbags had deployed, but the primary blow was from the side. Nigel's head drooped toward the side window.

Maddison was alert, but he was unsure of her injuries. Her head hurt, and she was scared. She continued to sob. Ben unbuckled his seatbelt and reached around to inspect his granddaughter. He had to brace himself so he would not fall on Nigel. He couldn't assess her injuries. He asked her if she was okay, but she didn't stop crying enough to respond. He knew Nigel was unconscious.

Ben pulled on the handle of the door and found it would open, but it was hard to push it open. He put his foot on the console between the front seats and could open it enough to climb out. Maddison's door also opened, and he reached into the car and held her with one hand and unbuckled her seatbelt with the other. He lifted her out of their car, and she clung to him.

Maddison was reliving her other accident when her father died. She could not do this again. She would not lose another family member. She could see her pop was not moving. It was so similar to her father. Please, no. I'll promise anything if my pop can live.

Ben watched as the truck sped off over the rise. Bastards. He had to get an ambulance for Nigel. Ben didn't know how long before anyone would come by. He wasn't sure where they were. He wondered if he had any cell phone reception.

Maddy was inconsolable and asked for her other grandfather. Ben had to put her down and attempt to find his or Nigel's phone in the car. As he jumped up on the side of the car, he felt the car tip. Could he pull it over by himself? The position in the ditch that gave him leverage. He tried rocking it and could almost get it right. He saw Nigel was still alive but not responding. There was no sign of a fire.

"Maddy, darling? I need you to go into the car again and get a phone. Can you do that for me?"

Maddison nodded in between gulps. He lifted her into the car, and she leaned down to the console and reached for Ben's phone, which was charging. The car was still running. There was no way to turn it off. Ben dialed 911. There was no response. He remembered it was a different number in Australia. "Maddy, what do I dial?"

"Triple zero. Is Pop going to be okay?" She was now only whimpering.

Ben hated lying. "Yes, he's going to be fine." He dialed 000 and found he had no cell service. He searched on his phone to see where they were. Despite the limited phone reception, it still displayed the map. He was near the town of Minlaton. He was about three miles north of the town. He hated the idea, but he had to do something fast. He leaned into the car. "Nige, I'm going to get help. Please hang on, buddy. Maddy needs you."

Ben picked up his granddaughter and walked back toward the town. He saw a long driveway to a farm. He couldn't see much, but he had to try. If anyone came along the road, they would see the car on the side of the road with the open doors. He turned and, holding Maddison, walked toward the farmhouse. As he approached the structures, a man walked out.

"Sir, my name is Ben Taylor, and I've had an accident. My friend is still in the car, and we need an ambulance and some rescue people." Ben was shaking. He knew this man? He was one of Lindy's clients.

Maddison turned to face the man and immediately wanted to be released from Ben. She ran to the older, stocky man and hugged his legs. "Mr. Butler, please come and help my pop. He's hurt terrible bad." Colin Butler ran to the house and yelled at his farmhand to call the police and Emergency Unit.

Colin returned and signaled for Ben and Maddy to get into his truck. "Which way?"

Maddy sat in the middle. No one had seatbelts. "Farm truck" is all Colin said. He turned north out of the driveway, and they were back at the accident in less than a minute. Colin and Ben both peered into the vehicle and saw Nigel was breathing, but he was still unresponsive.

Ben rocked the car again. "I think we can pull the car upright. I could almost do it myself."

"Mate, help will be here in a minute or two. Let's wait in case he has a broken neck. How long have you been waiting?"

"Maybe ten or fifteen minutes. I saw a truck pull away. I think it T-boned us."

Both men looked down at Maddison. Colin went to Maddison and examined her face. "There are some bad actors around here. My guess is they were on something."

"We were asleep and coming back from Innes. We didn't see it." Ben felt horrible that he was not the driver.

"I think I hear a siren." They stared up the road and over a rise saw both an ambulance and a police car heading toward them.

Maddison was in shock. She clung to her grandfather and buried her head in his neck. While several people attended the overturned car and Nigel, a paramedic wanted to examine her. She refused to allow them to take her from her grandfather's arms. A trickle of blood came from a small superficial wound above her ear. The wound was cleaned, and a thin bandage was applied.

She kept asking if her pop was okay. Ben assured her he was still alive, and the paramedics were doing everything they could. "But what if he dies?" she wailed.

"Your pop isn't going to die, darling." Ben knew this may not be true. He prayed it was. Ben had abandoned formal religion when his wife died without ever knowing the fate of their son. Still, he wanted to give God another chance. Let this man live, and I'll reconsider you.

"Why doesn't he say anything? My daddy did that too, and he died. How do you know?" Maddy turned toward more oncoming vehicles with their sirens blasting.

Colin Butler was probably close in age to Nigel and Ben, but he was involved in helping to right the vehicle. A paramedic had climbed into the car, assessed Nigel, and placed a collar around Nigel's neck. He stayed in the vehicle while several people slowly rolled the car into an upright position.

The driver's side door was pried open with a jaws-of-life apparatus. Nigel was taken from the car and placed on a stretcher. He was immediately reassessed, and Ben could hear them discussing a helicopter retrieval. When Ben peered into the back of the ambulance, he noticed Nigel was now intubated.

Maddison wanted to go over and see her grandfather, but a woman who appeared to be in charge shook her head as she stared at Ben holding Maddison. Colin had informed the rescue officers who worked on Nigel that this little girl's father had recently been the last person killed on the YP. Two of the officers were involved in that accident and groaned.

Ben rubbed Maddison's back and watched while sitting on the edge of the ambulance. More personnel arrived. Another paramedic asked to assess Ben again. Maddison clung to her grandfather and only let go of Ben when Colin came and asked her if he could take her for a moment. He distracted her by talking about the horses they'd seen last week.

Ben was bruised, but his vitals were within normal limits. The paramedic who examined him quietly said it was touch and go with Nigel. They would send him by helicopter to the Royal Adelaide Hospital on the mainland.

In the meantime, Nigel was going to the Kadina hospital until the retrieval copter arrived. The car was totaled, and Colin offered to drive them to the hospital. The sun was setting, and Ben was trying to comfort Maddison. Colin put her in his truck, and they drove back to the farmhouse to change automobiles. "Do you boys have another car to use?" Colin turned down the long driveway to his farmhouse.

"Yeah, I kept my rental and was going to turn it in and maybe look for a junker, since it looked like I was going to be here for a while. Well, that's on hold. I may need to buy a Hummer." He stared at Colin.

Ben set Maddison between the men as they approached the house. He dialed Lindy Smart. He received a voice message saying she was not available. He left a message anyway. He didn't want to say too much in front of Maddison. When they arrived at Colin's house. Ben asked Maddison if she needed to use the bathroom. He knew the signs.

"Yeah, I'm busting." She headed toward the bathroom.

Colin tapped her shoulder as she walked past him. His mobile phone rang. "Collie, it's Lindy. What's happening?" Colin stepped into the other room. He quietly explained the situation and hung up.

He returned. "Let's get to the hospital where they took your friend, and we'll meet Lindy Smart there. She's going to drive you to Adelaide, where the hospital's located. Mate, you don't look too good. You okay?"

Ben gingerly felt his head. "No, I'm fine. It's just a hell of a situation. Thanks, Mr. Butler."

"Colin, mate. Mr. Butler is only for kids. I think we might just have a second opinion about your assessment. Maddy, hop in the back seat."

They pulled up to the hospital's emergency entrance, where the ambulance sat with open doors. By then, Ben had a black eye. He said he felt fine, and they went into the corridor and asked about Nigel. "Is he awake?"

The attendant said he was in a room where they were assessing him. "I haven't had any updates, but I know he's still alive."

A woman emerged from the room and asked Ben and Colin if they were relatives. "She's his granddaughter. I'm her grandfather, so I guess we're related. How is he?"

"There's no change. We're somewhat limited, and he'll get a full assessment when he gets to the RAH, but he has a broken collarbone, and his right cheek has a couple of fractures."

"Is my pop going to live?" Maddison wanted the truth.

The woman bent down to Maddison's level. "I remember you. You were here before. Honey, we are doing everything we can, and so far, he's still with us. Would you like to see him? You can't go into the room, but they're bringing him out to go to the airport, and you can see him when he comes out of the room."

Maddison didn't reply. The gurney came out of the room and was quickly rolled toward the ambulance. Maddison got to watch her grandfather as he rolled past. He had an endotracheal tube and an intravenous line. He appeared to be breathing on his own. Ben quickly lifted her so she could see him, but it was only a second before he was placed back in the ambulance and driven away.

Colin went outside. He phoned Lindy. "It's not looking good. How far away are you?"

"Ten minutes tops, Collie." Lindy was in shock.

"The ambulance is leaving the hospital. I'll take Maddy and her grandfather out to my car and meet you at the emergency entrance. This poor kid has had way too much drama for a little girl."

"Yeah. I thought her troubles were over when her grandfathers showed up. I'll do my best to help. I called Fiona Harding. She wanted to come too, but she's going to have to wait until tomorrow. She's on call for any domestic violence issues on the YP tonight."

Fifteen minutes later, Lindy drove up in her father-in-law's SUV and hugged Maddison as the little girl ran to her. Maddison turned to Colin and said she would not be able to ride again until her grandfather was home from the hospital. "Please give the horses a carrot from me on Christmas Day."

"Maddy, I sure will, and they'll be here when you're ready again." Colin was choking back his last words. "You take care, darling."

Chapter 50

How Can I Help You?

Ben, Maddison, and Lindy entered the late model Land Cruiser and took off for the mainland after a brief stop at McDonald's. When they were close to turning onto Port Wakefield Road, they looked back at the sign showing the number of days since the last fatality. Maddison had fallen asleep. Daniel was the last to die in a vehicular accident. The days were increasing. Both Lindy and Ben prayed Nigel would not be the one to change the sign.

They didn't want to discuss Nigel's condition for fear of Maddison overhearing the conversation.

"How can I thank you?" Ben touched her arm.

Lindy considered her response. There were so many ways to answer this. She could ask him to come and work with her and Baz. She could ask him to relinquish custody of Maddison. She could—ask him to take her in his arms and kiss her. "Have you learned anything more about house cleaning?"

"Huh?" Then Ben remembered the conversation where Lindy mentioned his skill set. "Oh, yeah. I'm sorry. I've been a bit busy. It's at the top of my to-do list, but I'm so occupied with kid wrangling and learning about the child custody laws in Oz. I'll get onto it next week."

"It was nice to have the boys home. Apparently, they think you'd make an excellent addition to — She didn't finish the sentence as a kangaroo jumped in front of the Land Cruiser, and she had to suddenly brake.

Once the drama was over, she never finished her thoughts. "Damn, they're going to revoke my citizenship. You know I've never hit a roo."

"Is that part of the citizenship requirement?"

"Of course. By the way, when does your visa expire?"

"Damn, I don't even remember. This wasn't how I thought things would go. I better check." Ben wondered how people who overstayed their visas were treated.

"How much longer to the hospital? Do you want me to drive?"

"No. I mean, no thanks. An hour and forty-five minutes. Have you thought about...?" Lindy didn't finish the sentence. She glanced into the rearview mirror. She saw Maddison was still sleeping when a car's headlights illuminated her face.

Ben turned back as well. He knew she meant his long-term plans if Nigel didn't survive. "No. I'll cross that bridge when I'm..."

Lindy finished the sentence. "Not knee-deep in crocks?"

Ben still wanted to know what Lindy's boys were alluding to. He knew he should think of Nigel. But... "I'll order a Good Housekeeping subscription."

They arrived at the Royal Adelaide Hospital shortly after 9 p.m. and woke Maddison. They entered the foyer and were taken to the emergency department.

Nigel was being assessed. If he needed surgery, he'd be taken upstairs. It would be hours before they knew if he would regain consciousness. An ER doc came out and informed them he would get an MRI in a few minutes, and they might as well get a motel room. The doctor suggested they call the hospital in the morning before returning.

"Can't we wait here?" Ben wanted to stay. He and Maddison could stay in the lobby. Maddison took Ben's arm and pulled him down so she could whisper. She needed to go again. He saw the women's bathroom and pointed.

"Can you come with me?" she whispered.

Ben shrugged and took her to the men's bathroom in case there was someone in the women's. Lindy had stepped away to call her vet friend, who lived nearby.

When Maddison and Ben were alone, she whispered, "You and Dr. Smart can leave, and I'll hide here until you're gone. Then I'll wait and find Pop, and then I can stay."

Ben was astounded at her plan. "Great idea, Maddy, but that's a big NO. Not gonna happen, darling. We'll get a motel room and wait for a call. Your pop will call us in the morning when he's awake." The idea was ridiculous, but maybe this would soothe Maddison's worries.

They returned to find Lindy talking to a nurse, whom she seemed to know. "Hey, Ben. This is my sister-in-law, Kelly." Ben shook her hand.

Kelly seemed concerned. She glanced up at several monitors. "You guys need to leave. It's not safe. With security and the local issues, I recommend getting away from here. The only place that's open is the ER, and it's no place for anyone, let alone a child, to hang out. I'd lend you my place, but my son is home, and I'm pretty sure he's invited a few friends for the evening. The closest motel is across the street. You don't want to stay here." Kelly rolled her eyes.

"That's okay. I have a place for tonight." Lindy took Maddison's hand and pointed to the exit door. "Maddy and I have a date with a vet friend."

Kelly nodded. "Okay. You staying with Carly?"

"Yep. Call me as soon as you know something. Promise?"

They locked little fingers. Ben had done this with Maddison and was told it was a pinky promise, which was a vow that can't be broken.

"I get off at seven, but I'll make sure someone takes over on the promise. Go get some sleep."

The three left the hospital. Lindy drove to the outskirts of the town of Gawler, which was forty minutes away. On the way, Lindy had briefly informed Ben about Carly's son and his battle with a brain tumor. The long-term prognosis was not good.

On the outskirts of Gawler, they turned onto a long driveway of a veterinary clinic. The set-up was unusual with three large structures. Lindy explained Carly's house and clinic used to be a glider factory where the planes were built. She pointed to a dark field where Ben could see a railing.

"It used to be an airport, but now it's a trotting track. The former owner is an American horse vet who retired. She was an innovative top vet in her day. She liked to fly fish, and she moved to Georgia to write books about horse vets now. She sold it to Carly when she retired."

The residence had a porch with covered vines. The evening was hot, and Ben heard an AC unit going as he was ushered into the unusual house. It was huge. Maddison's eyes widened when she saw the interior. There was a loft and a circular slide that was an option for descending from upstairs. There was also a netball net and two scooters. The kitchen and dining area rested above a painted cement floor.

"Ben, this is Carly Langley. Don't worry. She's been cleared of all charges, and she's not going back to jail anytime soon."

Carly had long blonde hair and was probably in her mid to late thirties. She wore shorts and a shirt that showed her athletic build.

A man in his early thirties emerged from the bedroom. He put his finger to his lips. "He's asleep."

Lindy hugged him. "Ben, this is the godsend who helped me when Jamie was so sick."

The man shook Ben's hand. "Rich Hamilton, I heard you had a..." He stared down at Maddison. "Need a place to park tonight." He obviously didn't say what he had intended in Maddison's presence.

Ben noted Rich was of medium build, with short, dark hair and a hint of gray at the temples. He had dimples and a crushing handshake. Rich's smile was genuine. "So sorry to hear about your accident, but you know you're in excellent hands at the RAH. We're sadly familiar with the place."

Carly was divorced from her husband, who was a doctor at a private hospital in Adelaide, but most of the little boy's treatments were done at the Women's and Children's Hospital. "You're in luck. The girls are visiting their father, so we have a few beds available. Let me show you to your rooms. Two of you are going to have to sleep together."

Ben and Lindy looked at one another and both blushed. Maddison didn't hesitate. "I'm sleeping with my grandfather."

Ben was pleased and relieved. He and Maddison were shown into a bedroom with a queen bed. "Do you need to use the…" Ben hesitated. "The loo? Is that what you call it?"

Maddison stretched her hands skyward. "Well, you're learning. No, I'm just tired. Are you coming to bed now?"

Ben helped her onto the far side of the bed. He had older men's needs and preferred to sleep near the bathroom. Maddison was a heavy sleeper. "I forgot about Tag. Grandpa, we need to go back home."

"Honey, Lindy called the Smarts. They've already medicated him tonight, and he's staying with them. He'll be fine. I'll be back in a minute. I'm going to say goodnight to everyone. Don't fall asleep before I get back." As if she could stay awake for another minute.

Ben was so pleased Maddison chose him. He thought about where they would live once Nigel was better. He'll get better, or I'm going to kill him. He returned to the large front room. Everyone was having a glass of wine and heading out to the veranda. It had cooled and was almost pleasant.

"Too late for skeeters," Carly announced.

Ben remembered she was from the States and her accent had changed little. Skeeters.

Ben sipped his wine but felt guilty sitting and enjoying the company of fellow countrymen and professional colleagues, as Nigel might die alone with strangers. Ben had grown to like the man more than he would have expected. He's never been much of a man to seek company with other men when his wife was alive. He kept thinking of the events that led to the accident. What if he'd insisted on driving or stayed awake? What if he'd remained at the beach one more minute?

Ben pulled out his phone and opened his stored pictures from the day. He thumbed through the images of the last pictures taken at Dolphin Bay. There were three of them on the steps leading back to the car. He was so glad he'd stopped to take several while trying to get a shot that showed the beautiful beach in the background. As he flipped through the photos, he found one that he hadn't realized he'd taken. It was a wonderful shot of the three of them, but in the background were the two women wading back into the water with no swimsuits once again. Ben was near tears until he realized what he'd captured. O-M-G, you bastard. You better live so I can show you this picture.

Everyone was staring at him. He was laughing and crying at the same time. He handed his phone to Lindy, who intently gazed at the three of them, and shrugged. She handed it to Carly, who quickly glanced and then handed the phone to Rich Hamilton.

Rich saw it immediately. He used his fingers to expand the picture. Despite the autofocus, the women were easily captured in their "altogether." He laughed and handed the phone back to Ben. The women were perplexed.

Lindy reached for the phone. "Let me see that again." She scrolled through the images and asked about the pictures of Ben and Maddison swimming with the dolphins.

"They're on Nigel's phone." That sobered everyone.

"I'll bet the police have the phone. I'll contact them in the morning."

"Duty calls." Carly stood up, and Rich followed her as they went to the barn to examine a hospitalized horse. As they stepped off the porch, the house door opened.

Maddison emerged and climbed onto Ben's lap. She stared at Lindy and then closed her eyes as she was enveloped by her grandfather's arms. Ben stood holding her and quietly whispered, "The sandman calls. Wake me if you hear anything." Lindy opened the door to the front room as Ben carried the child to their assigned bedroom.

"You too, Ben. Pleasant dreams, if that's possible."

Chapter 51

Waiting to Hear

Lindy walked out to the barn, where they had a horse in the crush, receiving intravenous fluids. "Colic? Don't you like the word 'crush' better than the American terms?"

"You mean stanchion or chute? Yeah, I do." All three vets were from America.

"We could have had a branch meeting of the American Vet Medical Association with Dr. Delicious a few minutes ago. Jesus, Lindy. He may be old, but he ticks all my boxes."

"Naw. He's still married to his deceased wife. And we all know I'm not looking."

"Well, neither am I, but sometimes ya gotta make exceptions." Carly winked.

Rich smiled. "Go ahead, put on a glove. You won't have to get your elbows dirty. It's a ripper."

Lindy reached for an obstetrical glove Rich held and performed a rectal examination on the colicky horse. She barely had her hand in the rectum, and she could feel the tip of the cecum full of hard dry feces. A couple of moist fecal balls pushed their way to her hand, and she removed them as she withdrew her arm. "I don't envy you. That impaction is one for the record."

Carly smiled. "I'm hoping for a colic free day for Christmas. My nurses are on it. They're masters at moving mountains."

"Yeah, but that feels more like a continent." Lindy removed her glove.

"I'll take our colic problems for your problems." Rich picked up a stomach tube, and with no one holding the horse's head, ran the tube into the horse's stomach. "How old is Maddy?"

"Six going on twenty-six. She's probably in the genius category, but she's so worldly. She's had it tough. Her mom is a druggie, and we think her father took Maddy away when she was a baby to protect her. They lived on a station in Western Australia until earlier this year. Her dad was on the spectrum. He was intelligent, but I don't think he gave Maddy much in the way of emotional support. That's why her grandfathers are so important to her. They're normal guys. You know, Ben's an incredible surgeon. He's so humble. He talked Gaz through the surgery to fix Maddy's Kelpie. We would have suggested euthanasia with the multiple fractures. Ben insisted Gaz was the hero."

Rich gave the oral fluids with stool softeners to the horse through the nasogastric tube and removed the tube. "So, what's not to like?"

"Nothing if I wanted to date." Lindy looked at the house. She imagined Ben in bed with his granddaughter. She knew he'd probably never experienced the joy of comforting a child by the simple act of sleeping next to them.

The three vets returned to the house. Rich went to Carly's bedroom, and when he shut the door, Lindy glanced over at Carly and smirked. Lindy knew Rich had carried a torch for Carly for years. Carly had resisted because of their age disparity. Then there was her speculation that Rich would want to have children of his own and her personal opposition to having any more children. She had four children—two older girls and younger twin boys — all by her cheating ex-husband. She was done.

"He wore me down. Damn caring S.O.B. The kids were on his side the whole time. When he left to do locum work at other clinics and a stint back in the States, the kids were miserable."

"And you weren't?" Lindy considered her own life. What was it going to be like when Ben left? It had to happen.

Lindy wanted to ask about her son and his brain tumor. The long term was not good. So far, his developmental progress had been normal. He and his twin brother, Harry, were equal, minus a few speech issues. Lindy was disappointed not to see the older girls during this visit. She knew they were stressed about going from one house to the other during the school holidays. She didn't think she would be so gracious to her husband under the circumstances.

Carly's ex was great with the children, but he was a cheating bastard, and Lindy had no time for him. Thankfully, it was not Lindy's family. Lindy raised her boys with Jamie until his death. By then, they had grown and moved to the States.

"My boys were here for my birthday. I miss them, but life is good. I wouldn't change my life right now for anything." Lindy knew she was less than honest with herself, but saying it out loud helped her to deny any feelings that she knew were emerging. She was falling in love with Maddison. Her grandfather was icing on the cake.

Lindy received a text message during the night from her sister-in-law that Nigel had been moved to the surgical ward and was undergoing surgery to relieve pressure on his brain from a large blood clot that had formed under his skull. He was headed to recovery, where visitors weren't allowed. She had no other info and left a number for them to call for an update.

At dawn, Lindy rose and went out to the front room. There was coffee and a note to say both Rich and Carly had treated the horse an hour ago and had gone back to bed. "Help yourself."

Lindy took a cup of coffee and went out and sat on the porch. She'd slept in her clothes and would have killed for clean undies, but if that was her biggest problem, she was doing well. She texted Fiona about what was happening. Fiona hadn't responded.

Lindy waved to Julie and Emma, the vet nurses who worked for Carly. They were phenomenal. They were trained by the original vet and knew how to care for horses with colic.

The colicky horse emerged from the barn as the nurses walked him to a round pen, where they would jog him to stimulate the intestines to propel the feces and relieve the impaction. As they rounded the corner of the barn, the horse lifted its tail and sprayed diarrhea. Lindy smiled, thinking Carly just might get her colic-free Christmas day.

Lindy sat on the porch feeling the heat increasing and waited for Ben and Maddison to emerge from the bedroom. She listened to the birds in the surrounding trees. There was a grassy oval between the residence and the barns. She watched magpies eating insects from the recently watered lawn. She observed a black cat stalk the birds. That cat was ancient. He'd been here when Carly moved in. He was called Cheese because of his insistence that he be fed cheese every morning before the office staff could begin their day.

The door to the house opened, and Ben came out to the veranda and touched Lindy's shoulder. He sat down and set his coffee cup on the table. "Any word?"

"Nigel was taken to surgery and had a craniotomy to remove a blood clot. I have a number to call. Nigel's in recovery. How are you? Your shiner is a ripper."

"I played football in college. I've had worse mornings." Ben rubbed his face. He was stiff and sore. He hadn't slept well. "I don't know how Maddison is ever going to keep a partner. She runs marathons in her sleep." His bedmate tossed and turned and poked him all night.

"Starfish." Lindy laughed and stood to refill her cup.

"Is that what you call it?" Ben smiled. He was still pleased Maddison had asked to sleep with him.

Ben wanted to call the hospital before Maddison emerged. His phone was charged, and he copied the number and stepped away from the porch to make the call before Maddison woke.

The number was for the ICU nurses' station. Ben was prepared. "Hi, I'm Dr. Nigel Buckby's brother. We were in an accident yesterday, and my brother was flown to the mainland from the Yorke Peninsula. I'd like to speak with him if he's awake or at least get an update on his progress."

"Oh, his sister, Fiona, called a while ago. Maybe it would be easier for you to talk with her?"

Ben smiled. "Yeah, I didn't realize she'd called. Is he awake? Can we come and see him?"

"No, and no. We're in a changeover. How about you call your sister and get the update? Dr. Buckby will be reassessed in the next hour, and then we can let you know if there's been any improvement. These things can take time."

Ben thanked her and returned to the porch. Maddison was sitting next to Lindy. Ben held her in front of him for a moment and examined her abrasions. She was remarkably unharmed, except for a few superficial cuts and scrapes.

He said nothing in front of Maddison. "Maddy, how about we go get some breakfast? I'm guessing they have a place here in town. How're you feeling this morning?"

"I'm okay. How's Pop?" Maddison stood. She felt the side of her head. It was sore as she felt the crust of the abrasion. Sadly, she would not have a shiner this time.

"He's in the intensive care unit, so we can't visit him yet. We can call later to get an update."

"But he's going to be okay?" Maddison's eyes brimmed.

Ben put his arm around his granddaughter. "Yes. So far, he's okay. There're some sick horses out in the barn across the lawn, and I'll bet the nurses would let you watch them. We'll leave in a few minutes, but do you want to see what they're doing?"

Lindy walked around to the front of the house, where a vegetable garden grew. She was talking to Fiona. Ben joined her as she hung up her phone. "Fi said it's touch and go. They have him in an induced coma and on a respirator. They are doing an EEG this morning to determine his brain function. They won't know until later this morning. He won't be receiving visitors until the assessment is completed. She was told to wait."

Ben knew Lindy would need to get back to the YP. "You need to get back. How about we go get something to eat, drive back to my place, and then you can go home? I can return and wait for Nigel to wake up."

"It's Christmas Eve today. Damn, this is not how I hoped Maddison would spend her Christmas." Lindy turned to Ben, and they hugged. It was a friend comforting another friend with a hug—until it wasn't. It lasted longer than a friend hug, and there was no mistaking the electrical charge that ran in both directions.

Ben was confused. He wanted to stay like that forever. He felt something he hadn't felt in years. He tried to deny the feeling, but it brought such pleasure. He finally let her go. She hadn't resisted, and she hadn't been the one to start the separation. He knew it was mutual. Or maybe he just wished it were.

Lindy woke up. She'd been emotionally dead since Jamie had passed. She was going through the motions. She'd carefully planned to live out her life until the end. It was a well-charted ending to a past life. She'd work until she was unable. She'd finally move into one of the houses that her in-laws owned on the cliff above the beach. She'd sit on the veranda every night and remember her life with Jamie and the kids. And then she would die.

Lindy didn't want the embrace to end. The shot of emotion ran from her heart to her legs. She blushed and turned away. She was confused and so happy. She didn't want Ben to see her if he didn't feel the same way. "Oh, it's sure getting hot."

"Yeah. Maybe we should get going." Ben felt guilty for having a moment of pleasure when Nigel was fighting for his life. "Lindy? I —"

Lindy knew what he was thinking. "Not a great time to…." But she didn't finish the sentence.

"Yeah, a terrible time. I'm so sorry." Ben was confused. Was she politely rejecting him?

"I'm not really…" she wanted to say, "rejecting you," but Carly opened the office door near where they were standing. Lindy didn't finish her thought.

"Any word on your friend? Breakfast will be ready in fifteen minutes. Can you guys bring in a few strawberries? My boys are up, and Rich is making bacon and pancakes. Where's Maddy?"

Ben turned away from Lindy. "She's out learning how to treat colic." He quietly whispered to Lindy, "Or telling the staff how to do it."

This made Lindy laugh. "We'll be right there, and then we're heading back home."

Maddison resisted leaving the nursing staff. They had her collecting the diarrhea that had shot out of the colic. "You can see I'm busy. I'm on the clean-up team. I'm working my way up to the treatment crew."

The nursing staff were smiling and winking at one another. Emma was writing in a medical record and looked up at Lindy. "Sorry, Dr. Smart. She's ours now. You can have her when she becomes a teen, but until then, she has to stay. We'll put her on a bus when she talks back to us. Oh wait, she's already telling us what to do."

"Maddy, we need to get back home. I'm sure Tag misses you." Lindy tried to hide her mirth.

That was enough. Maddy stepped out of the stall and handed her scoop to Julie. "Sorry, I have to leave. Thanks for showing me how to treat colic. Maybe I can skip that class when I go to vet school." Maddison turned to them and then waved goodbye. "I'm kidding, you know."

Emma didn't look up. She quietly turned to Julie. "I doubt it. My guess is she'll teach colic treatment in less than five years." The nurses knew this gifted child was going places.

After breakfast, Ben, Lindy, and Maddison left for home. Maddison knew enough not to say anything in the house when she observed Carly Langley's little boy with the large scar on his head. After they turned onto the road home, she asked about the boy. "What's going on with little Georgie?"

"He had a growth on his brain. The doctors opened his skull and removed the growth."

"A growth? I hope he's going to be okay."

Lindy spared her the cancer diagnosis. "Yeah." Lindy thought about her own family and the death of her husband. It was a painful recollection, but suddenly she realized her feelings had changed. Somehow, it wasn't a crippling pain. The pain was there, but it had moved down a notch in her mind. Maybe two notches.

Ben thought about Tania. He missed her, and if he could have her back here enjoying their grandchild, he would choose that first. But he couldn't, and somehow, he was okay with that. He glanced over at Lindy, who was smiling. It was so nice to see her smile. Really nice.

"Grandpa, it's Christmas Eve today. I hate thinking Pop is in the hospital and alone. Can we come back?" Her voice was wistful, and Lindy glanced at the rearview mirror and saw Maddison had tears.

"When we get home, we'll call the hospital again. We'll go back if they let us. I promise you." Oh, God. Please let him be conscious. Ben reached back and touched Maddison's knee.

They were silent as they passed the electronic sign showing the days since the last vehicular death on the YP as a reminder for drivers to drive with care. It had changed to one.

CHAPTER 52

STILL WAITING

Both Lindy and Ben stared at the sign. Thankfully, Madison hadn't noticed. Lindy immediately called Fiona. She had to leave a message. "Hi, Fi. How are things? We are all in the car and should be back within the hour. Maybe you could text me with any news?"

They drove on and waited for a text message, which never came. They eventually drove up to Ben and Nigel's beach house. Maddison ran next door to the Smarts' house to retrieve Tag. He was asleep on a mat on the veranda and stood and limped over to Maddison. His tail went full speed, which caused his pelvis to rotate, and amplified his pain. Tag put his head under Maddison's arm and would not leave her side.

She hugged the Smarts and thanked them for caring for Tag. They didn't ask about Nigel until Lindy took Maddison in to help her bathe while Ben took Tag's bed and medication. He gave them the update and asked if they knew anything about a fatal last night. Lindy prayed it wasn't Nigel.

"Yeah, mate. The kids who hit you went on and rolled their car. One was killed. I think the other's in awful shape, but he'll live. I hear they were on something. Bloody idiots. How's Nigel?"

"We're waiting for a report. It turns out Nigel has a sister named Fiona Harding, and they are only releasing info to her." Ben pursed his lips. "We have to be careful with info, considering Maddy's needs. It'll be tragic if she loses another close relative at this stage. I'd better get back. No doubt Lindy has scalded the kid."

"Huh?" Doug didn't know about Maddy's insistence that the water was too hot when she bathed.

Ben's phone rang. He signaled to Doug. "Later. It's a great story."

Ben answered his phone as he carried Tag's bed and medication next door. "Hi, it's me. Can we talk?" Fiona's voice was halted, and Ben could tell she was crying.

"Is he still alive?" Oh, please, God, let him be alive.

"Yeah, he's alive. They say he's in an induced coma, and it may be a day or two before they wean him off. It's touch and go."

"We're back at the beach and getting a change of clothes. We'd like to head back, but we haven't been told if we can see him. Do you know if they're allowing visitors?"

"No," Fiona whispered, "I planned to do the same. I'm at home. I wanted to go over, but they said they would call within the hour. How are you and Maddison?"

"Bruised and sore, but we're fine." Ben heard the bathwater draining. "We'll stay here, and then if you want, we can go together. After all, we're family." He laughed.

"Yeah. Okay. I'll call you as soon as I hear something. I'm so sorry for poor Maddy."

"It's a hell of a thing. I'd give him a kidney. He's really a great guy. This will kill Maddy. She's had a tough life, but she's so bright and worldly. She'll never want for anything in life, except a decent family. That reminds me. Have you heard from her mother?"

"Not a word. She seems to have disappeared from the earth again. Strange, and of course, I didn't tell you that, did I?"

Ben knew Fiona had to be impartial. "Not a word. So, will we recommence the Family Court hearing after the Christmas break? I mean, is there any point?"

"Not unless she surfaces again. As long as she's out of the picture, and you and Nigel can agree on Maddy's custody, there's nothing to stop us recommending either of you as permanent guardians."

Ben almost cried when he heard this. "God, I'm praying for an almighty custody fight. I've found my brother."

"I've got a call coming in. It's the office. I'll call as soon as I hear from them. Give Maddy a hug for me and thank Lindy for helping. She thinks the world of Maddy."

Ben hung up as Lindy and Maddison emerged from the bathroom. Maddison smiled and said, from now on, she would only let Lindy do her bath.

Lindy replied, "Not gonna happen, little one. I'm going to make sandwiches while your grandfather showers." She pointed to Ben. It sounded like an order. Ben recalled his deceased wife's insistence that he shower after a hot day. He saluted her and mentioned Fiona had called, and she was waiting for a call from the hospital about whether Nigel was allowed visitors.

"I'm heading home to shower and change, and if you're heading back to Adelaide, I'll take Tag. I can get his radiographs and get his staples removed."

Both Ben and Lindy saw the concerned look on Maddison's face. Tag was by her side as she sat at the table eating a Vegemite sandwich. They ignored the pieces of sandwich that went under the table.

When Ben emerged from the shower, he heard Lindy on the phone, talking to the office. "I'll be over in fifteen minutes." She hung up.

Ben knew the look. "Duty calls?"

"No, they want to close early on Christmas Eve. I need to take Tag now."

Maddison stood. "I'll come too."

Lindy and Ben both shrugged. Ben knew his expertise would shorten the visit. "Let's all go. How about we meet you there at the clinic? We can bring him home and then be ready to head back to the hospital. I'm going to run next door and talk to Doug and Janet. I don't know if we're going to be here for Christmas dinner." Lindy left as Maddison took Tag out to give the dog a quick moment out on the grass.

Ben knocked on the door, but they were gone. He returned and wrote a quick note to his neighbors to say he was unsure of his plans for the night. They loaded Tag into the SUV and headed to the vet clinic, where they met the whole team. Gary Hancock was keen to see if the fixation plates held. A veterinarian from the university was visiting Gaz for summer break.

Ben was surprised to learn they were classmates in vet school. She did relief work when she wasn't teaching. She was spending the week with Gaz and his family, as she was from the UK and the vet school was closed for the holidays.

She was introduced to Ben and Maddison, who wore her clinic scrub top for the visit. "Gaz can't stop talking about you, Dr. Taylor. He said you're a bloody talented surgeon. I'm Jacinta."

"Nice to meet you. Did he mention I only handed Garry—Gaz as you say — the instruments?" Ben deflected the compliment.

"Yeah, but I think we all know who called the shots." Jacinta Thomas explained she taught small animal internal medicine.

"Well, let's see if we're on a winner or not. Maddy, you're going to have to wait outside." Ben lifted Tag and carried him to the back, where they radiographed his pelvis and hind limbs. The digital system they had was not state-of-the-art, but it was adequate for what they needed to see.

All four veterinarians stared at the computer screen. Lindy patted Ben's back. "Brilliant job, mate." Ben and Gaz shook hands, and Ben had a tear. Jacinta examined the original radiographs, and as she stared at the screen, she was amazed at how well the bones were still in perfect alignment. There was some evidence of early bone healing.

Tag would probably lead a normal life, and in time, could go back to work.

Ben went out and brought Maddison into the room to see the radiographs. He was taken aback when Maddison correctly anatomically named the bones. He pointed to the other bones on the radiograph, and she named most of the bones. "You missed one, Grandpa." She pointed to a small linear calcification in the groin area. "That's called the os penis. Mrs. Donovan told me about it. It's in other animals too."

Lindy laughed and turned to Ben. "So much to teach you and so little time. I hope Maddy can keep you current on anatomy."

Jacinta was trying not to laugh but failing miserably. "You know the vet school needs a new anatomy instructor. Maddy, are you available in a month when school starts back?"

Maddison looked at her grandfather. She thought they were serious.

Chapter 53

Friends

Ben's phone vibrated. "Excuse me." It could only be about Nigel.

He stepped outside the clinic and realized it was an unlisted number. "This is Ben Taylor."

"Ben, it's Trevor Hutchinson. I met you on the tram when the young lady went into labor."

"Oh, yeah. Hi. Uh..." Ben paused. "I'm not sure what I should call you. Your honor?"

Trevor cleared his throat. "Only in court. Mate, Adelaide is a small town. I heard about Nigel. I'm wondering if there's anything I can do. I live close to the hospital, and if you need a place to stay, Marilyn and I would be glad to have you."

"Uh huh." Ben tried to think of what to say. "Trevor, how did you hear about Nigel?"

"Our neighbor is one of the hospital administrators. We're good friends, and he recognized Nigel's name and knew the story. We'd love to help, mate."

Ben thought the offer was kind. "To be honest, I'm waiting for a call. We still haven't received updates on his status. You can probably understand we're anxious to hear any news. Do you know anything?"

"No, mate. I only know that he's in the ICU. I'm going to text you my number if I can help. Marilyn and I are leaving to be with our daughter, but we can hide a key for you, and you could use the house as a place to stay and be nearby. Our dog is going to a kennel, so the house is safe for your granddaughter's dog."

"How did you hear about the dog?"

"Court filings. I can't say any more." Trevor knew his involvement in the custody case was done, but he still had to appear to be impartial.

"Trevor, I can't thank you enough. I think I'll take you up on that. I'm trying to get through the next twenty-four. Maddy hasn't had a real Christmas in a few years. Nigel and I were trying to give her one. According to Maddy, Santa missed her last year, and we sure don't want that to happen this year. I'm torn." Ben's voice was choking.

"I get it. I'll text you our address and number. The house is yours, mate. We won't be back until after New Year. Good luck. It's a hell of a time for you all. Any word on the mum?"

"No. I guess that's a blessing. At least we don't have to contend with her. Thanks again, Trevor."

Ben returned to the clinic. He saw Lindy had moved to the hallway, and she was whispering. She held up a finger when she saw him. He returned to the radiology room and helped move Tag to the floor. The nurse had removed his staples, and Maddison was telling him how brave he'd been. "Tag, I'm so proud of you. You're the bestest dog in the world. You need to be quiet for one more month. Can you do that for me?" Tag peered up at Maddison and licked her hand.

The office manager, Sandy Brown, told everyone to get out of the building. "You're all off the clock. We're ending on a high note. Oh, there're presents for the staff on the desk." Ben guessed they were Christmas bonuses. The nurses, along with the kennel and barn help, all had a quick bite of Christmas cake. Ben could smell alcohol on their breath. "Maddy, there's an envelope for you too." Sandy patted Maddison's shoulder.

Maddison raced to the staff room and returned with the envelope. She gazed at Sandy, who told her to open it. Inside the envelope was a notice of a subscription to Horse and Rider Magazine. Maddison glanced around the room and thanked everyone. She was uncharacteristically lost for words.

"Maddy, we thought about getting you a subscription to the Australian Veterinary Journal, but we thought you might enjoy that more in a few years." Gaz patted her head as she hugged him and everyone in the room.

Ben was so pleased they thought enough of his granddaughter to go to such lengths to make her feel welcome. "I still get JAVMA. She can read my journals." And I'm sure she will.

"What's JAVMA?" Maddison searched her grandfather's face.

"Journal of the American Veterinary Medical Association, but maybe the Australian Veterinary Journal would be more appropriate."

"How about both? But I like Horse and Rider. Thank you." Maddison was overcome with emotion. She turned and buried her face in Ben's leg. He, in turn, was caught in the moment. The culmination of events had finally overwhelmed his ability to control what the world saw. He had to wipe his eyes. Damn filter...

"Sorry." He was embarrassed.

Gaz broke the awkward moment. "Yeah, a good radiograph does that to me, too." Baz grinned as his eyes brimmed. "I guess you realize we aren't letting you leave the country. You better have those journals redirected to Australia."

Lindy had been on the phone and finally returned to the departing staff. She gave Ben the look and cocked her head toward her office. Ben patted Maddison on the shoulder. "Honey, I need to talk to Dr. Smart. Can you take Tag out in case he needs to go?"

"Yes sir. I saw his bladder in the radiograph. He's busting."

Ben shook his head. Who is this kid? He followed Lindy into the back office. He saw pictures of her boys when they were children. There were some with Lindy and Jamie. He was ruggedly handsome and had a wonderful smile.

Lindy pointed to a chair, but Ben declined. "Ben, I spoke with Fiona. It doesn't look good. He's on a respirator, and his brain activity is minimal. They advise not to come to see him, and they especially won't allow a child in the ICU. Fi's going, but she thought you should have Christmas at the beach and maybe go over in the afternoon after the festivities are over. I can keep Maddison here. Fi's heading over now, but she's going to stay with a friend." Lindy stepped closer to Ben. "I know this isn't how you planned your Christmas, and I'm so sorry." She hugged Ben again and, once again, the hug lasted longer than a simple, friendly hug.

Ben considered her suggestions. "You know, a month ago, my plans for Christmas were to be on a tropical isle and scuba diving. But more likely, I'd eat a frozen turkey dinner and just watched college football. As bad as it is, this is so much more than I could have ever imagined."

"It's so much better than I could conceive, too. But in case you forgot, I need to get home and shower. How about I take Maddy with me? I have chores, and I'm guessing you need to get the place ready for Father Christmas."

"You're coming to dinner, too?" Ben and Nigel were invited to the neighbors, and Ben assumed Lindy was coming.

"Yeah, the 'outlaws' have commanded my presence. I'll call Janet and tell her what's happening. By the way, your shiner is a beauty. Try some make-up, so you don't scare the large jolly one away tonight."

Chapter 54

The Fat Man Cometh

Ben returned to the beach house after stopping for cookies and carrots. He remembered putting out carrots for Santa with Daniel. He went to great lengths to ensure his son understood Santa was real, even paying one of the clinic nurses to bring goat poop to leave on the lawn.

There was never snow, so Santa landed on the grass. Ben would drag a heavy pole through the lawn to make sleigh tracks and leave a pile of feces and half-eaten carrots to set the scene. He remembered one Christmas Eve when Daniel announced his father didn't have to go to such lengths to pretend Santa came.

"Dad, it's physically impossible for Santa to come to all the kid's houses. I get it."

Tania had to turn away to hide a smile. "So how do you think all the presents come?"

"It's magic. I don't know, but it isn't a sleigh." Daniel was so matter of fact with no signs of emotion or doubt.

Tania and Ben quietly glanced at one another. At least he still believed it, but the next year, he announced there was no Santa. "A kid in class told us all." Apparently, Daniel had not conveyed this information to Maddison. Ben was pleased to see some humanity in his son. Why didn't he have a present for her last year?

Ben remembered his first Christmas after Tania passed. Not knowing his son's whereabouts, he hoped Daniel was alive and with someone having Christmas dinner. Ben would never wonder about his son again. Ben was on the precipice of emotion. He hadn't allowed himself to grieve over his son's passing. He wished he could have talked to Daniel just one more time and told him how proud he was to be his father and now a grandfather. Despite all of Daniel's shortcomings, he's raised a beautiful daughter, and he would have loved to see the two together. Was there a picture of them together?

Ben arrived home and let Tag roam. Tag smelled an incursion on the property and had to re-mark his territory and make the place safe again. Ben unloaded the groceries and went next door to give Doug and Janet an update of the plans. Doug gave Ben the key to the shed where the presents were stored. "See you later, mate. So sorry about all this. Janny and I'll do anything we can to help you."

Ben returned to the house and cleaned the kitchen and living room. He turned on the Christmas tree lights and sat on the sofa to rest. He was beyond exhausted. An hour later, he woke when his phone rang. It was Fiona. She had to step out of the ICU to make the call. "No change. I'm here, and they're going to let me stay with him until later tonight. I can hardly recognize him. His face is so distorted. Oh, Ben," Fiona cried. She then regained her composure. "He's in an induced coma, and they won't know much until they wean him off the drugs. He has a fractured collarbone and upper jaw. His cranium has a hole now, and the doctors say it's touch and go. I'll call you if there're any changes. How are you and Maddy?"

"Bruised and sore, but we're fine. Please call anytime if anything changes. I'll be down tomorrow after lunch. I'm so sorry I wasn't driving. One second later, and none of this would have happened. I'm sure the families of the kids who hit us are having their worst Christmas ever."

Fiona was tearful. "I have a son, and he's like those kids. Christmas can be horrible for dysfunctional families. At least little Liam will have a good Christmas."

Ben knew how close the Child Protection Department had come to getting an outcome that was not in the child's interest. "Is his mother out of jail?"

"Of course, she's on bail, and she'll front the court after the new year. They let her go interstate to be with her parents. We normally would not support that, but it gives Liam's father some breathing room. I feel awful about how we were fooled by the mother. How's Maddy coping?"

"You know how stoic she is. It's hard to tell. She's with Lindy, so I can do a little preparation for Santa. Nigel had it covered, and I'm sorting out the presents. I hate to have another tragedy in her young life. I'm praying he pulls through." Ben realized he needed to do a few things before

Maddison returned. "Gotta go. Call me whenever there's a change or even if you just want to talk. You know, Nigel means the world to me."

Ben took all the presents that were stored next door, placed them in the garage tool shed, and locked it. He was taking no chances. The presents were store-wrapped and better than any of his. They had cards with names, including some for Tag. Most were from Santa, but there were some with both Pop and Grandpa. Ben sat down and cried.

As he waited for Maddison's return, Ben thought about Nigel. This guy was a saint. If he could do anything to bring him back, he would. If there was a custody dispute, he would let Maddison live with Nigel. He'd be glad to live nearby. New Zealand wouldn't be so bad. He'd learn to fish. Ben returned to the house and heard Lindy's car enter the driveway. Ben washed his face and prepared to greet them.

One look from Lindy, and he knew his momentary lapse of self-control was not lost on her. Maddison went straight out to the porch and hugged Tag. She popped her head inside and announced she was heading next door to help with the dinner preparations. Tag followed her.

Lindy turned to Ben. "What have you heard? It couldn't be good?"

"No, it wasn't. I need a drink. Are you on call?" Ben headed to the kitchen.

"No. Not technically. I'm up for a beer. It's hot as Hades out there. Want to take a walk on the beach? Dinner won't be for another two hours." Lindy had on a light silk flowered shirt and three-quarters length pants. She'd put on perfume.

Ben's emotional status was like a yo-yo. He felt guilty, but Lindy was so beautiful. "The beach is quiet this afternoon. Sounds great. You look nice, by the way. You smell good too."

Lindy blushed. "You can thank your fashionista granddaughter. She directed the evening preparations."

Ben bent down and kissed her cheek. "That's my kid." He handed Lindy a beer, and the two went over to the Smart's veranda. "Hi, Mum. Unless you need us, we're going to walk on the beach. Anyone want to join us?" Lindy smiled and quietly gave Maddison the thumbs up.

"No, we're busy. Mrs. Smart and I are whipping cream. You know, the meal doesn't cook itself. Can you smell the turkey?" Maddison then gave Ben and Lindy a swooshing motion with her hand. Ben saw her smile and wink as she turned to Janet. They were co-conspirators. For once, Ben didn't mind.

When they reached the beach, they walked along the water's edge. There were a few lingering families, but most were packing up for the evening and the seafood dinners, which were traditional for many Australians.

From a distance, Ben noticed a familiar dog. The red and tan kelpie was chasing a ball thrown by the owner. The owner was also holding the hand of a small girl who might be three or four years old. He'd seen the dog walking with its owner several times since he'd arrived at North Beach. Ben glanced over at Lindy, who was walking in the water while holding her shoes. It was still hot. He considered joining her. He smiled and pointed at the dog bringing the ball back to the owner.

Lindy cupped her right eye to see what Ben was pointing toward. She seemed to be intent on the scene. Ben looked back and realized the woman was staring at Lindy and waving. This must be one of her clients.

The two women met and hugged. Lindy bent down and patted the dog that was only interested in the ball, which rolled back and forth in the shallow surf.

"What the hell? I thought you moved back to the States. What are you doing here?"

"I'm out visiting my kids. This is my granddaughter, Abby. This is her dog, Dotti."

"Are your kids still in SA? Do you come back often? Oh, where are my manners? Elizabeth, this is Ben Taylor. Ben is a dog vet, and he's over here sorting out some family members. He's from South Carolina. Ben, this is the woman who owned the clinic where we stayed last night." They shook hands.

Ben was surprised the woman he'd observed on the beach for several days was a vet and used to own the clinic where he'd stayed last night. "Wow, what a setup. I loved your mural."

"Yeah, the one piece of art I couldn't take with me."

Lindy kneeled down and patted the dog standing next to the shy child, who had her arm around her grandmother's leg. "Hi, Abby. Please say hi to your mother for me."

"Lindy, how are things? I heard about Jamie. I'm so sorry."

"Yeah, well, life goes on. It's taken a while, but I'm doing fine. And you? Are you still fishing and writing books? I love your books, by the way."

"Samo-samo. Thanks. Hey, we better go. The whole family is here, and we're going to have dinner soon. Nice to see you."

The women hugged, and Lindy watched as Elizabeth and her granddaughter walked away. She stared at Ben, who was watching the ocean. "I better move back to the States. You guys aren't aging as fast as us Aussie vets."

Ben was surprised. "You don't look a day over fifty."

"Ben, I'm forty-eight." Lindy tried to keep from smiling.

Ben blushed. "Oh, I'm sorry. I thought—"

Lindy interrupted him. "But seriously, I would never have thought you were in your mid-seventies."

Now Ben knew he was being teased. "Yeah. Me either. Thank God for my daily hyperbaric oxygen chamber and Viagra. Oh, and the weekly derm visits don't hurt either." He had to look away as he grinned.

"I may have to join you in the chamber. Is it big enough for two?"

"It will be a tight fit, but I can probably accommodate you."

"I'm a horse vet. I'm used to tight squeezes." Lindy looked down. She realized her wedding ring was still on her wedding finger. Ben's ring was on his right hand. Quietly, she took it off her left ring finger and placed it on her right. "I'd race you to that rock, but it might kill me."

"Me too. The anti-aging stuff isn't all it's cracked up to be." He wanted to hold her hand. Should he just take it, or should he ask her? He wanted to kiss her, but he thought maybe just holding her hand would be a start.

Lindy put her hand on his back to steady herself as she put her shoes back on. "I don't remember when I could stand on one foot and not fall."

"There are exercises you can do to regain your balance." Ben took her hand for the second shoe. He didn't let it go when she was done. She didn't resist either.

Chapter 55

Wishful Thinking

Fiona Harding sat in the waiting room outside the intensive care unit. She was asked to leave Nigel's bedside so they could attend to his tracheostomy incision and other personal needs. He was still not responding. She was sure he was squeezing her hand when she talked to him, but she could see the attendants were not convinced. She ignored their eye rolls and lip purses.

She thought about the circumstances that had led her to something she would never have wanted or entertained anymore. How did this cultured man find her attractive? Yeah, sure, she was above average in the "looks department," but she always had to add the qualifier "for a woman her age…"

She went to the gym at least twice a week. She was trying to keep her tummy muscles in check. Her hairdresser was an artist in keeping her hair looking natural. Her skin was showing her age despite her best efforts.

Fiona didn't prevent the aging process. She only wanted to hide it a little. Her job required her to dress well and "look smart." She laughed after she read that in the advertisement when she transferred to the Kadina office. Her boss certainly set the mark. Swimming this time of year is easy, but Terri swam in the winter and only used a short wetsuit. Granted, Terri was a few years younger than Fiona, but still, for her age, she was model material.

Fiona resented her when they first met and worked together, but over the last few years, they had become a team. They occasionally disagreed, but Terri usually allowed Fiona to resolve a crisis without interference, and they developed mutual respect. Terri had insisted she work over Christmas so Fiona could help with Nigel's care.

Fiona thought about the implications of a potential relationship with a client. Bad move, Harding. It's so unprofessional of you—danger, danger, danger, and remember your vow of no more men.

The worst part was he came with a small child. Until she met Maddison Taylor, she was immune to the antics and guile that a small, manipulative child could add to her life. She thought about her first interaction with this poor girl, who was grieving for a father who could never give her the physical attention that all children need to develop into healthy adults. Maddison was a child living as a responsible adult. She'd fed herself, woken her father, and then walked to school on her own.

Fiona had received the little girl's report card. She read it and the accompanying recommendation of a transfer to an inland school, which catered to exceptional children. Miss Osbourne said one more year in her current school would not harm the child, but why not start over now as Maddison's circumstances had changed?

Maddison was wise beyond her six years. She had her grandfathers wrapped around her finger. It was obvious. When each man arrived, the last outcome each considered was to care for a young girl at his stage of life. One "meet and greet" and their resolve was gone. They were hooked on a six going on twenty-six-year-old woman who never asked for anything, but who now had them doing handstands to make sure she had what she wanted and, more importantly, needed.

On reflection, Maddison's father was the last person she would have wanted to raise a little girl, but despite his inability to give Maddison physical and emotional love, he had done a wonderful job in making sure Maddison had role models who would show her how to be a normal and productive citizen. Thank God for Mrs. Donovan and thank God for the dog.

A nurse emerged from the ICU. "You can go back in with Dr. Buckby. He's resting. You'll have to leave at eight tonight, though." The nurse smiled that smile when they knew the outcome would not be good. It was a going-through-the-motions smile. Fiona had been through this when her mother passed. It seemed everyone had given up, except for her, when her mother had a stroke.

Fiona had brought her mother's dog to the small rural hospital, and the dog sat on the bed while Fiona's mother rhythmically touched the dog with her good hand. When the dog was removed from the room, there was a change. Fiona knew her soul had departed. Her mother passed a day later.

Nigel's condition was not like her mother's. She felt it in her bones; he was inside this sleeping body, and he would wake up. She dozed for a few minutes when a nurse came over and tapped her shoulder. "There's someone out in the lobby wanting an update on Dr. Buckby. Are we allowed to talk to them, or would you like to speak to them?"

Fiona wasn't sure. She didn't want to get nabbed for pretending to be Nigel's sister, but she didn't want to be forced to leave. She bit her lip and went to see who wanted to know about Nigel. "I'll go. I guess it's time to go, anyway."

Fiona kissed Nigel's cheek and squeezed his hand one more time. This time, there was no mistaking the response. He squeezed back. She turned to the nurse, but the nurse was gone. As soon as she dealt with whoever wanted information, she would call Lindy or Ben and give them an update.

A woman was leaning against the drink machine, staring at her phone. Fiona coughed, which brought the woman to attention. "Hi. Are you after some information on Dr. Buckby?"

The woman came to attention and smiled. "Uh, yes. I'm sorry to bother you. Kate Kilroy sent me. Are you Mrs. Buckby?"

Fiona had to decide how to answer this. "No. How can I help you?" Kate Kilroy was an institution. Even Fiona had previous dealings with the savvy older reporter over the years.

"I'm Millie Thermopolis. We'd like to know if you would mind a short story about his accident for the Tiser? We received a bucket load of likes and responses to that article where he and his partner helped a woman. We'd like to do the same for him. Does he need anything? We can start a blood drive. It's just a courtesy visit."

Fiona didn't want to blow her cover. "No, thanks, Millie. Probably the best you can do is pray for him. He's fighting for his life." Or a few synapses...

Millie asked if Fiona had a picture of Nigel. She shook her head. It was true. She had no pictures except his passport photo back at the office.

"No, not with me." Fiona could feel the noose tighten.

"We hear he was over from New Zealand on a custody issue. Can you tell me anything about that?"

"I think you know I can't discuss that because of ongoing family court issues. Listen, Millie, Dr. Buckby is a good man, and he's fighting for his life. It's touch and go, but that is probably all I can talk about. It's Christmas Eve. Don't you have better things to do?"

"I wish. Nope, I'm on call tonight unless all hell breaks loose. I'm out trying to find something heartwarming to write about."

"I'm afraid there isn't much heartwarming in this story. You know, the kid who ran into Dr. Buckby's car crashed his truck a few hours later and is dead. Maybe a story about teens and driving on rural roads would be good?"

"No, I think I have all I need. Have a good Christmas, Mrs. I didn't get your name. Is it Buckby too?"

Gulp. "Gotta go. Have the best Christmas you can and pray for us." Fiona walked out the electric doors and went to the parking lot under the hospital to her car. She hated lying. She hated being here on Christmas Eve. She hated everything.

Fiona's phone vibrated as she emerged from the underground parking lot. It was from her son. Fiona hated this, too.

The message read, Merry Christmas. She didn't respond. The next message was the real reason for the contact.

Any chance you could send me some money?

Luv

Justin

She wanted to throw her phone out the window. There was no one behind her. She stared at the message. She'd been receiving these messages for two years. Terri had coached her in the response. Still, it was like sticking a toothpick under her nail.

Justin,

I love you. No, I will not give you money. I will buy you a plane ticket home.

Love

Mum

Fiona wanted to ask how he was doing, and if he was going to return from Victoria, but she had asked at least a handful of times, and he never replied.

Fiona turned out of the parking structure and headed to her friend's apartment. The traffic had decreased in downtown Adelaide. Most people would be home, having their Christmas Eve dinner, or out searching for the best Christmas light displays.

Fiona didn't have far to drive. Her high school classmate lived in a neighboring suburb. Fiona had called her earlier and asked if she could crash there for the night. Adriana was single once again, and her children had flown the coop. She was delighted to have company for Christmas.

Adriana had a glass of wine for Fiona when she opened the door. "So, Fi, what gives?"

Fiona clenched her fists. "Forgive me, Sister, for I have sinned. I may have broken a pinky promise."

Adriana ushered her into her perfectly appointed apartment with colonial decorations. A small Christmas tree with vintage ornaments sat in a corner of the living room next to the divan. Adriana smoothed her dark, straight hair and pointed to the nibbles on the coffee table. "I only remember two. One was chastity until marriage, and we all know that one was broken. What was the other one?" Adriana then smiled and pointed to Fiona. "O-M-G, you've bloody fallen in love. You're an idiot."

Chapter 56

A One-Eighty

Isla and the BF had a parting of the ways. He insisted she seek custody and had his solicitor friend get an urgent court appointment for an interim application to get temporary custody of the child. It was all set, and the court date was two days away.

But Isla was having second thoughts. The image of her daughter cowering at Daniel's funeral burned into her mind. How bad had her existence become that her presence scared her only child? Was there to be a course correction?

Had she reached the bottom of her decades-long downward spiral? Had she hit bottom? Could she reverse course? She'd gone drug free for the last eight months of her pregnancy with no help from anyone. Could she do it again? Was she capable of raising a child on her own and not fall back into the abyss she was in?

Early the next morning, she left the apartment where she and her current partner had crashed. She walked to the rehab facility her friend had suggested. Would this be her last attempt? Would this be the moment she would return to her previous life that included family and the commitments of motherhood? Would her family even take her back? Maddison's reaction to her presence at Daniel's funeral was seared into her memory. So much to consider and so little time to make amends.

With methadone on board, thanks to a walk-in clinic, Isla still had enough money to catch a bus to the Yorke Peninsula. She then hitch-hiked to the caravan park where Daniel had worked.

Isla wanted to stay there for a few days and offered to work in exchange for rent. She had "borrowed" money from her latest ex as she slipped out of the house. It wouldn't last long. Harry Grant was desperate for help at the caravan park and hired her. He advanced her enough money for groceries. He could see she was coming off something, but he didn't want to know. He would give her a week and no more. If she didn't meet his expectations, it was easy to take her up to Kadina, where she could catch a ride back to Adelaide.

After one day, Harry knew he was onto a winner. She was better than anyone he'd hired in the last few years. She was up early, fed the cat that now slept in her small cottage, and even did Harry's laundry.

Isla only had to hold the course and stay off the hard stuff, and she knew she was headed out of the hellhole she'd lived in for years.

She planned to work for six months at least and then maybe arrange a visit with her daughter. But then Harry informed her of her father's accident.

Chapter 57

The Setup

Ben left Lindy next door and went into the house to retrieve a bottle of wine and cheese with crackers. He checked his phone for a message from Fiona. There was a single message from his staff in South Carolina wishing him a wonderful Christmas and asking for pictures of his granddaughter. He'd never thought to send one of Maddison, and he pulled out the picture of the three of them on the stair landing at Dolphin Bay with the two young women swimming without their suits on. He laughed to himself and then sent another that only showed the women with their heads above the surf.

He would send his brother-in-law the first picture. The bastard will be so jealous. Ben sat down and took stock. Last Christmas, he'd spent the day at home and only had leftovers from the office Christmas party. He'd cried once when he thought about Tania and Daniel. He spent most of the day studying diving equipment and online skin-diving travel adventures. Oh, how my life has changed.

He thought about Nigel and the unfairness of life. He knew this was going to tip the balance in his favor. He could take full custody of Maddison and return to the States. Who was he kidding? He was smitten with Lindy, and any chance of going further would only be if he stayed here on the Yorke Peninsula.

Would Lindy accept the total package? He knew she liked Maddison, but the thought of raising another child was never something he would have chosen a month ago. Why would she agree to it? This was a summer romance and nothing more. He knew life as he had planned it was over. There was no way he would ever leave that child. As soon as he let Lindy know his commitment to raising his grandchild, he would be kicked to the curb.

Ben checked his phone once more and headed next door, where he met his granddaughter. Maddison was so excited to be part of a family meal. She'd helped Mrs. Donovan, but she was young, and her role was to set the table and greet the other station hands and their families. This time, she had cooked the dinner rolls, whipped some cream, and helped make the stuffing.

Maddison met Ben and announced she was changing into her Christmas outfit. "Go on. I'll feed Tag and be back in a minute. You're going to sit next to Dr. Smart, Grandpa. And I won't be happy if you try to sit anywhere else." Ben received "the look."

"Yes, ma'am." Ben smiled, but it was forced. The chances of Lindy and Ben successfully having a long-term relationship were questionable. Would he do the same if Maddy belonged to Lindy? He hoped if Nigel recovered fully, they might do a kid-share, but Ben knew the chances of Nigel fully recovering from a traumatic brain injury without regaining consciousness in the next few days were improbable. Just get through the next twenty-four and then think about the future.

Ben had put on long pants and a green Izod shirt. He'd never worn a short-sleeved shirt at Christmas and felt he was underdressed, but Doug still had on shorts and sandals. Ben kissed Janet and handed her his contribution to the dinner's festivities.

Doug held up his hands. "Ben, if you try to kiss me, it's all over, mate."

"No prob." Ben smelled the turkey, which was sitting on the counter. "I can dissect the turkey, if you like."

Janet looked at Doug. "Uh, no thanks. I always let Dougy do the honors. It makes him feel important."

Doug walked behind her and playfully smacked her. "I can think of other ways you can make me feel important, darling."

Lindy smiled and turned to Ben. "These two rabbits have been like this since the day I met them."

Ben checked his phone again and saw no messages from Fiona. He'd call her after dinner and see if she was available for a report. Janet reminded Ben he needed to leave cookies and carrots out for Santa and his herd of reindeer.

The sliding glass door off the lanai opened, and Maddison entered wearing a smocked cotton sleeveless red dress. She was beaming with pride. It was not a simple store-bought dress. It appeared to be handmade.

"Who is this little elf?" Doug reached over, lifted Maddison, and twirled her.

"It's me, thank you. I love the dress, Grandma." Both Lindy and Ben heard the reference and glanced at one another.

Janet smiled as Maddison dropped from Doug's arms. "It was my daughter's, and then one or the other of the grandchildren wore it. I'm so glad it fits, darling. Now would you like some fizzy drink?"

Ben nodded toward Janet and realized she had a tear in her eye. He mouthed, "Thank you."

"Yes, please. Are you all sufficiently liquored up? Can we eat now?" Maddison crossed her arms.

"Where did you hear that expression?"

"At the pub out near the station. That's what Mr. Gilbert, the bartender, would say when he kicked the drunks out."

The dinner was served, and everyone sat down in their assigned seats. Lindy and Janet were the last to sit. "And to think I have to do this all over again tomorrow?"

Ben gave her a quizzical glance. Lindy sighed. "The rest of the Smarts are meeting tomorrow for Christmas Day lunch after church. Doug, are you doing the honors?"

Doug gave a blessing, and the dinner began. Everyone was careful not to mention Nigel's injury or prognosis. When his name came up, Maddison was visibly upset. "I wish he were here."

Lindy took her hand. "We all do, darling, but you'll get to see him tomorrow, and he'll probably be mad he didn't get any turkey and stuffing."

"May I take some home and take it to the hospital tomorrow?"

"Sure, you can." Janet gazed at the child and felt sorrow for all the things she'd suffered in her life.

Ben put his arm around his granddaughter and hugged her shoulder. "You know it's getting late. We need to prepare for a late arrival."

"Who's coming?" Maddison was surprised.

Everyone spoke at once. "Santa, Father Christmas."

"Oh yeah. I guess Tag will have to sleep with me and Grandpa tonight."

Ben sat up straight. "Uh, we may need to make other arrangements, Maddy."

"Well, I thought it was good for a chance. Tag probably wouldn't want to share the bed with you, anyway."

After dessert and a final brandy for the adults, everyone stepped outside where Tag was resting. Janet had prepared a small plate of food for him. Tag wagged his tail and ate the food. He walked over to Lindy and inched his head under her arm.

Maddison was quick to admonish the dog. "Hey, come here, you mongrel. That's not how we planned this."

"Planned what?" Ben glanced toward Maddison and Janet.

Janet secretly pointed at Lindy. Lindy was bent and petting Tag and unaware of the interactions. Ben blushed and turned to his house. "Come on, you two. We need to get ready for Santa."

Lindy smiled and turned to everyone. "I better get home and prepare for the fat, old boy, too. Thanks, Janet." She hugged the Smarts and went with Ben and Maddison to her car, which was parked in their driveway.

Ben asked Maddison to change and brush her teeth while he said goodnight to Dr. Smart.

Maddison winked and told him to take his time. She whispered, "You know, it's okay to kiss her."

Ben stared at this beautiful, precocious child. "Gee, thanks."

"Well, get out there before she leaves. Sheesh, Grandpa, she's going to be halfway home before you get the job done." Ben lifted his finger, and without a word, she ran to the bathroom.

Ben went out to the driveway as Lindy was backing out. She stopped and rolled down her window. "Man, it's still hot. What I would give for a real Christmas. I'd like some snow."

"I don't know. Nigel aside, I think this is one of the nicest Christmases I've had in years. Thanks again for all you've done for us. I can't tell you."

"Ben, I..." But she didn't finish the thought. "Call me when you get any word on Nigel." She then reversed her car and was gone.

Ben watched her, knowing he'd been dismissed. He returned to the house where Maddison had already put out a plate of cookies and milk near the Christmas tree.

"How about the carrots for the reindeer?" He stared at this beautiful small child.

"Uh, well, duh. Grandpa, you realize the reindeer won't be in the house. I put some on the patio. How'd it go with Dr. Smart? Did you kiss her?"

"None of your business, young lady."

Maddison searched his face. "I'll take that as a no." She was obviously disappointed.

"We need to work on your mating skills. You're out of practice."

Ben shook his head. "Who are you? Get to bed before I reconsider the no spanking rule."

"That would be child abuse. The only person who can spank me is Mrs. Donovan."

Where did she get that? "Yeah, thank the Lord for Mrs. Donovan. I'd hate to think what you'd be like without her."

Ben tried Fiona's phone, but she never answered. He wanted an update and realized he would have to wait for any news until the morning. He broke his no-praying rule.

Chapter 58

Christmas Morning

Maddison was the first to wake. Ben stayed up until two in the morning, ensuring the presents were displayed under the tree. He filled the stockings with small toys for Maddison and Tag, and he ate bites from the cookies and carrots. Nothing was left to chance.

Ben heard his granddaughter making coffee. It was early, and only a small amount of light crept through the gap in the curtain. He heard her feed the dog and let him out onto the veranda. She squealed when she opened the door. He lay in bed for another minute and then heard knocking. "Grandpa, get up. Hurry, please. Santa came. No kidding, he really did come. He gave me a bike. Hurry up."

This alarmed Ben. A bike was not on the list. This was a complication he could do without. Who did this? Ben stumbled out of bed and threw on a robe. He opened the door to find Maddison holding a cup of coffee.

"It's about time. You're going to have to lift your game if you expect to be chosen as my guardian." Maddison looked at her grandfather and then laughed.

O-M-G, this kid... "You know, Mrs. Donovan told me it was okay to spank you when you needed it." He took the coffee and walked out to the living room. He feigned shock when he surveyed the presents. "Where's the bike?"

"There's reindeer poop, and Santa brought me a real bike. I didn't even ask for one."

Nor did I. "Where's the bike?" He realized the Smarts must have brought it. Neither he nor Nigel had discussed a bike. It wasn't on the radar.

Ben went out to the porch and found a brand-new red bike parked under the pergola. Maddison went over to it and stroked the handlebars and the seat. She looked at her grandfather and cried. Ben went over and picked her up. "Hey, darling, Santa wouldn't want you crying. Shall we go inside and see what else he brought you?"

Maddison shook her head. "No." That was all, just no. She held Ben's neck, and he sat on a patio chair and continued to hold her. He waited. Finally, she turned her head and gave him a kiss. "Can we wait to open the presents until Pop is back home?"

Ben sighed. This wasn't the Christmas morning either he nor Nigel envisioned. "Sure, honey. I think that's a good plan. And how did we ever get so fortunate to get such a kind and caring granddaughter?"

"Just lucky, I guess."

Ah, a dose of reality. The real Maddy has emerged. "Okay, let's have some breakfast, and then we'll call to see how your grandfather's doing and if we can go see him. Why don't you wear your dress again today? I washed the gravy off, and it's hanging in the laundry. Pancakes okay?"

"Can I wear my shorts and have a go on the bike? I'd rather try riding than eating." Maddison stared at her grandfather. His black eye was peaking. "You need makeup if we go to the hospital."

Ben went to the bathroom and saw his shiner—so ugly. He threw on a nice shirt and pants. Even if they weren't allowing visitors for Nigel, he planned to go to the hospital. Lindy had agreed to take Maddison if need be. Ben remembered Trevor Hutchinson, the judge, had offered his house as a place to stay near the hospital.

"Hey, I want you to eat a pancake, and then we'll go to the hospital. Do you want syrup or Nutella?" He stood over the fry pan and sipped his coffee and waited.

"Vegemite, thanks." Maddison had returned to the kitchen and retrieved the Vegemite from the pantry. "It's gonna be a scorcher today. Do you think Father Christmas is still out delivering presents to children on the other side of the world?"

"For sure. It's a busy day for him. Want more orange juice?" Ben ate his pancake and sipped his coffee.

They devoured their breakfast, and Ben guided the bike through the house and out onto the street. He adjusted the seat so Maddison could reach the pedals and then held the back of the seat and ran along beside her as the little girl wobbled down the street. It was early, and no cars were coming down the road. Ben thought about his attempts to teach Daniel how to ride a bike. It was brutal. He could die doing this, and then Maddy would be on her own again. This is not an old man's gig.

Maddison kept trying, and when Ben said that was enough for today, she begged for more. She finally rode the bike without help and screamed with joy. Doug came out and joined them. Ben asked him to take a picture of Maddison and him with the bike. He handed Doug the phone. He sent the picture to his office email group. It would have been a treasured moment if he hadn't thought about who missed this momentous occasion—Nigel, and even Daniel, were in his thoughts. That brought Ben back to reality. He watched Maddison ride up and down several times, and then his phone rang. The silent number didn't register. "Benny-boy, it's Gill. Hey, where are you?"

Gill was Ben's brother-in-law with the large, blended family, and the bastard who made Tania's life miserable with the family Christmas cards. Ben gritted his teeth. "Australia. I'm visiting my family here." Ben was reluctant to share the details. "I have a granddaughter, and I'm visiting her. Hey Gill, sorry, but I need to go. Nice talking to you. I'll send you a picture." He hung up before Gill could ask any questions. He'd send it later.

The next call was from Fiona. "I'm at the hospital. No change. Sorry about last night. My phone died. They suggest you wait until tomorrow to come. You can do what you like, but there isn't much to see or do, and to be honest, he's a mess. I wouldn't bring Maddy." Fiona waited for a response.

"It'll break her heart. Are they assessing his brain activity? Is he still on the respirator?"

"He's still on the respirator, but they have said little about his brain waves. I doubt they're doing anything today. There were several admissions that were critical according to the nurse in the ICU. I thought he was responding last night, but maybe it was just wishful thinking."

"Damn, this is going to kill Maddy. She didn't want to open her presents until Nigel could be there. Any chance things will change later? We've been offered a place to stay near the hospital."

"Who knows? Oh, by the way, your picture is back in the newspaper. The Tiser ran a story about Nigel."

"Oh great. Maybe this will bring the wayward daughter back to the pack." Ben really hoped it didn't bring her back, but he had to pretend he was all for family unity. He admitted he now felt he, Maddison, and Nigel were a family unit. That was all he wanted. Well, maybe Lindy and Fiona might make acceptable additions in the future. How would that work?

"How am I going to break this news to the munchkin? She's getting ready to leave." Ben glanced over his shoulder at his granddaughter, putting food out for Tag in the vehicle.

"It's your choice. Hey, I've got to go. The doctor's here." Ben could hear Fiona greeting the attending doctor before the phone went dead.

Ben turned to Maddison. "Hey, great news. Your grandfather's doing well. He's still sleeping, and the doctors think we should let him sleep today. I think we'll wait before going to see him. How about you and me go for a swim on the beach?"

"No." The response was predictable—arms crossed and lower lip protruding. The tears followed. "If I sit with him, he'll feel better. I know."

"Yes, and I know that, but the hospital staff need to sit with him, too. They're only letting one person visit him at a time, and right now, that's Ms. Harding. She's the only one who may stay in the room."

"That's not fair. I'm his granddaughter."

Fair? Did Daniel ever talk about fairness? Did he ever express a desire to see someone? While Ben agonized over his granddaughter's distress, he found reassurance that Maddison was normal in every way. She could express her sense of fairness. Daniel's response would have been a meltdown.

Janet Smart appeared on the patio. She smiled and went to water her small garden. Thank-yous were exchanged, and Maddison hugged her and asked if Santa was as good to them as he was to her. Maddison mentioned she was waiting to open her presents when her pop could be there.

"Really?" It was hard for Janet to watch the distress on Maddison's face.

Ben clarified they could not see Nigel today, and they were going to have to wait until tomorrow.

"Did you see my new bike? I can already ride it." Maddison asked her grandfather to show Janet the picture. Janet praised her and asked them to come later for drinks.

As she walked toward her house, Ben asked if the bike was from them. "Not us. We love her, but we didn't get her a bike. Maybe it was Lindy?"

Chapter 59

Making the Most of a Bad Situation

"We'll go for a quick swim and then reassess the trip to town. Hurry." Ben stood in his shorts and tee shirt. He knew there was a new swimsuit for Maddison from Nigel, but it was still wrapped and under the tree. She was growing so fast. He knew her current suit was tight and chaffed at her.

"Can we bring Tag?" She stared at her grandfather with pleading eyes.

"Not yet. It's too early. His incisions are healed, but it's too much activity for the pin and plates. You'll understand this when you're in vet school. It'll be another four weeks before he can do anything that strenuous." The dog amazed Ben. His recovery was miraculous, and Ben would not jeopardize this by allowing him too much activity and pressure on the repair so early in his recovery.

When Ben and Maddison entered the water, it was already warm. As they moved farther from shore, the temperature dropped. Maddison clung to Ben for warmth and protection.

Ben watched as Maddison performed several strokes and dove to retrieve objects on the ocean floor. She was experiencing an exponential increase in her confidence.

"I'm tired. Can we go back home?" It had been an hour, and Ben was happy to return to the house. By the time they were cleaned up, the phone rang.

Fiona reported she knew he was responding to her commands. "He squeezed my hand several times, and he opened his eyes and looked around. The nurses asked me to leave so they can do some obs, and they want to do another scan on his brain. I think I'll go back home and let you take over."

"Okay, we're on our way. I think we'll bring Tag and plan to spend the night at the judge's house. He heard about the accident. Did I already tell you?"

"Yes, you did. You have a lot on your mind."

"Yeah. Okay, I'll let you know when we get there. I hate to ask you, but did you get Maddy a bike?"

"Not me. She got a bike? Maybe Nigel arranged it?"

Ben hadn't considered this. "Yeah, maybe." That would make sense. Except it doesn't. The two men had discussed the presents, and both agreed they would get nothing that couldn't be easily transported overseas.

"Maddy," Ben yelled. "We're going to Adelaide. Let's pack a bag and get some food for Tag."

Ben stepped out the back door and saw Doug watering his garden. He repeated Fiona's good news.

As they backed Ben's SUV out of the garage, they noticed Lindy had driven up to Janet and Doug's driveway. Ben wanted to talk to her, but after last night, it was awkward. Had she blown me off? Damn, it's hard to read her.

Maddison rolled down her window and yelled, "Merry Christmas, Dr. Smart. I got a bike from Father Christmas. We're going to see my pop."

Lindy waved and grinned. She hesitated, then opened the door on the passenger side, brought out a tray covered in aluminum foil, and started for the gate to her in-laws.

Ben drove off without stopping. What the hell was I thinking? I'm too old. I'll probably be the caregiver of a six-year-old, and I'll take her back to the States, where she can get an education that will stimulate her and allow her to reach her full potential. Eyes forward, old man. You've had enough love in your life. Reset required. Eye on the game...

It went on until Maddison shouted. "Grandpa. We forgot Tag's leash and bowl." This jerked Ben out of his pity party. Damn. He turned around and stopped outside the gate to their house. He ran onto the back veranda, retrieved the items, and then headed back to the car when Lindy shouted over the fence. "Merry Christmas, Ben. Good luck and give Nigel my best. I'll be thinking of you and Maddy all day."

This was a surprise. "Thanks, Lindy. We're spending the night in town. Have a wonderful Christmas. If there's any improvement, I'll let you know. By the way, do we need to thank you for the bike?"

"Not me. Did she get a bike?" Lindy had moved closer to the fence but could not see over the top.

"Yeah. I don't know who brought it." Ben paused.
"It's obviously Santa Claus. Safe travels."
"Thanks, darling." O-M-G, did I just say darling? Please tell me I didn't say that. Ben quickly went to the car and left. He was so embarrassed. He hit the steering wheel with the palm of his hand, which frightened Maddison.

Maddison said nothing. She'd never seen either of her grandfathers show any kind of overreaction. She sat silently in the back seat. When they'd driven for several minutes, she finally asked the obvious. "Did she blow you off?"

"Blow me off? Where did you hear that expression?"

"At school? Maybe on television? I don't know. Did she?"

Ben considered his conversation with Lindy. "No." He waited for a minute. "No, she didn't at all." Ben smiled. "She asked us to let her know about Nigel." On the other hand, I was an idiot.

They arrived at the address of Trevor Hutchinson's house two hours later. Palatial was the only way to describe it. It was colonial, but modernized over the years. There was a large backyard with fruit trees and a tennis court. The house was cool, and there was a note from Mrs. Hutchinson letting them know any food in the house was theirs and to feel free to use the house as if it were their own.

Ben set up an area for tag, and then he and Maddison drove to the hospital. They went to the underground parking lot and saw the lot was almost full. They eventually made their way up to the foyer and were directed to the intensive care unit.

The staff was all busy, and no one would even stop to talk to them. Maddison was becoming more distressed by the moment. Ben regretted bringing her and suggested they come back tomorrow. As he put his hand on her shoulder to deliver the bad news, someone in a suit stared at him and smiled.

"Dr. Taylor?" The man appeared to be someone of authority. He had a lanyard hanging from his neck. "I'm Baz Miller. I'm Trevor Hutchinson's neighbor. He said to expect you."

Ben stood up and placed a hand on Maddison's shoulder. "Dr. Miller?"

"No, just Baz, it's short for Barry. I run the place. Are you here to see this young lady's grandfather?" Baz Miller looked down at Maddison, who wiped away tears.

"Yeah. I understand how busy you all are, and if we can see Dr. Buckby for even a minute, it would make us so happy." Ben remembered his black eye and reached up and rubbed it with his free hand. "Sorry, I look a mess."

"Has anyone assessed either of you?" Baz peered down at Maddison and smiled.

"No, we're fine. We only need to step in for a moment. We're staying at Trevor's house, and we're only a short distance away." Ben then realized Baz would know if he was a neighbor. "We understand how busy everyone is, and we'll only stay for a minute."

Baz turned to the nurses' station. "I'll get the nurse who is caring for him, and he can escort you into the room. Wait here."

After a minute, Baz Miller returned with a nurse, who appeared to be annoyed. He briskly said nothing more than, "Follow me."

They walked down the hall and entered a room where Ben and Maddison received the shock of their lives. Isla sat holding her father's hand.

Isla turned and stared at them. She stood and gazed at Maddison. She smiled and looked at the nurse, who was retreating. "Hi, Maddy. It's nice to see you again, darling. Come over and see your grandfather. We think he's waking up. He'll be so glad to see you."

Isla appeared sober and had on clean summer clothes. Ben would never guess this was the same person who had shown up for his son's funeral. He was wary. He'd known drug addicts who had fooled him before. A vet nurse he'd hired had stolen narcotics for several months before anyone discovered her in the drug cabinet.

"Hi, Isla. I'm Daniel's father and Maddy's grandfather. We weren't introduced." He held out his hand to shake hers as Maddison clung to his leg and stayed away from her mother. "How's Nigel?"

Ben didn't expect a medical report from the woman, but she rattled off his vitals and showed him a tracing of his brain activity and said, while he hadn't spoken, he squeezed her hand on command.

Nigel's face was distorted, and his head was wrapped. Ben worried this would upset Maddison, but she appeared to be more worried about approaching her mother than her grandfather's appearance. She hung back and made sure she was protected by her grandfather.

"Maddy? Do you remember me? I'm afraid I was a bit of a mess the last time I saw you. I'm getting some help, and I'm doing okay now. I'm so sorry about it all. I came when I heard about Daddy. I'm staying at the caravan park where you used to live. I have your father's job now. I clean the cabins, and I even let Cheese sleep with me. What did Santa bring you for Christmas?"

Ben tried to ease his granddaughter's concerns. "Maddy, how about you and I walk over so you can sit on the bed? Then you can tell him how much you love him?" Ben felt Maddison's hand pulling at his pants.

Maddison didn't budge. She saw Nigel's contorted face, and as everyone predicted, it scared her. Her mother's presence didn't help. Maddison turned to Ben and extended her arms, asking silently to be picked up. Ben obliged and stood watching Isla and the monitors that showed Nigel was alive and seemed to be stabilized. Ben patted Maddison's back.

"His heart rate and oxygen levels look good." Ben tried to think of something to say, but he was so shocked by Isla that he was lost for words.

"The nurses say it's a miracle. He hasn't spoken, but he does occasionally open his eyes, and he will squeeze your hand when he's asked. I need to step out for a minute. Would you like to sit next to him? I can return in thirty minutes?"

Ben couldn't get over how much the woman had changed in such a short time. He wondered how a transformation could be achieved in less than ten days. She was well dressed, although her clothes were old, and her hair needed a cut. She wore long sleeves, which Ben thought might cover the telltale signs of needle tracks. Was this just another attempt to fool everyone into giving her money to feed her needs?

Ben knew she was leaving Nigel's bedside to let Maddison have a moment with her grandfather without fear of her mother's presence. He wanted to know more, but his worry of losing Maddison to her mother could not be denied. Could this Christmas get any worse?

Chapter 60

And Again

Isla stepped out of the room, but Maddison stood by Ben and only approached Nigel with Ben holding her hand. Ben sat in Isla's chair next to the bed and put Maddison in his lap. He talked to Nigel as if Nigel was aware of his surroundings and could hear what he was saying. Ben had no illusions that Nigel could hear or understand, but he wanted to calm Maddison's fears.

"Mate, this place is not what I envisioned for Christmas. You need to wake up so we can go home and get back on the program. You would not believe all the presents Santa Claus has left us, and we're waiting for you to get home before we open them. So, let's get this show on the road."

Maddison would not reach over and take Nigel's hand. She just glanced once or twice and then buried her head in Ben's shoulder. Nigel didn't react. His heart rate stayed the same, and there was no sign he was hearing what was being said.

"Can we go?" Maddison was clinging to Ben and refused to look at Nigel.

"Yes, I'm sorry. I..." Ben didn't finish the sentence. He hated himself right then. He needed to be a better guardian to this fragile child with a rock-hard exterior. Ben took Nigel's hand, leaned over, and kissed Nigel's cheek.

He felt Nigel move away. He was sure Nigel had responded. "Hey, mate. Squeeze my hand." Ben felt Nigel's hand grip ever so slightly.

"Do it again." Ben waited, but there was no squeeze. "Squeeze my hand two times, or I'll kiss you again." This time he felt two weak squeezes.

"Did you feel anything, Grandpa?" Maddison stood and avoided her grandfather's face but watched his legs and body.

"Move your toes, you bastard, or I'm going to plant one on your lips." Both Ben and Maddison watched the end of the bed.

"Say it again, Grandpa." Maddison reached out and moved the sheet that covered Nigel's toes.

"Last chance, mate. Move your toes." Ben leaned toward Nigel, took his finger, and touched Nigel's lips. There was no mistake. Nigel's toes moved.

Ben almost cried. He held back the tears for Maddison's sake. Ben remembered seeing his father cry and how much it upset him, and he inhaled deeply as Maddison hugged him, and he lifted her back onto his lap. "How about I hold you, then you lean over, and squeeze his hand? You can keep your eyes closed."

Maddison tentatively reached for Nigel's hand, careful not to look at his distorted face. She squeezed it, and Nigel's fingers closed over Maddison's small hand. She reached into her pocket with her free hand. She placed the shell she'd found while swimming into Nigel's outstretched hand, and in a barely audible voice said, "Merry Christmas, Pop."

Ben shifted and continued to hold Maddison. She left her hand in Nigel's. After thirty minutes, Isla returned with a popsicle for Maddison. "Eat it quick before anyone sees it."

Maddison glanced at Ben, who nodded, and she took it. Ben announced Nigel had wiggled his toes, and apparently, the best way to get him to respond was for a man to threaten him with a kiss.

Isla laughed and moved to the other side of the bed. She stared at Maddison and smiled. "I can leave again. Do you want some more time here?"

Ben shook his head and glanced back at Nigel. "No. We need to get back to the house where we're staying. We left Maddy's dog there, and he'll need us to reassure him he hasn't been abandoned." As soon as Ben said it, he regretted it. He didn't mean to imply anything. Or did he?

"Oh, no. I understand. Will you come back tomorrow? I'll stay as long as I'm allowed." Isla stared at Maddison, whose head was tucked in her grandfather's chest.

Ben thought about inviting her to stay, but he knew the judge wouldn't be happy. "Yes. We'll come tomorrow. Do you have a place to stay tonight? Do you have to get back to work?" Ben hoped he could spend time alone with Nigel. He wanted to talk

"I need to return tonight. I'm back on duty tomorrow morning. My boss would barely let me come here today. You know Christmas is the busiest time in a caravan park. Anyway, it was so nice to meet you, and thanks for allowing me to see Maddy."

Maddison didn't acknowledge her and walked out of the room holding her grandfather's hand as soon as she finished her popsicle. She pulled on his hand to get away quickly and kept glancing back to see if Isla had followed them.

Ben was encouraged. He wanted to call the Smarts, but they would be eating their family Christmas lunch. He rang Fiona when they returned to the North Adelaide house, and Ben was alone while Maddison went to check on her dog.

He reported the toe wiggling and Isla's presence. "She appears to be clean and sober. Did you know she's working at the caravan park where Daniel and Maddison lived and worked?"

"No. We haven't heard from her."

Ben sensed the surprise in Fiona's voice. "Hey, did you get a present for Maddison?" Ben was still wondering about the mysterious bike.

"No, why?" Fiona knew personal gifts were against the government policy. She wanted to get something for Nigel, but she knew it was too risky in case there was a pending court case. No man is worth losing a job.

"Someone left a new bike for Maddy, and I don't know who it's from."

"Are you thinking Isla gave it to her?"

"Don't know. How would she know where we live?"

"Not a clue. Hey, I'll come over tomorrow. Will Isla still be there?"

"She said she has to work tomorrow. Maddy and I'll come back. I won't stay long. It probably wasn't my smartest move bringing a six-year-old here. It frightened her to look at his face—bad grandfather moment."

"You'll have to learn to say 'no' again." Fiona coughed.

"No." Ben paused. "I mean, yes."

"Practice makes perfect. I have a call coming in from the boss. Maybe I'll see you tomorrow."

"Thanks, Fi." Ben hoped using her abbreviated name wasn't going too far.

Maddison returned to the house and took Tag out to the backyard. She reported a swimming pool inside an enclosed corrugated iron fence. She said there was a tennis court as well. She saw some books and magazines scattered on a table. They were mostly novels. One was of a woman riding into the sunset.

"Is it okay if I read this?" She handed the book to Ben.

He recognized it from Carly Langley's veterinary clinic, where they'd stayed two nights ago. He realized it was the vet who he'd met on the beach yesterday. She'd sold the veterinary clinic to Carly Langley and had returned to the States. He wondered if she was any good as an author.

He opened and read the first few pages and knew it was too old for Maddison, but he handed it to her and asked her to read a sentence or two. He was surprised when Maddison could read most of the first few lines. "I'm a vet."

He listened to her recite other lines, but when the phrase "celebratory activities" came up, he took the book from her. "I'm not sure this is a good book for you, Maddy."

Maddison was hooked on the "I'm a vet" opening sentence and asked Ben to continue to read it to her. Ben knew he could read and skip anything that wasn't age appropriate. He read the entire first chapter and wanted to continue on his own. Maddison had fallen asleep. Her head was in his lap, and he didn't want the moment to end.

Never once had he had such an experience with his son. He thought about his wife, and how much she would have enjoyed this moment. Curiously, it wasn't as painful as it might have been. He continued to read to himself and then fell asleep as well. His phone was on vibrate, and he felt it pulse. He gazed down at the screen. It was Lindy. His heart skipped. He didn't want to wake his granddaughter, so he didn't answer. As soon as it stopped vibrating, he sent her a text message to say he would call her in a few minutes.

Ben slowly lifted Maddison's head off his thigh and took the phone out to the patio. He called Lindy, who answered immediately. "Hi. Sorry, I didn't want to wake Maddy. How was your luncheon?"

"Great. Seafood and grog consumed, the annual cricket match played—by the way, we won. Oh, and presents were opened. A great day was had by all. And you?"

"Who do you think gave Maddy the bike? I sure would like to know." Ben knew it was not her now, but maybe she could think of someone.

"I wish it were me, but no, it's not. How's Nigel?"

"Improving. He's a mess, but he squeezes your hand on command, and he wiggled his toes when I threatened to kiss him." Ben could hear Lindy snort.

"Well, that answers a lot of questions. We've all wondered about you two. Don't worry, I'll still love you even if I'm not on the same team."

Ben accurately guessed Lindy regretted that quip.

"I mean respect you."

"Oh darn. I liked the love idea better. No, sadly, we aren't inclined that way. I'd consider it, but I think I'm too old to change teams. The big surprise was Maddy's mother. She was sitting with Nigel when we got there."

"You're kidding?" Lindy sounded shocked.

"I wish I were. You know, she appeared to be on the straight and narrow and was even gracious. Maddy was having none of it. Bringing the kiddo was a big mistake. Nigel's condition scared her, and then her mother scared her more."

"Sounds like a shitshow. What are your plans?"

"I'll stay tonight and see Nigel in the morning and then head back. I'll figure out what I can do with Maddy in the morning. Maybe I can run her back up to the vet clinic. Hopefully, she can stay there while I spend some time here. Maybe I can meet the doctors and get an accurate assessment of his prognosis. Can you text me Carly's number? Would that be too imposing considering it's Christmas?"

"No, not at all. That sounds like a good plan." Lindy paused. "Ben?"

"Yeah?" Ben held his breath. He waited for the shoe to fall.

"About the dinner and walk on the beach."

Here it came. Ben braced himself. "Lindy, you don't have to say anything. I understand."

"Well, I'm guessing you don't. I wanted to tell you I liked it. I'm struggling, but I think I'm coming out of a deep hole. I liked the feel of holding your hand. Half of me wants to run away and crawl into a hole, but the other half of me doesn't want it to end."

Lindy paused, and Ben didn't know what to say, but he knew this was a tremendous breakthrough for her. The silence was deafening. Ben's heart was pounding.

"So, Ben?"

Ben stammered, "Y-yeah?"

"I'm a work in progress. I need time, and I know we have little in common, but..."

"I think we do, Lindy. We're both widows. We're both vets. We have our American backgrounds. I'm guessing neither of us ever wanted or considered raising any more children at our age. But here we are. I don't know what will happen, and I have to say, I'll kill myself to give Maddy the best outcome that I possibly can. Everything else has to come behind that. If I must move here, I will, and if I have to move somewhere else, well, that may have to take over my personal wants and needs, but I'd like to get to know more about you and see where things go." Ben knew he'd gone over the line. Why hadn't he kept his mouth shut? Kill me now.

"Are you done?" Lindy was laughing.

"Yeah. I think I mangled that response pretty well. Can you pretend you didn't hear all that?"

"Uh, probably not. Hey, I'm pulling into my place, and I can see the sheep are out. Gotta run."

O-M-G, what the hell have I done?

The thing was—he didn't really care.

He received a text from Lindy with Carly's number and the message: To be continued.

Ben returned to the house. Maddison was still asleep. Ben called Carly, and he explained the problem. He didn't know anyone else, and he wondered if Carly was available to babysit Maddison while he went to the hospital for a few hours tomorrow.

"It's colic central as per usual here. Is she prepared to give intravenous fluids and drench horses? Seriously, Ben, I'd be happy to have her."

Ben said he would confirm it in the morning and bring her up to the clinic. He returned to the house and saw Maddison had woken and must be in the bathroom. When she returned to the living room, he asked her if she would like to spend the following morning at the horse clinic. He told her allowing kids in the intensive care unit is not usually allowed, and since it looks like her pop is going to recover, they wouldn't allow her back in the room. He knew Maddison would search for an excuse to avoid what she experienced today, but then maybe she would like to see her mother again?

"Can I go to the vet's place again? That place was so much fun. Will the nurses still be there? Oh, wait. I don't have my clothes and boots."

"Maddy, I'm guessing with all the kids Dr. Langley has, she'd have something you could wear. Okay, well, let's see how things go tonight. You know, I thought you were very brave at the hospital. Honey, it was hard for me to see your grandfather like that as well."

Ben sat down and patted his lap. "You can tell me what you think, but from now on, I'll decide what's good for you. I have some questions. Would you like to see your mother again? I can arrange for you to see her back at the caravan park."

"I don't know. I can see she's better, but how long will she be better? I know you're not very used to taking care of kids, but you're always there when I need you. I don't want to live with her. My dad was not always good. I loved him, and I knew he would never leave me if he could help it."

"Darling, I can't promise you anything for sure, but Pop and I will do our best to take care of you and be there for you."

Maddison snuggled against her grandfather and cried. This was such a rare moment. It was something he'd never experienced with his son. It was only much later he realized he hadn't thought about Tania.

Chapter 61

Touch and Go

Fiona returned the phone call when she'd finished with a client the next day. She was exhausted. Ben relayed the events and Maddison's reaction to seeing Nigel and her mother. Ben explained he would not take Maddison back to the ICU the next day. He said he'd leave Maddison with Lindy's friend, who has the vet clinic in Gawler. Ben planned to drop Maddison off at the clinic early, then head back to the hospital, and maybe get an update on Nigel. He hoped to talk to the doctor. He knew Isla wouldn't be there this time.

It was still an official holiday in Australia. Ben had researched the derivation of Boxing Day and knew it had various historical explanations. He thought the idea of giving boxes of leftovers to the servants of noblemen was the most logical, but who knew for sure?

Ben dropped Maddison off at the clinic and drove back to the Royal Adelaide Hospital to attend his friend's bedside. Maddison was so happy to stay at the clinic, she barely said goodbye. She ran from the car to the barn, where a single nurse was helping Dr. Langley with a colicky pony. She turned and waved to her grandfather and immediately picked up a rake. Ben waved and gave her a thumbs up as he drove past the barn. "I won't be long."

He found Nigel had been moved to a room and was off the ventilator. Some staff members were standing around Nigel's bed. He guessed this was hospital rounds, and several of the people were medical students. They turned, and then one of the women approached him and asked who he was. He said he was Nigel's brother-in-law, which made the attendant suspicious. "Visiting hours aren't until ten."

"When can I get an update on Dr. Buckby?" Ben would stand his ground as long as he could.

"I'm not sure you're allowed." Ben could see this guy was a "play by the rules" kind of guy.

"Okay, I know you're trying to do your job. I'll get the info I need from the director. So sorry to interrupt." Ben stepped out of the room and asked a man folding towels if the director was here today.

"Not a clue, mate." The man had on a lanyard that showed he was a nurse. He pointed down the hall and said his director's office was around the corner. "Good luck."

Ben thanked him and went to the hospital director's door. It was locked. He returned to the foyer, and as he was waiting for an elevator, he heard his name being called. It was Baz Miller, the director. Baz signaled for Ben to follow him to the room where Nigel was resting. "You go in and wait for someone to come and give you an update. I just got here, and Tony said you were looking for me."

Ben and the director stood in Nigel's room. Two attendants were unhooking probes from Nigel's head. They were laughing, and it appeared they were communicating with Nigel.

"Sorry, mate, the probes are torture to remove sometimes."

Ben saw Nigel wave his arm. Nigel tried to respond, but his voice was garbled. The door to Nigel's room opened, and a woman with a lanyard showing she was a neurologist smiled at the technicians and then used her finger to summon Ben. She took him out to the hall and introduced herself. "I'm Dr. Lucy Griffen, and I understand you're his brother?"

Ben almost choked. "Ah, well. I'm his brother-in-law." Kinda.

Dr. Griffen stared at Ben. Ben knew he hadn't fooled her, and he could see she was deciding how much information she could release. "And you're friends with Baz?"

"No. Not really. I'm staying at his neighbor's house. You know it's complicated. To be honest, Dr. Buckby and I have a granddaughter in common." A little truth might grease this wheel.

"So, you're not from the press? I know there is interest in Dr. Buckby because of his efforts to help a woman in distress on a tram. Do you know about that?"

"Yes. I was there on the tram. She was in labor, and we were heading into Adelaide for an appointment regarding our granddaughter."

"Okay, I think you're safe. As you know, he has a traumatic brain injury, and he had a bleed into the brain, which set up more damage and..." The doctor paused. "Am I making sense?"

"Dr. Griffen, I'm an orthopedic surgeon. Though my patients are the four-legged kind, I know about brain injuries."

"Oh! Sorry, well. Despite the odds, he's improving rapidly, and his neurological function and brain wave patterns are returning to normal. He has trauma to his face and swelling, so communication is a challenge. He responds to commands, and he even tried to smile today. It's quite remarkable. I understand he lives out on the Yorke Peninsula. He may even be able to go home at the end of the week, but if he still needs help, we may send him to our rehab facility."

"Whatever it takes. If you need a payment or something, please let me know."

"Nice to know, but he's a citizen of New Zealand, and we have the financials sorted. We're good on that end. How long do you plan to stay today?"

"I'm not sure. I don't want to get in the way. I farmed our granddaughter out with a vet clinic up in Gawler. If she isn't running the show, I'd be surprised. I can't leave her there too long. Thanks again, Dr. Griffen. This is great news."

"My dad was a vet. Call me Lucy. My pleasure. We always take special care of local heroes. Baz wouldn't be happy if we didn't do our best."

Ben went over to the bed. Nigel appeared to be asleep, so Ben sat down in a chair and opened his phone. He had several messages. Fiona, the Smarts, and Lindy all wanted updates. Ben replied things were looking up, and the clinicians were even talking about moving him to a rehab facility. Ben received several replies with emojis showing prayers and good luck charms.

There was another email from his brother-in-law asking for the promised picture of Ben's granddaughter. He thumbed through several pictures he'd taken and found the one of the three of them at the beach and one of her on her new bike. He sent them on and remembered he still didn't know who had put the bike outside. He then remembered Colin Butler. It had to be him. Ben sent a message to Lindy asking for Colin's phone number.

She sent the number and a question mark. He mentioned it might be Colin who'd left the bike. He dialed Colin's number, who answered after one ring. Ben gave him an update on Nigel and asked if he'd given Maddison a bike. "Not me, mate. I would have, if I'd known she didn't have one."

Ben thanked Colin again for his help and hung up. There was only one conclusion. It had to be Isla. She must know where they live. At least she hasn't tried to show up unannounced. Maybe there's hope for her.

"Hey, Nige. Piss poor way to see the Christmas holiday." Ben watched Nigel's face contort in a smile. "Maddy was here yesterday. It was a little too confronting. I shouldn't have brought her. Fiona was with you for most of Christmas Eve. I think you've got a great friend in her. Someone gave Maddy a bike. I'm guessing it wasn't you, mate?"

Nigel didn't respond. He'd gone back to sleep. Ben continued to hold her hand. He felt his phone vibrate. He pulled his phone out of his pocket and with one hand and the phone in his lap, he scrolled through the apps. There were several emails and text messages from friends. His favorite was from his brother-in-law. All it said was:

Lucky Bastard.

Fiona and Lindy had both left text messages thanking him for the update.

Nigel squeezed his hand and alerted Ben he'd woken. Ben knew he had news that would probably delight Nigel. Ben explained Isla had come to the hospital and was with him most of yesterday. "Who knows, but she seemed clean and sober."

Ben explained there was a "good news" story in the newspaper again about our tram drama. She must have seen it and come over from the YP, where she's taken over Daniel's job at the caravan park. Nigel was awake, but he didn't respond.

"Anyway, she saw Maddy and was kind to her and didn't get too close to Maddy or suggest she would try for custody again. Oh, and I have something that will make you smile. I don't know where your glasses are, but maybe you can see this." Ben opened the camera to the pictures of Ben, Nigel, and Maddison when they were leaving Dolphin Bay. Nigel nodded, and then Ben expanded the camera, which showed the topless girls standing behind them in the surf. Nigel smiled, but Ben wasn't sure he could see the complete picture.

A nurse entered the room and announced they were taking Nigel down for more scans. He suggested Ben come back later in the day. "So, Nige, you need to get better fast and blow this joint. You can't expect Maddy and me to just hang around in a hospital all day. She's hanging out at Lindy's friend's vet clinic. I need to leave and rescue the vet clinic from Maddy. I'm sure she's running the show. How about I come back this afternoon?"

Nigel squeezed Ben's hand and attempted to smile, but he shook his head. Ben understood. Nigel was protecting his granddaughter.

"Okay, I'll be back tomorrow?"

Nigel nodded.

Chapter 62

Respite

Maddison was teetering between heaven and hell. Another person in her life might die, but here was the family she'd always dreamed about. In truth, this was so far beyond anything she'd ever considered.

The two older girls, Casey and Faythe, had returned from a visit with their father. They took her into the bedroom they shared. It was decorated with wallpaper with horses running across the walls. Even the lampshades had ponies on them.

"Do you like to be called Maddison or Maddy?" Casey was in charge. Faythe was quiet and played a game on her iPad. Faythe glanced up from her game as Maddison considered her response. Maddison had a favorite new name, but it was only for her grandfathers.

"I guess Maddy is best. My father…" Maddison didn't finish the sentence. The Langley girls knew Maddison's father had recently died. They didn't respond. They knew about the anguish of lost relationships. Their father had been the perfect father until he wasn't. He had to go away, and they didn't see him for over a year. Casey was six and knew he'd gone to jail, but the reason was still a mystery to her. Faythe only knew he was gone. No one ever talked about that time in his or her life. That's when they moved to their current house, and the twins were born. Rich had taken over their father's role.

But that was all in the past. Now they lived in this enormous house and had ponies to ride and a slide in the house. They worshiped Rich and were delighted he'd returned and had moved in for good, according to their mother.

"Would you like to ride our ponies?" Casey and Faythe accepted babysitting duties. The nurse had gone home, and the hospitalized pony was ready to return to its owner.

"Yeah, maybe. I've only ridden horses. Are ponies good to ride? Do you ride every day?" Maddison could only dream of riding on a regular basis. She wondered if either of her grandfathers would move to the country so she could have a horse of her own.

"No, not every day, but most days. Our ponies are good. Mum got them when someone owed her some money. Tango is a bit old, but he really gets around. He used to do games at Pony Club. Missy is a show pony."

Casey held up a ribbon. "I won first place at the Gawler Show last year. I take lessons from Julie. She's our clinic nurse, and she's also our instructor."

"Wow, you guys are lucky. I hope I can have a horse when they decide where I'm gonna live. I used to ride with Mrs. Donovan."

"Where was that?" Faythe glanced up from her game.

"On a station. It's a long way away. That's where I wanted to stay but not anymore."

Casey gazed at Maddison. "I'm sorry about your dad."

"Yeah, thanks. I miss him, but my pop and grandfather are pretty nice. I guess I'll probably live with them until I start vet school."

Faythe was now interested. "So, who will you live with?"

"I don't know for sure. Maybe one or both? Everyone's trying to decide. I may have to leave Australia."

"Do you have a favorite?" Casey knew she shouldn't ask that question, but she wanted to know.

"Mrs. Donovan is my favorite, but she says she's too old. I like them both. They're not very good at raising kids, but I'm teaching them. They have a lot to learn. It's a job and a half, but they're getting better all the time."

Maddison didn't mention her mother. She felt guilty that she didn't want to see her. The new bike was from her. She knew it. It smelled like her mother. She wouldn't tell anyone. When she saw her mother in the hospital, her mother was scary, but nice. Madison had seen people before at the pub near the station. They always fell off the wagon, as Mrs. Donovan said. Maddison had little hope that this would last with her mother.

Casey turned and stared at her guest. "I'm going to be a vet too. Rich even lets me cut stitches when he does surgery. Maybe we could work together when we're vets."

"Yeah, maybe. Can we go see the ponies? I don't have any riding clothes or boots."

"We have tons. Faythe, get your pants that you said were too small."

Maddison was dubious. But then she saw the jodhpurs and riding boots. She'd only worn Western clothes. She was in heaven. Then she thought of her pop, and heaven vanished.

Chapter 63

Decisions

Ben arrived at the equine clinic, where the kids were all in swimsuits and were sliding down a makeshift slip and slide. He noticed two older girls who must have returned from their father's place in town. Ben was amazed they all had red hair. Rich Hamilton was standing on the grass spraying the plastic sheet so the children could run and then slide to the end of the slide.

"Watch me," Maddison shouted to her grandfather. Ben waved and watched her slide about halfway down the sheet. She shrugged and then got back in line to repeat the process.

Ben went up on the porch where Carly was bringing out drinks and sandwiches for the children. Ben helped with the table settings. "Quiet day?"

"Thankfully. We're down to one sickie. How's your partner today?" Carly sat down and poured a glass of lemonade for the both of them both.

"Now that they're taking him off the drugs that suppress his brain, there's a meteoric improvement. He's going to make it. I'm sure. He's a mess, but he understands what I said, and he can communicate by hand gestures. His face is so swollen it's hard to understand what he says." Verbalizing this made Ben tear up. He stood up and turned from Carly, who immediately stood and put her arm on Ben's shoulder.

Ben coughed. "I think the lemonade went down the wrong pipe."

"Yeah, I believe you." And then Carly quietly added, "But thousands wouldn't."

"He's quite a man." Ben watched Rich's interaction with the children.

"Yeah. It took me a while to believe he would sacrifice a need to have a child of his own."

Rich told the kids they were done for the morning. When the wails subsided, they asked for sandwiches. Ben observed Rich drying the small boys and handing the towels to the girls. He watched Carly as she came and went from the house to the porch with food. There was no question these children treated them as their primary parents. The interactions reminded him of his own parents. He'd forgotten how families interacted.

As Ben sat on the porch, Maddison climbed onto his lap wearing a wet swimsuit she'd borrowed from one of the girls. He watched Maddison as she observed the interactions. She was taking it all in. But in it all, she leaned into him and quietly put her arm under his. "How's Pop?"

"He's fine, darling. He's getting better every hour. Your pop will be fine," Ben said this with conviction and knew it to be true. Ben planned to return to the judge's house to care for Tag, then go to the hospital for one more conversation with Nigel, and then he and Maddison would head to the beach and their home.

Rich cocked his finger at Ben, asking Ben to follow him. They went into the big shed with the mural painted on the front. Inside were more stalls and a crush where they could treat horses. There was a horse in one of the stalls and a small black pony in the neighboring box.

"This is Chocko. He's our resident babysitter. His job is to be a companion to the sick horses in the hospital. He plays a vital role at the clinic."

"Nice." Ben wondered why Rich had asked him to come out here.

When Rich finished auscultating the horse's abdomen, he stepped out of the stall and wrote in the horse's record.

"Just a guess, but I'm thinking you're wondering about your life and what you'll be doing in the next few months." Rich cocked his head as he stared at Ben.

"And?" Ben wasn't sure what Rich was getting at.

"It's not a bad life here. Would I like to return to the States? Probably, but I couldn't leave these kids for anything. Not even one of my own. And we won't go into their mother. Ben, it's a great life here. It's retro and frustrating at times. I miss my family back home, but this is my home now. No regrets."

How far I have traveled, thought Ben as he nodded toward Rich. He'd already made that decision. Ben knew his life would be different. He knew he'd remain in this rural spot. Ben wouldn't make any changes with Maddison until Nigel was back on board. He'd contend with Maddison's mother and Nigel's needs. They would remain at the beach until the time Maddison would need to change schools. Maybe he and Lindy would be together in the future. Maybe Nigel and Fiona would be as well. But for now, this would be his life.

Ben lingered and watched the kids resume their water activities, and then he asked Carly to care for Maddison while he attended Tag before returning to the hospital. He needed to speak to Nigel. On the way, he called Lindy. "Hey, Lindy, it's me. How are you?"

Lindy sensed Ben wanted a serious discussion. "I'm fine. How's things?"

"Good. Really, really good. I think Nigel would say, bloody fantastic. I'm staying," Ben announced.

"I thought you would. I'll let the 'outlaws' know you won't be back tonight."

"No, that's not what I mean. I'm going to live here. If it's okay with Janet and Doug, I'll rent the place for the next six or so months until Nigel is fully recovered, and then we'll decide how to share Maddy. Maybe we'll live here together or get houses side by side, but I'm staying. So, I want you to know it's not just Maddy who makes me want to stay."

"Yeah, those endless paddocks of wheat stubble will get you sucked in. I can't say I blame you."

Ben imagined Lindy smiling. Lindy did the same.

Ben turned into the parking structure. "I'm headed back to the hospital to see my housemate. He's compos mentis enough to understand. Who knows about Isla? I'm not counting on her. Maddy will get what she needs. She'll have choices and opportunities, or I'll go down trying."

"Hey, Ben?" Lindy paused.

"Yeah?" Ben prayed for the response he wanted.

"She needs a horse."

Ben laughed. "O-M-G, are you already taking sides?"

"Sides were drawn when I met you. I'm just letting you know the boundaries."

"I'm at the hospital now. I'll call you later."

Ben walked into Nigel's room. He was alone and asleep. Ben moved his chair next to Nigel's bed. He dozed and woke when he felt Nigel's hand brush his. Nigel pointed to the phone and twirled his finger. It took Ben a second to realize Nigel wanted to see the pictures on his phone. Fortunately, he'd taken a few of Maddison on the slip and slide. He started with the last picture taken and scrolled all the way to his first picture of Maddison.

Nigel nodded, and Ben wiped away the tears. He cleared his throat. "Nige, old man, I'm going to live here, and since you're not in a position to make any decisions, I'm taking over. First, I'm staying for good. I'm hoping to rent our current house for the foreseeable future. Second, we'll live together until one of us wants to move out. Conjugal visits will be tolerated, but keep in mind, we have an impressionable young lady in the house. We can renegotiate the living arrangements when you're well, but until then, it's you and me and our Maddy. You have no choice. We'll see how your daughter responds to this, but a slow and controlled introduction to reacquaint Maddy and Isla will be considered. Squeeze my hand if you're okay with that."

Ben didn't have to wait for the response. "Hell, you have no choice. I'm in charge. Prepare yourself. I run a tight ship. You better get your voice back, old man. I'm already missing your accent."

Ben heard a garbled response from Nigel. It sounded like can or cane. Ben shrugged. "Gotta go, mate. See you tomorrow."

He drove over to Trevor's house to retrieve Tag. Tag greeted him like he were the best person in the world. Ben loved this dog. Tag was the icing on the cake. He picked up all of Tag's food and bowls and walked past a coffee table with magazines that he and Maddison had searched through. He spotted it instantly—Michael Caine. That was what Nigel had tried to say. He sounded like Michael Caine. He even had a faint resemblance to the actor.

Ben picked up Maddison from the vet clinic. Carly's parting words were to suggest Ben either get some makeup to hide his shiner or hide out for a few days. "You look like you've been in a knockout fight."

"I have. Ten rounds—but I finally scored an uppercut, and I won." Ben felt his bruised face. It would heal, and so would his heart. He was on the upswing. His life had irrevocably changed. Who would have thought?

As they drove back to the YP, Maddison thanked him for letting her play with the kids. Ben wondered if Maddison would resent having to live with two old men with no chance of siblings.

Ben's plans took form. He would call his office and ask Sarah to put his house on the market. Of course, he would return to collect his belongings. Ben would consult with an immigration lawyer or a solicitor. Damn, he was going to learn to talk like an Aussie.

Then there's Lindy. For the first time since his wife passed, Ben felt his heart race when he thought of her. Doug and Janet would be easy. He knew Nigel, and he could remain in their oceanfront home for the near future. Nigel could move into Maddy's bedroom for the initial recovery period.

Ben will speak to Fiona tomorrow about his plans and Maddy's mother. He hoped Nigel and Fiona could continue their friendship once the custody was decided. He knew he and Nigel would be awarded custody. While that was significant on a legal basis, the important thing was Maddy would be protected. If Isla's recovery from addiction continued, he and Nigel would be there to protect their granddaughter until Isla proved to be worthy of the responsibility of caring for a child. So much to consider, but so much time to plan.

Maddison sat quietly in the back seat. "Grandpa?"

"Yes, darling?"

"Can they be my cousins?"

Ben was relieved she didn't ask to live with them.

"You know, Maddy, we're going to make some decisions about all this. I guess it's only fair we ask you what you would like." Ben steeled himself for the response.

"Well, first, can you roll down the window? Tag's farting, and I can't breathe."

We're going to have to modify this kid's vocabulary in the future. Ben laughed and waited. "Anything else?"

"I like it when you call me Maddymeister. It's okay for you to call me that."

There was a pause, and Ben wondered if she'd fallen asleep or was considering her response.

"Promise me I can live with you and my pop for the rest of my life?"

Ben reached back with an extended pinky finger. He knew he wouldn't outlive his granddaughter, but he would die trying. "Pinky promise, Maddymeister." Or at least for the rest of my time. How my life has changed!

Maddison sat forward and tapped Ben's shoulder. "You know, it's not that long, Grandpa. I'll be going to vet school someday, and you and Pop are going to have to live without me. You can't expect me to take care of you forever. I have my limits."

"Your limits? I'll keep it in mind, Maddymeister."

Ben, Nigel, and Maddison's lives had irrevocably changed. But so had the lives of many on the YP.

What was it about this precocious child that ensnared so many in her universe?

Nigel had a moment of clarity. He laughed, thinking of the photo of the three of them at Dolphin Bay. He knew he had a difficult road ahead. How lucky he was to have a granddaughter who led him to Ben Taylor! How would this work? Ben said he had it covered, but he was shy on details. As he drifted away, the door to his room opened, and in stepped his daughter. He tried to smile, but it was so painful. He nodded as she bent over to kiss him.

As the plane ascended from Charles de Gaulle Airport, Jim Donovan patted his wife's hand. "You're missing Maddy, aren't you, old girl." Jim knew how Laura grieved when Maddison and Daniel left the station.

"I suppose I am." She glanced out the window when the plane shuddered as the landing gear retracted.

"Chook, as much as I want to be near our boys, I think we might be happier on the YP. Doug Smart and Collie Butler might transition off the land a little easier."

"From what I've heard from Janet, Ben's going to have his hands full with Nigel's rehab. We could rent a place nearby until we see how it goes. So you think she pulled her bathwater trick on them?" They both chuckled.

"Yeah, and after we received that picture from Innes with the sheilas swimming nearby, I'm going to have to check out Dolphin Bay regularly." Jim knew what was coming. "Ouch, what was that for?"

"I have my limits." Laura Donovan smiled. Course corrections achieved. Laura Donovan had a plan.

Thank God for Mrs. Donovan.

Cast of Characters

Yorke Peninsula: The Yorke Peninsula, in South Australia, is a rugged coastal region known for its sweeping beaches, historic fishing villages, and spectacular ocean views where the Southern Ocean meets golden farmland. Beloved by anglers, surfers, and beachcombers alike, it's a place where life slows down and every turn of the road offers a postcard-perfect vista.

Daniel Taylor—Maddison's deceased father

Maddison Taylor—precocious 6-yr-old orphan

Tag—Kelpie (working dog) companion for Maddison

Dr. Ben Taylor—Maddison's fraternal grandfather, retired veterinarian from South Carolina

Dr. Nigel Buckby—Maddison's maternal grandfather, a retired professor of reproduction living in New Zealand

Fiona Harding—caseworker assigned to care for Maddison through the Dept. of Child Protective Services

Terri Barber—Fiona's boss at Dept. of Child Protective Services

Dr. Lindy Smart—local veterinarian, widowed daughter-in-law to Janet and Doug Smart

Dr. Gary Hancock (Gaz)—Smart's veterinary partner

Isla Taylor Buckby—Maddison's mother

Doug and Janet Smart—Neighbors to Ben and Nigel and in-laws to Lindy Smart

Jim and Laura Donovan (Mrs. Donovan)—station owners where Maddison resided with her father

until moving to the Yorke Peninsula

Jarlee Yarran—classmate

Ruth Yarran—Jarlee's mother

Harry Grant—Caravan park owner where Daniel and Maddison lived and worked

Dr. Carly Langley—expat American Horse vet from Gawler, a primary character in Small Town Secrets

Dr. Rich Hamilton—expat American Horse vet from Gawler, a secondary character in Small Town Secrets

*Colin Butler—Farmer living on the Yorke Peninsula

*In real life Colin is my former client and friend from my veterinary days. I used his name and character with his permission. I miss his cheerful disposition and knowledge of life on the YP.

Acknowledgements

I would like to express my deep gratitude to my core readers, who have helped me over the years. They include, but are not limited to: Candace Fox, Brendalea Packer, Nancy Aronoff, Wendy Wilson, Denise Pigott, Petra Mckerlie, Sharon Spier, Lesley Pickford, Pat Wake, Sandra Fletcher, Beth Spurling, and Ila Rice Hennig, who also did the first edit.

Thank you to my editor, Chris Hall from the Editing Hall, as well as others who have helped in the editing process. Special thanks to Kathy Baldock from Kathy's Pet Portraits in South Australia for painting the cover, and Cathy Walker of Cathy's Covers for the formatting of my original vision for the scene that inspired me to write this book.

Finally, a big thank you to the residents of North Beach and the Yorke Peninsula of South Australia. I have so many wonderful memories of veterinary calls and trips to Innes

National Park. Special thanks to the two unknown young women who really swam au naturale at Dolphin Bay while I fished. Those and many other memories inspired me to write this book.

Colin Butler was my client and friend. He gave me permission to use his character in the book. I think I have portrayed him accurately. He is a kind and knowledgeable farmer, and a wonderful source of humor.

I encourage you to visit the Yorke Peninsula. The town of Minlaton has both a chocolaterie and a bakery that had the best sourdough in all of South Australia.

Thanks to Lucy Harris for the last pass through and edits. My high school English teacher, Mrs. Hastings, can rest in her grave. She has been replaced.

Finally, I would like to pass on my sincere gratitude to those of you who take the time to review my books and send me feedback. I thank you from the bottom of my heart.

BOOKS BY ELIZABETH WOOLSEY

Horse Doctor Adventure Books:

Small Town Secrets

The Travels of Dr. Rebecca Harper Series
Book 1 A Matter of Time
Book 2 Troubled Waters
Book 3 Lauren's Story
Book 4 Past and Present

Catch and Release series
Book 1 Catch and Release
Book 2 Catch and Keep
Book 3 Match the Hatch

A Man's Worth

Other books
Parkside Veterinary Clinic: I want to be a Vet
Horse Doctor: An American Vet's Life Down Under
Jack's War: Letters Home from an American WII Navigator
AI poetry from a Horse Doctor's Life

Note: The first chapter to all the books can be found on elizabethwoolsey.com
Amazon links to all books
https://bit.ly/4jba85s

Elizabeth Woolsey
DVM

Elizabeth Woolsey, DVM, grew up in postwar California. Sure, she was the daughter of Roy Rogers, she spent her youth emulating him. Sadly, DNA evidence has proved her wrong. Thus, she followed in her other father's footsteps into equine veterinary medicine. She subsequently migrated to Australia, where she practiced near Adelaide, South Australia, until her retirement in December 2020.

She began writing about her experiences as a horse vet and published her first book, Horse Doctor-An American Vet's Life Down Under, in 2005. A few years before her father's death, she discovered a treasure trove of personal and historically significant letters. She knew this would make an influential book not only for her family but also for WWII enthusiasts. She published Jack's War: Letters to Home from an American WII Navigator in 2015. While veterinary medicine has been her passion, fly-fishing, horseback riding, and writing occupy her leisure time. Her new books include stories about women in equine practice. Small Town Secrets: Horse Doctor Adventures 2021 is her latest book. She now lives in North Georgia, where she follows her passions.

She loves to hear from readers! ewoolseydvm@gmail.com

Elizabeth is available for book clubs via Zoom.

https://www.facebook.com/elizabeth.woolseydvm

https://elizabethwoolsey.com/

https://amzn.to/3dPAoGc

www.ingramcontent.com/pod-product-compliance
Lightning Source LLC
Chambersburg PA
CBHW052027030426
42337CB00027B/4893